A BEAUTIFUL CHILD

*A True Story of
Hope, Horror,
and an
Enduring Human Spirit*

MATT BIRKBECK

BERKLEY BOOKS, NEW YORK

THE BERKLEY PUBLISHING GROUP
Published by the Penguin Group
Penguin Group (USA) Inc.
375 Hudson Street, New York, New York 10014, USA

Penguin Group (Canada), 90 Eglinton Avenue East, Suite 700, Toronto, Ontario M4P 2Y3, Canada
(a division of Pearson Penguin Canada Inc.)
Penguin Books Ltd., 80 Strand, London WC2R 0RL, England
Penguin Group Ireland, 25 St. Stephen's Green, Dublin 2, Ireland (a division of Penguin Books Ltd.)
Penguin Group (Australia), 250 Camberwell Road, Camberwell, Victoria 3124, Australia
(a division of Pearson Australia Group Pty. Ltd.)
Penguin Books India Pvt. Ltd., 11 Community Centre, Panchsheel Park, New Delhi—110 017, India
Penguin Group (NZ), Cnr. Airborne and Rosedale Roads, Albany, Auckland 1310, New Zealand
(a division of Pearson New Zealand Ltd.)
Penguin Books (South Africa) (Pty.) Ltd., 24 Sturdee Avenue, Rosebank, Johannesburg 2196,
South Africa

Penguin Books Ltd., Registered Offices: 80 Strand, London WC2R 0RL, England

While the author has made every effort to provide accurate addresses, telephone numbers, and Internet addresses at the time of publication, neither the publisher nor the author assumes any responsibility for errors, or for changes that occur after publication. Further, publisher does not have any control over and does not assume any responsibility for author or third-party websites or their content.

A BEAUTIFUL CHILD

A Berkley Book / published by arrangement with the author

PRINTING HISTORY
Berkley hardcover edition / September 2004
Berkley mass-market edition / August 2005

Copyright © 2004 by Matt Birkbeck.
Afterword © 2005 by Matt Birkbeck.
Cover design by Pyrographx.
Book design by Kristin del Rosario.

ISBN: 0-425-20440-5

BERKLEY®
Berkley Books are published by The Berkley Publishing Group,
a division of Penguin Group (USA) Inc.,
375 Hudson Street, New York, New York 10014.
BERKLEY is a registered trademark of Penguin Group (USA) Inc.
The "B" design is a trademark belonging to Penguin Group (USA) Inc.

PRINTED IN THE UNITED STATES OF AMERICA

10 9 8 7 6 5 4 3 2

"Suffer little children, and forbid them not,
to come unto me: for of such is the kingdom of heaven."

MATTHEW 19:14

PROLOGUE

Oklahoma City, Oklahoma
April 1990

The thunderstorms that swept through the southern Plains left the region damp and misty, the spring moisture adding a heaviness to the air and to the darkness of the early morning hours, which made driving somewhat more difficult for Delbert Ray Collins and his two companions.

They had just exited Interstate 35 and were driving slowly along the poorly lit service road toward the Motel 6, which beckoned just a few hundred feet ahead. It was late, and the men were tired.

After passing a truck stop, one of the passengers, Shawn Peters, saw a small object in the middle of the road. His friend Roy Kibble saw it too. As the car passed it by, the two men turned around to look out the back window, straining to keep their eyes on the object. It was blue—with a high heel.

"Looks like someone lost a shoe," said Shawn.

As the two men stared out the rear of the car, Delbert Ray drove two hundred feet down the road and then called out, "Is that a body?"

Roy and Shawn quickly turned around and saw Delbert Ray pointing toward the right as he eased on the brake, slowing the car. There, on the edge of the road, was what looked like a young woman lying facedown in the gutter, her body convulsing, her arms and legs twitching in different directions.

Delbert Ray pressed his foot firmly on the gas pedal and sped into the Motel 6 parking lot. He jumped out of his car and ran into the building, telling the night watchman to call the police.

The 911 emergency call came into the Oklahoma City Police Department at 12:55 A.M.: A pedestrian was lying on the side of the east service road of I-35, just south of the northeast 122nd Street exit.

The I-35 highway is a major artery that cuts through the heart of Oklahoma and the capital city that bears the state name. Take the interstate north and end up in Kansas. Keep going south and face the flatlands of northern Texas.

Along its length through Oklahoma City, other highways intersect with I-35. Interstate 40 slices through on an east–west route, directing motorists toward either Arkansas or the Texas Panhandle. A northeast passage, I-44 leads to Tulsa and southern Missouri.

By the time Oklahoma City police arrived on the scene, paramedics had already taken the woman downtown to Presbyterian Hospital. She was still alive, though unconscious, and was apparently the victim of a hit-and-run accident. She was young, probably in her early twenties, but had no identification. Found on the road near where she lay were a loaf of bread, two containers of milk, a package of cookies, and two bottles of Dr Pepper. Scattered among the groceries were a broken radio antenna, a windshield wiper, and flecks of red paint, believed to be from the suspect vehicle, along with a pair of headphones and a portable radio, which apparently belonged to the victim.

While the ground and grass off either side of the road were still moist from the day's rains, the road was relatively dry, and there were skid marks forty feet before and after the presumed point of impact, which was determined by a shoe scuff on the road. The victim apparently had her headphones on, was listening to music, and couldn't hear the vehicle coming from behind.

Police interviewed several people at the truck stop, which was a few hundred feet north of the accident. A clerk at a mini-market there said the woman had come into the store to purchase groceries around 12:30 A.M. It appeared that she was walking toward the Motel 6 when she was struck.

Employees and the few patrons at the Kettle restaurant, which was across the street between the accident scene and the truck stop, said they didn't see or hear anything, not even the sound of a car screeching to a stop. The eatery was close to where the victim was found, about fifty feet away.

When the victim arrived at Presbyterian Hospital she was moaning, calling out, "Daddy! Daddy!" Her extremities continued to move uncontrollably and her eyelids opened and closed, though not on command. The paramedics had tried to talk to her during the ride to the hospital, but she was unresponsive, with the exception of rubbing her forehead and grimacing on occasion.

At the hospital, she was given medication and the jerking motions stopped almost immediately. Soon she was resting quietly, and doctors removed her clothing and began their examination.

They gently pulled back each eyelid. Her pupils were dilated but unresponsive to light. She had several thin scratches and older, faded bruises on her torso. Similar contusions were found on her legs, arms, and head. Injuries from the accident were relegated to three spots, with fresh bruises on the back of each leg, about twenty inches high and just below the buttocks. A much larger hematoma was found at the vertex of the head. Judging by their conversation with the paramedics and where she was found on the street, the doctors surmised the car apparently hit her from behind, the bumper striking her legs and the impact forcing her to roll backward over the hood, tumbling onto the windshield and up and over the rear of the car. At some point, the back of her head was severely bruised.

Remarkably, she had no broken bones, major skin cuts, or any noticeable blood, a rare occurrence in a motor vehicle accident of this type.

She was listed in stable, but serious, condition.

The following morning, Clarence Marcus Hughes arrived at the hospital.

Clarence was the husband of the victim, whom he identified as Tonya Hughes, twenty-three years old. He was forty-one. He was of medium height, wore blue jeans and faded sneakers, and when he spoke he appeared to have a southern accent. Clarence told police that he, his wife, and their two-year-old son had traveled down I-44 from their home in Tulsa to Oklahoma City on Wednesday afternoon so Tonya could keep an appointment to see a gynecologist. They checked into the Motel 6 around 3 P.M.

Sometime after midnight Tonya decided to leave their room and walk down the road to the truck stop convenience store to pick up some groceries. She called fifteen minutes later from a pay phone in the store to say she couldn't find any baby food and would be returning with some milk and other items. Clarence said he then fell asleep and didn't learn of the accident until the morning when he drove down to the truck stop, inquired about his wife, and was told by a clerk that a woman fitting her description was found on the side of the road early in the morning and taken to the hospital. Clarence called the police, who met him at the motel. He told them that his wife was a professional stripper who danced at a club in Tulsa called Passions. He said she liked to meet men, and he was used to her being gone most of the night, so it didn't concern him that she hadn't returned to their motel room, even in a strange city.

Before leaving the hotel, police examined Clarence's dark blue Oldsmobile 88. The car had no damage and the radio antenna was intact.

The police brought Clarence to the hospital and into Tonya's room. He appeared unmoved at the sight of his young wife, who was lying still but breathing easily. Wires and thin tubes protruded from her body. Her blood pressure was still high, 155/105, but her other vital signs were stable.

She appeared to be in a very deep sleep but in fact was in a coma and unresponsive to any spoken commands, though she did mumble a few words, particularly "Daddy."

The major concern, said the doctor, was the hematoma on the back of her head. Her brain had been severely bruised and all anyone could do right then was wait. Given that her vital signs were stable, doctors expressed cautious optimism that she would, in fact, pull through over the next day or two.

Clarence stood still as the doctor delivered his report. He displayed little emotion, nor did he try to comfort his wife by touching her body or whispering something soothing and heartfelt into her ear. Instead, following the update on his wife's condition, Clarence politely asked the nurse for a pen, a notebook-sized piece of paper, and some clear tape. The nurse, somewhat puzzled, left the room but quickly returned with the items.

Clarence asked the doctor and nurse to leave, saying he wanted a moment or two alone with his wife.

When they returned several minutes later, Clarence was gone, but he had left a sign taped to the outside of the door.

It read, NO VISITORS.

CHAPTER 1

Forest Park, Georgia
November 1983

The wide halls of Forest Park High School were crammed with teenagers, all moving in slow motion as they bumped and grinded their way to class. It was late morning and, despite the sluggish pace, a buzz was in the air. The Thanksgiving holiday was fast approaching, and the impending week off gave the students something to look forward to after three straight months of school.

Teacher Terry Magaro tried to navigate through the human mass, politely calling out to students ahead that she was "coming through." Magaro was rushing to a scheduled 11 A.M. meeting in the guidance office and had but thirty seconds to find her way through the crowded hall, down a staircase to the first floor, and into the school's main office. Magaro had twenty years' experience and moved like a football halfback, darting back and forth through the congestion, finally making it to a stairwell. From there it was one flight down and into the guidance office.

Waiting for her were Warren Marshall and his fifteen-year-old daughter, Sharon. The Marshalls requested the meeting with Magaro following a recommendation from Linda Harris, a teacher at nearby Riverdale High School. Sharon had completed the first semester of her sophomore year at Riverdale, but was now considering a transfer to Forest Park. The Marshalls were eager to see the school and learn more about the advanced programs.

Sharon came into the meeting sporting an impressive IQ of 132 and a report card that featured mostly A's and a few B's. A math whiz, Sharon had scored perfect marks in geometry at Riverdale and in math classes at Baldwin High School the year before. Baldwin was in Milledgeville, about one hundred miles east of Atlanta, and served as Sharon's school for the spring semester after she transferred from Northside High School, which was on the northern fringes of Atlanta.

Magaro entered the office and offered an awkward apology to the Marshalls. Warren extended his hand and Magaro grabbed it and shook, continuing to apologize, blaming the long walk from the other side of the building for her tardiness. Magaro invited them to sit in two chairs directly in front of a wooden desk, behind which Magaro took her seat. She smiled as she scanned the father and daughter.

Warren was of medium height and build, with a pleasant but nondescript face. He looked to be fortyish. His hair was thin and scarce near the dome, but full and neatly trimmed around the ears and back of the neck. He wore a blue sport jacket over a white shirt and blue slacks. Across the front of his waist was a large silver belt buckle with the word *Painter.*

Sharon appeared to be just a couple of inches over five feet tall, with shoulder-length blond hair that curled inward toward the neck. Her magnetic blue eyes lured Magaro, who stared just a second or two longer than was comfortable. Sharon was dressed impeccably with a white sweater buttoned to the neck and dark blue skirt that fell just below the knees. Sharon smiled and only nodded when Magaro said hello during introductions. Sharon remained quiet, sitting with her back straight and hands folded neatly on her lap as her father thanked Magaro for the meeting and explained that he and his daughter wanted to see the school and meet some of the teachers before enrolling Sharon at Forest Park.

Warren's voice was distinctly southern, clear, and succinct. He voiced his displeasure with the quality of education at Riverdale, particularly the classes for advanced students.

"Sharon is a special student, very bright, and we want to make sure the quality of the advanced and gifted classes here at Forest Park are up to our standards," said Warren.

Magaro was pleased to tell Warren that Forest Park offered advanced classes in many subjects and also offered a variety of extracurricular activities that Sharon would find attractive. Warren was less interested in the after-school programs than he was in the advanced classes, which were offered in nearly every major subject at Forest Park.

As Magaro boasted of the benefits of Forest Park, Warren seemed pleased and his already friendly demeanor became downright giddy. He even pulled out one of his business cards.

"You ever need a painter, you give me a call," he said.

Magaro changed the subject, politely asking about Sharon's family life.

"Her mother died when Sharon was a child. I've raised her myself and I've done the best I could as a single dad. I think I've done a pretty good job," said Warren, leaning toward his daughter and smiling. "She's a good girl. We go to church on Sunday, she studies hard in school, and she takes care of her daddy."

Magaro was impressed with Warren's commitment to his daughter. She was sadly familiar with far too many fathers who were either absent in body or in mind, or both.

It was plainly clear that Mr. Marshall was different.

Sharon was quiet through the meeting and remained that way when Magaro turned and asked what questions she had. Sharon didn't reply. Instead she focused her pretty blue eyes on her father, who laughed loudly, saying he had already asked the important questions and he liked what he was hearing.

"This school seems like a good fit for Sharon!" he bellowed. "I believe she'll do very well here!"

Magaro agreed, acknowledging that Sharon's previous semester at Riverdale was indeed impressive, given her high marks. Magaro failed to notice that Sharon was about to register into her fourth high school in twelve months.

"Forest Park is a fine school, Mr. Marshall, and I'm certain that both you and especially your daughter will be happy with what we have to offer," said Magaro.

Warren rose from his seat, and Sharon followed.

"I believe we will be very happy here," said Warren, looking down at his daughter. "Don't you agree?"

Sharon looked up, smiled, and nodded.

They walked toward the door, and Warren thanked Magaro for the meeting.

"We'll be making our decision on the transfer in a day or so," he said.

Magaro said good-bye to Sharon, who smiled in return, but left the room without saying a single word.

The next day Sharon Marshall enrolled as a student at Forest Park High School.

The sizzling Georgia sun bore down hard on the dozens of teenagers waiting in line to enter the Grand Ballroom of the Krannert Center on the campus of Berry College.

It was Sunday, July 15, 1984, and the high school students were at the college campus in Rome, Georgia, for a summer leadership workshop. Throughout Georgia, students from freshman to senior classes elected their own council, and the representatives from the dozens of schools assembled each summer for a weeklong seminar prior to the new school year. The seminar was regimented, with classes entitled "Things You Need to Know," "Parliamentary Procedure," and "Group Dynamics." Each day started early with breakfast at 7:30 A.M. and ended late, around 11 P.M.

Jennifer Fisher from Stone Mountain, Georgia, was among those standing in line. Stone Mountain was a suburb northeast of Atlanta, and Jennifer was entering her freshman year at Tucker High School. Six weeks earlier, as her junior high school year came to a close, she was elected to serve on the freshman student council.

The students were each handed a pencil and sheet of paper entitled "A Fun Thing," and the first order of business on their first day was to make new friends. Underneath the title were directions for each student to "Find a person (not from your town) who fits the descriptions below and have them write their name on the line opposite their attribute. Do not use the same person more than once. GO!!!!!"

Each student was expected to pick someone out of the crowd to sign next to the description that fit them best. There were forty-seven descriptions in all, which varied from "lives at least one hundred miles from you" to "with glasses" to "wearing a Timex watch."

Jennifer was friendly, but like most teens her age she was short on confidence and self-esteem. With brown hair that curled down the sides to her neck, Jennifer's features were pleasant in a way that announced a certain sweetness. But as she stood on line with hundreds of other students, most of them older, Jennifer felt a tinge of nervousness. She entered the ballroom, looked down at the paper, and saw a description for a "preppie dresser—boy." She spotted a skinny teen wearing a crisp polo shirt and clean jeans.

"Hi, I'm Jennifer. Think you can sign for me?"

The boy smiled, looked down, and scribbled in "Kevin."

"Thanks," said Jennifer, her confidence rising as she scoured the room for more signatures. After twenty minutes, thirty-two people had signed her sheet. Most were brief introductions, but the contact was somewhat awkward and uncomfortable, the conversation forced. This was her first student council camp, and she hoped to meet someone, really anyone, to engage in conversation. Looking out over the ballroom floor she let out a deep sigh as other students appeared to be talking and laughing, then she felt a tap on her shoulder.

"Hi, I'm Sharon. Do you think you can sign my sheet?" she said.

Sharon had the bluest of eyes and perhaps the nicest smile Jennifer had ever seen. She was the same height, just a wisp above five feet, and she was thin and attractive, even model-like.

"Sure," said Jennifer, signing the line that read "is 5' 2"—eyes of blue."

"Can you sign mine?" she said.

Sharon took the paper and signed line number 29, "planning to attend college."

Jennifer looked at the signature. Sharon's last name was Marshall.

"What college do you want to go to?" she said.

"Georgia Tech," said Sharon. "I'm going to be an aerospace engineer and work for NASA."

Jennifer was impressed.

The two girls started talking, and as the signature exercise came to an end twenty minutes later, they were still standing where they had met, giggling, laughing, and talking away as if they had known each other since birth. Their conversation focused on various subjects, from school to boys to their families. Jennifer's father was a pilot for Eastern Airlines, her mother a housewife. Jennifer had an older brother, Butch, and a younger sister, Susan.

Sharon was an only child. Her mother had died when she was seven, killed in a hit-and-run accident. Her father, Warren, was a painter. She said she attended Forest Park High School and had finished the school year with A's in each of her six subjects. She had entered Forest Park midyear, but had caught on quickly, was popular among her classmates, and by May had been elected to serve on the junior student council.

Walking out of the ballroom, they decided to attend the next class together, and as the week wore on, Sharon and Jennifer were inseparable, meeting for breakfast, going to workshops together, meeting again for dinner, and remaining with each other through evening activities. One night they joined a group making a human pyramid, and they all laughed hard when the teenage pile fell to the ground.

By the end of the week, on a sunny Friday morning when it was time to say good-bye, the two girls stood near a bank of vans and cars ready to take the students back to their respective schools.

They hugged each other and began to cry, thinking perhaps this would be the last time they would see each other. They didn't want to let go of the bond that had formed.

"Sharon, give me your phone number and I'll call you. You can come visit me at my house," said Jennifer, wiping away the tears from her cheek.

Sharon paused a moment.

"I can't give out my home number. I'm not allowed to," she said.

"Your father won't let you give out your phone number?" said Jennifer, somewhat surprised.

"Well, it's just . . . I just can't give it out," said Sharon, who appeared to be uncomfortable. Jennifer moved quickly to help her new best friend. She reached into her bag and pulled out a pen and small piece of paper, wrote down her phone number, and instructed Sharon to call her.

The smile returned to Sharon's face, and the two girls hugged, holding on tight for several more seconds.

Sharon watched as Jennifer boarded her van.

"You make sure you call me, OK?" said Jennifer.

"I will," said Sharon, waving good-bye. "See you."

Nearly a week had passed since Jennifer returned home to Stone Mountain from the student council camp, and she had yet to hear from her new friend, Sharon Marshall. Jennifer couldn't stop talking about Sharon, telling her parents how well they got along together and how they laughed and talked and laughed and talked. Sharon was pretty and outgoing and had a sense of confidence Jennifer admired. Sharon seemed so sure of herself in many ways, a rarity for a teenager, and Jennifer was certain that a friendship had blossomed between two young girls on a college campus far from home.

Jennifer hoped she'd get a call the day she returned home, or over the weekend at the latest, and became more disappointed with each passing day and still no call from Sharon. Jennifer thought she'd found a friend, a close friend. Maybe Sharon had lost her number? Jennifer decided something wasn't right, and if Sharon wasn't going to call her, she'd call Sharon.

After dinner Jennifer went upstairs to her brother's bedroom and closed the door. For some reason her older brother had a phone in his room, which was a cause of some friction between Jennifer and her parents. She fingered through the paperwork she took home from the student council camp and pulled out the directory, which listed students' names and, to Jennifer's relief, their phone numbers. She followed down the list of names to M and found Sharon Marshall, whose number was listed. Jennifer eagerly picked up the phone and dialed.

After two rings someone answered, "Hello?"

Jennifer instantly recognized the voice, and shot out "Sharon, it's Jenny from student council camp!"

Jennifer was thrilled. She had found her friend.

Sharon, though, seemed less than pleased.

"Jennifer? How did you get my number?" said Sharon, who spoke softly but clearly sounded disappointed, if not angry.

This wasn't the reaction Jennifer expected. She was thrilled to find Sharon's number and was ready to tell her how she missed her new friend. But Sharon didn't sound happy to hear from Jennifer. Instead, she sounded odd.

"I went through the student council directory. Your number was there. Are you all right?"

"You weren't supposed to call," said Sharon. "My number is not supposed to be listed, and you weren't supposed to call."

Sharon's voice now had a nervous shrill to it. This wasn't the confident, happy girl that Jennifer had met at student council camp.

"Sharon, are you OK? Is anything wrong?"

Sharon didn't answer, but Jennifer could hear a voice in the background, an older, male voice, screaming loudly, with Sharon giving panicky responses.

"Who is that on the phone?"

"It's a friend, Daddy. A girl I met at camp last week."

"How did she get this number!"

"I don't know Daddy, I don't know. I didn't give it to her. I didn't give it to her. I'm sorry, I'm sorry."

Jennifer heard what sounded like quick and heavy footsteps, then the phone being handled and slammed down on its cradle. Jennifer was startled. She stood there for several seconds, unsure of what had just occurred, then put the phone down and slowly walked downstairs to the kitchen, still trying to figure out what had just happened.

Five minutes passed when the kitchen phone rang. It was Sharon, and she sounded calmer, apologizing for what had happened earlier.

"My father was upset. I'm not allowed to give my number out. He didn't understand where you found our number, but I'm glad you called me," said Sharon.

Jennifer quickly forgot the previous exchange, and for the next hour the two girls chatted away, the weirdness from the first call vanishing quickly as the girls picked up where they'd left off at camp.

They talked about their week, and boys, which would become a favorite topic. Over the next two years they would spend half their conversations talking about boys: movie stars, teen idols, boys in school, athletes, whomever. If it had anything to do with a boy, they talked about it.

At the end of the conversation they agreed to talk again the next day at the same time, and Jennifer made the call. This time a male voice answered the phone. It was Sharon's father.

He introduced himself as Warren and, despite the yelling she'd heard the night before, Jennifer decided he actually sounded nice.

"I've heard so much about you, I can't wait to meet you," he said. "You have to come over and stay a night at our home."

Jennifer was thrilled with the invitation. Things were fine now. The two friends could talk, which they did nearly every night for the next month.

By the middle of August and a week before the start of a new school year, Jennifer received permission from her parents to invite Sharon to spend a night at the Fisher home. All Joel and Sue Fisher had heard Jennifer talk about lately was her new friend, and her parents were intrigued.

The invitation was extended, and Sharon Marshall arrived on a Saturday morning, standing in the driveway, gawking at the four-bedroom Tudor home set on a finely landscaped property.

"Oh my God! It's huge!" yelled Sharon as Jennifer bounced out the front door to greet her friend. They hugged and smiled and giggled. Standing behind Sharon was her father, Warren, who was as impressed with the Fisher home as his daughter. The house was set on a wooded acre and a half, had a two-car garage and matching toolshed. Warren parked his muddied pickup truck in the driveway, behind the Mercedes 75 300D that belonged to Jennifer's mother. On the front bumper of Warren's car was a sticker that proclaimed, HE WHO DIES WITH THE MOST TOYS WINS.

"My daddy wants to meet your parents, OK?" said Sharon, whispering into Jennifer's ear.

"That's fine," she answered.

Sharon turned around to her father.

"Daddy, this is Jennifer," she said, pointing to her friend and smiling proudly.

"Hello, Jennifer," said Warren. "I'm really happy to finally meet you."

Warren had a pencil-thin mustache and was slightly bald with short, dark hair on the sides. He wore blue jeans, sneakers, and a red St. Louis Cardinals baseball T-shirt. Jennifer returned the greeting and invited Sharon and Warren inside, where she introduced them to her parents.

"And this is Sharon," said Jennifer, proudly.

Mrs. Fisher gave Sharon a hug and commented on her clothing, a matching summer shirt and short pants outfit with short white socks and white sneakers so clean they appeared to be new.

Warren shook Joel Fisher's hand.

"You have a beautiful home here," said Warren, who told the Fishers that he was a painter and wouldn't mind painting some of the homes in this neighborhood.

"A guy like me could do very well around here," said Warren, reaching into the back pocket of his pants and pulling out his wallet.

"Here," he said, giving a business card to Joel.

It read MARSHALL PAINTING SERVICE in black letters near the bottom. Underneath, in smaller typeface, *Interior. Exterior. Residential. Commercial. Sober. Dependable. Trustworthy.*

"If you ever need any work or know anyone who is looking for a painter, I'm the man," said Warren, laughing out loud.

Joel took the card and slipped it into his shirt pocket. Warren said he'd pick up Sharon the next morning, said good-bye, walked to his truck, and drove away.

Sue and Jennifer took Sharon through their home, and Sharon's head darted up and down and from side to side, taking in all the elegant furnishings and colorful accents. Between the "oohs and ahs," Sharon whispered, "Wow!" into Jennifer's ear. Sharon was respectful toward Jennifer's parents, and proudly told them of her success in school and her dream of going to college. The Fishers were particularly impressed with Sharon's desire to study aerospace engineering, not to mention her bubbly personality. Sharon was electric, and the Fishers were drawn into her bright light, pleased that their daughter had found such a fine friend. Perhaps, they thought, some of her youthful idealism and determination would rub off on their own daughter.

Following lunch, Sue drove Jennifer and Sharon to the nearby Northlake Mall in Tucker. It was a gathering place for teenagers and the two girls spent the afternoon ogling nearly every boy who passed them by. In one instance Sharon stopped, grabbed Jennifer's arm, and said, "Oh my God, that guy is sooooo good looking!" She pointed to a boy who was standing about twenty feet away.

Jennifer looked at the boy, then leaned into Sharon's ear.

"Sharon, that's a girl."

Sharon giggled. "Are you sure?"

"Yeah, that's a girl."

"Wow!" said Sharon, who explained that she was near-sighted and didn't like wearing her glasses. She wanted contacts, but her father couldn't afford them, so from time to time she'd make some silly mistake, like seeing a girl for a boy.

The two girls laughed and joked about it as they continued their slow walk around the mall. They returned to the Fisher home at 5 P.M. and were greeted with a barbecue chicken dinner. Sharon easily joined the conversation and helped clean up afterward.

Following dinner the girls went up to Jennifer's room, changed into their pajamas, and soon realized that they'd spent half the night talking. Jennifer couldn't stop talking about boys. Sharon extended the conversation to other subjects, such as books, college, and careers.

Sharon liked to read Shakespeare and loved *Romeo and Juliet*. They decided to play out a scene, and Jennifer turned red with embarrassment. Sharon was actually good.

"Romeo, oh Romeo," said Sharon, who wrapped herself in a sheet but couldn't help but giggle at her poor English accent. Jennifer was enthralled. She had never known anyone her own age whose interests included Shakespeare and poets and philosophers.

She was glad she'd met Sharon Marshall.

Warren returned the following morning and offered a loud "hello!" Sue offered him a cup of coffee, which Warren readily accepted.

He asked Joel if he'd had a chance to ask around for any painting jobs.

Joel said no, reminding Warren that they'd just met the day before.

"Well, when you ask around, you tell your friends that I've been painting for over twenty years. Not gonna get anyone better than me," said Warren, who turned toward Sue. "And ma'am, you make some very good coffee."

Sharon returned to the Fisher home two weeks later, with Jennifer sporting a wide smile as she answered the door. Upon entering the house, Warren politely asked if he could speak with Jennifer's father.

"Is he home? I have some business I'd like to discuss with him," said Warren.

Jennifer called out for her parents, yelling out that the Marshalls had arrived and that Mr. Marshall wanted to talk to Dad. Joel and Sue walked in together from the kitchen, and Joel took Warren aside into the living room. Jennifer turned to Sharon and asked what was going on, but Sharon shrugged her shoulders, said she had no idea, and the girls ran upstairs to Jennifer's room.

The two men emerged some ten minutes later, and Warren said he'd be back to pick up Sharon the next morning, leaving Joel Fisher standing alone and shaking his head.

"What was that about?" said Sue, joining him.

"He wanted to borrow some money," said Joel. "He said he's doing some big painting job in the neighborhood but didn't have the money to buy the paint and supplies."

Joel turned down the request, even after Warren pleaded, saying he was desperate.

The request caught the Fishers off guard. It also left them confused. They had grown fond of Sharon Marshall in the short time they had come to know her. Her father seemed friendly and had produced a wonderful daughter. Sue suggested that perhaps Warren was in dire straits. After all, she said, he was a single parent.

CHAPTER 2

The new school year proved difficult for Jennifer Fisher, who struggled through most of her classes while trying to resume friendships with classmates from her previous year. The schoolwork was hard enough, reconnecting with old friends even harder. Sharon Marshall had become a positive force in her life, and with every phone call from Sharon, Jennifer's spirits peaked. Her good humor did not go unnoticed by her parents, who were happy to learn that Sharon would be visiting their home again.

When Sharon arrived in late September, she hugged Mr. and Mrs. Fisher, then joined Jennifer upstairs in her bedroom. Warren followed Sharon inside, offered his usual hearty hello, and then asked Joel if they could talk. Sue watched as the two men went into the kitchen, where Warren once again asked for a loan. He needed three hundred dollars and sounded like a used car salesman trying to close a deal. Again, Joel wouldn't budge, said no, and escorted Warren into the living room where he smiled weakly toward Sue, trying hard to mask his disappointment. He reached behind his back with his right arm and squeezed on his waist area and grimaced as if he were in dire pain.

"I've got a really bad back from a motorcycle accident a couple of years ago," he said. "I was on the bike and some guy hit me from behind and then took off. Caused all kinds of problems for me. I need physical therapy and money for a shrink, but the state won't help me. Can you believe that? I'm in pain and the state won't give me the money I need to get better."

Warren shook his head, then said he'd be nearby cruising through the upscale neighborhood, dropping off business cards and soliciting paint jobs.

"I'll be back later this afternoon for Sharon," he said.

Warren's financial problems notwithstanding, the Fishers adored Sharon, particularly Sue, who became deeply attached. It broke Sue's heart that Sharon had grown up without a mother. It was also clear to Sue that Sharon needed mothering, and her maternal instincts were always triggered during Sharon's visits. During one conversation as Sue was preparing lunch, Sharon eyed a plate of fresh broccoli.

"I never had this," said Sharon.

Within minutes, Sharon devoured the broccoli, stems and all.

"That was one of the most delicious things I've ever eaten," she declared.

Sue also noticed Sharon had a propensity for mood changes, particularly during the rare occasions when she talked about her father. Discussing Warren provoked nervousness and a slight stutter. Sharon would fold her hands together and squeeze. Sue didn't know what to make of it but didn't pry. Warren appeared careful with Sharon, and it was clear he was a disciplinarian. Given the Fisher's deep feelings for Sharon, Warren was tolerated, though Joel made it perfectly clear that under no circumstances would he ever allow Jennifer to spend a night at the Marshall home.

The invitation was extended in November, and Jennifer, excited about the possibility, received the bad news as soon as she asked her parents. A day later, after her father left town for a three-day tour, Jennifer begged her mother to let her spend the night at Sharon's house.

Sue Fisher gave in and, on a Saturday afternoon, drove nearly an hour from Stone Mountain through Atlanta to Forest Park. When they turned onto the Marshall's street, Sue was not pleased. The neighborhood was run-down, filled with small, ranch-style homes nearly all in need of fresh paint. Late-model pickup trucks were parked in short driveways, and toys and garbage littered the street. The Fishers were conspicuous in Sue's brown Mercedes, driving slowly toward the end of the dead-end block. The Marshalls lived in the last house on the right, the one in need of a landscaper, with weeds sprouting all around.

Sharon spotted the Mercedes as it pulled up her short driveway, and she flew out of the house with Warren not far behind.

Jennifer jumped out and the two girls embraced. Sue remained in the car, rolling down her window to say hello, then quickly backing out of the driveway as Warren yelled out, "Don't worry, we'll take care of her."

Jennifer was led inside the house, which seemed even smaller compared to the view from the road. Straight ahead against the wall was an old sofa beneath a shelf with several photos, including one worn, color photo of a woman.

"That's my mother," said Sharon. "Her name was Linda."

Sharon's mother had long dark hair, but the photo was somewhat blurry, making it hard to focus on her features.

Still, Jennifer blurted out that she thought Sharon's mother was beautiful.

"You must miss her," said Jennifer.

"Yes. I think about her a lot. But Daddy's taken good care of me," said Sharon, who continued the tour.

To the left was a small eat-in kitchen. To the right was a short hallway that led to Warren's room. Jennifer peeked inside and spotted dozens of black videotapes, one on top of another, lined up in rows against the wall. Warren was out of sight, but his arm reached out across the doorway and pulled the curtain, which served as a door. To the left was another room, but Sharon warned Jennifer not to go in there.

"No one is allowed in that room," whispered Sharon.

Jennifer didn't ask why as she was led into Sharon's room, which took up the right corner of the house. The room was as Jennifer had imagined, filled with plenty of fluffy stuffed animals, several porcelain figurines, dolls, and brown teddy bears set on shelves.

Jennifer also noticed all the novels, magazines, and dozens of copies of *Reader's Digest*.

"You must read a lot," said Jennifer.

"I *love* to read," said Sharon. "I just lose myself and imagine I'm part of the story or in some distant part of the world."

As she studied the room, it occurred to Jennifer that Sharon did not have a door. Instead she had a long curtain that hung in the doorway. None of the rooms in the house had doors, just curtains. It seemed odd, but Jennifer figured that Warren couldn't afford doors. She had heard her parents whispering one night about Warren asking for money or something.

Warren reappeared and announced that he was taking the girls to dinner. They jumped into Warren's pickup for the ten-minute drive to the Piccadilly restaurant. Jennifer sat in the middle, with Sharon to her right by the window.

They made small talk; Warren made a point of telling Jennifer she was attractive.

"You know, you're soooo pretty. Just like Sharon," he said.

Although somewhat embarrassed, Jennifer didn't mind the compliment. As they neared the restaurant, the girls told jokes, and everyone laughed harder when Sharon began to mimic her father.

"Oh, my back, my back hurts so bad!" said Sharon.

Warren enjoyed the moment, then announced he had a brilliant idea.

"Why don't we drive down to Peachtree Street and make fun of the prostitutes," he said.

"Dad, the prostitutes don't work there anymore. They're on Stuart Street," said Sharon. "And I don't really want to do that, Daddy. Why don't we just go eat?"

Warren agreed, but said he first had to stop for gas. He pulled into a service station, stopped the truck by the pump, and turned up the volume to the radio, which spouted out the first few chords of "Iron Man" by Black Sabbath. He opened the truck door, walked over to the gas pump, and filled up his truck, singing along with Ozzy Osbourne.

Sharon and Jennifer joined in the chorus, and they all clapped when the song ended. Queen's "Bohemian Rhapsody" came over the air as Warren turned the key to start the engine. The song was unfamiliar to Warren, but the girls sang in unison.

They enjoyed quiet conversation during dinner over chicken, mashed potatoes, corn bread, and vegetables. For dessert there were chocolate cake and ice cream to round out the meal. Warren paid the check. As they drove away from the restaurant, with the orange glow of dusk fading on the horizon, Warren announced he had another great idea.

"How about I take you girls dancing?"

The girls shrieked. "Dancing? Tonight? Wow!"

Jennifer was only fourteen years old and had never even thought of setting foot in a dance club. She was underage, and it was something her parents would never allow. She also didn't have any clothes to wear.

"What would I wear?" she said.

Warren calmed her fears. Sharon had plenty of suitable outfits at home, and he was sure she had something that would fit Jennifer.

They drove back to the Marshall house and the girls ran into Sharon's room, giggling as they rummaged through Sharon's dresser drawers. Jennifer was excited, so excited she didn't notice the lingerie, the nightgowns, the string bikini underwear and the crotchless panties that filled the dresser.

Sharon then went into her closet and pulled out a pink minidress with black tiger stripes. It was outrageous. And Jennifer loved it.

Warren walked by the room and Sharon held the outfit up high.

"What do you think, Daddy?"

"Yeah, you should put Jennifer in that nice pink and black dress," said Warren approvingly.

Sharon decided she'd wear an off-the-shoulder shirt and miniskirt. They combed their hair, put on lots of makeup, and announced to Warren they were ready to go—two young teens out for a night on the town.

"Boy, you ladies are something to see!" he exclaimed.

When they arrived at the club, the first thing Jennifer noticed was that it didn't look like a dance club. It looked more like some seedy redneck bar. Warren walked the girls to the front door, where they were met by a bouncer who was checking identification. It was clear they were underage, but Warren leaned over and whispered into the bouncer's ear, then turned to the girls.

"OK, let's go," he said as he ushered them into the club.

Inside it was dark, the only light coming from the bar to the right, and the reflections coming from the large, silver disco ball that hung over the small dance floor.

Warren walked them to the middle of the bar, then turned to leave.

"Ok, you girls have a good time. I'll be back later."

Jennifer was confused. "You're not staying with us?"

"Hell no, honey. You and Sharon have fun!" said Warren, who left them standing on the small dance floor.

Jennifer stood awkwardly, unsure of what to do. Sharon didn't waste any time and began moving her hips and waving her hand at Jennifer to follow her motions, and the girls started to dance. They remained there the rest of the night, dancing to the throbbing music. Jennifer had danced before, but at home, in her bedroom, alone. She was unsure of her movements and kept her eyes focused on Sharon, who moved easily with the music, her hips gyrating back and forth, her arms raised high. Sharon wasn't just good; she was sexy. Most of the men in the bar had noticed, and some of them had come onto the floor to dance with Sharon. They were much older, well into their thirties and forties, some with scruffy beards and bad body odor. All were poorly dressed, wearing faded jeans and T-shirts.

Jennifer was simply terrified at the prospect of dancing with a man as old as her father. Sharon made it clear she wasn't interested in dancing with anyone other than Jennifer and waved the men away.

Warren returned at midnight and informed the girls the night was over.

During the ride back to Sharon's house, Jennifer couldn't

help herself, blurting out what a good time she'd had, and how cool it was that Warren would take them dancing.

"I know what you girls like," said Warren.

When they got home, the girls went into Sharon's room. Warren stuck his head through the curtain, telling them to get ready for bed.

Sharon opened her dresser drawer and this time Jennifer noticed all the pretty and sexy lingerie.

"Where did you get this stuff?"

"My daddy lets me have this. He even buys it for me," said Sharon.

"Sharon," said Jennifer, "you have the greatest dad."

Changing out of their sweaty clothes and still high from a night of dancing, the girls laughed hysterically as they recalled the awkward attempts by some of the men in the bar to dance with them, and laughed even louder at how Sharon ignored them.

Jennifer was still giggling, pulling her nightgown over her head, when Warren barged into the room screaming, his face contorted in a monstrous glare.

Jennifer didn't hear what he was saying. She couldn't. She felt faint. Feelings of exultation and joy were replaced in an instant by fear and terror. She noticed the gun in Warren's hand, then looked over to Sharon, who stood naked from the waist up, wearing only white panties and blue, frilly socks. Sharon was trembling, staring at the floor and holding her hands together as her eyes welled with tears. Questions raced through Jennifer's mind: "What's going on? Can this be happening?"

CHAPTER 3

When the 1984 fall semester ended, Sharon Marshall earned near perfect marks, though she was disappointed with her first attempt at the college boards, or Scholastic Aptitude Test, on which she scored a respectable 1120 out of 1600. Her performance was good, but Sharon thought she'd failed miserably and could do much better. She planned to take the test again in June.

Along with her heavy course load, which included advanced classes in math and science, Sharon took part in a variety of extracurricular activities, including the Air Force ROTC and serving as secretary for the junior prom committee. The previous year, after finishing the spring semester with perfect marks in six classes, which included advanced literature, geometry, and the World Wars, Sharon also held a similarly heavy extracurricular schedule. Among the groups she joined were the Future Business Leaders of America club and the Math and Computer clubs.

For her junior year, Sharon dropped the Math Club but

remained with the Future Business Leaders and added the Strategic Gaming Society, the ROTC, the ROTC Rocket Club, and junior prom committee.

Sharon was popular in school, evident by her election to the student council. She was approachable and could chat with just about anyone, teacher or student. She rarely missed a class, always caught on quickly, never daydreamed, and remained focused on her teachers, class work, and after-school activities, particularly the ROTC. Of the sixteen hundred students enrolled at Forest Park, some two hundred students, from ninth to twelfth grade, participated in ROTC. Students were taught discipline, respect for the flag and country, ethics, and moral leadership. Every Tuesday ROTC cadets were required to wear their standard-issue blue Air Force uniform to school, neatly pressed with earned ribbons placed properly on the left lapel. Students were graded each week for their appearance.

As she did with all her other pursuits, Sharon excelled at ROTC, quickly rising to the top rank of lieutenant colonel. She impressed Earle Lewis, the ROTC instructor, with her leadership and intelligence, a rare combination, and she could drill the cadets, which meant forcing them to submit to her will. Sharon was self-motivated and barked out orders better than any of the boys when she presided over the weekly drills and drill meets with other schools.

Warren would even attend the drill meets, and took pride in Sharon's ability to lead the troops.

Popular and well-liked as Sharon was, some teachers at Forest Park noticed some unusual behavior.

No matter where she was or what she was doing, Sharon dropped everything to be home by 4:30 P.M. to clean the house and cook for her father. If something important came up and Sharon was asked to stay a few minutes longer, she'd decline.

And teachers such as Carol Worley noticed Sharon's clothing. Aside from that one day a week when Sharon was required to wear her Air Force ROTC uniform, she'd often dress in loud shirts and short skirts that suggested something more tacky and even provocative. And the colors wouldn't match. It was as if someone else short on fashion sense were dressing her. Worley and other teachers also discussed the fact that Sharon didn't appear to have any close friends at Forest Park. She was friendly and would always be seen chatting with someone, but never the same person day after day. And in casual discussions with other students, the teachers learned that not one person had ever been invited to the Marshall home or had ever seen her father.

Aside from his first meeting with Terry Magaro and attending a single parent-teacher meeting and several ROTC drill meets, Warren Marshall was a virtual ghost. The consensus among the faculty was that Warren didn't have any additional time for school functions. He was a single parent who worked as a painter. Given Sharon's performance in school, Warren was admired for his devotion to his daughter. Yet some thought he was too strict. And there was that one inconsistency concerning the death of Sharon's mother. During that one parent-teacher meeting he attended, Warren relayed that his wife had died of cancer. Terry Magaro recalled that he once said she'd died in a car accident, something Sharon validated on a number of occasions. The discrepancy didn't cause a stir. Everyone figured it was the Marshall's business, and if they wanted to set the record straight about Sharon's mother, then let them do it. With so many mixed-up kids and their dysfunctional families stressing already overburdened teachers at Forest Park, Sharon was the least of their worries.

While Sharon excelled, her friend Jennifer Fisher continued to be plagued with problems in school and by bouts of depression. Her parents often used Sharon as a role model, telling their daughter to emulate her friend, who pushed Jennifer hard to improve her grades.

"You're just not trying hard enough," was Sharon's typical lament to Jennifer.

During sleepovers at the Fisher home, Sharon engaged Jennifer in conversations that went beyond the usual mindless teenage fare, touching on everything from religion to politics. Sharon loved intellectual conversations—some of which Jennifer found too deep to understand or keep her interest. So Sharon would save the topical discussions for Jennifer's parents, particularly her mother, Sue.

One subject Sharon would never broach, however, was her personal life. Whenever Sue or Jennifer would ask a question about her past or her father, Sharon quickly changed the subject. On rare occasions Sharon would let something slip, such as when she told Jennifer that she had to massage her father every night to soothe his arthritis. But those insights were few and far between, particularly when they spoke on the phone. Sharon was far more restrained and kept the conversations centered strictly on school, boys, and other things that interested teenage girls. As Sharon spoke, Jennifer could always hear Warren close by, as if he were sitting next to his daughter monitoring the conversation. On occasion Warren would join in. Once Warren grabbed the phone to offer his commentary as Sharon and Jennifer talked about music. Sharon loved Pat Benatar and Prince, and knew by heart the lyrics to "Little Red Corvette" and "When Doves Cry." Warren favored hard rock.

"Iron Maiden and Black Sabbath. You can't go wrong with them, Jennifer," Warren said before giving the phone back to Sharon.

By Christmas, Jennifer knew to call Sharon during the late afternoon hours, before Warren returned home from work. She also knew never to accept another invitation to sleep over at the Marshall home. Sharon understood why, but Warren kept pushing the issue, especially during the holiday season. Instead, Jennifer extended an invitation for Sharon to stay at her home, and when she arrived that week before Christmas Day, Sharon came with gifts in hand.

Each present was carefully and colorfully wrapped. Sue was delighted with her thermos and teapot, and Jennifer loved her sweater. Sharon was proud of the gifts. They were inexpensive but heartfelt. Clearly, Sharon loved to give, and the Fishers enjoyed being on the receiving end, feeling the utter warmth and goodness in Sharon, who in turn was thrilled with their warm reaction. They shared hugs all around and wished one another a Merry Christmas.

Spring had arrived in 1985, and the Fisher family had just returned home from a trip to the mall. It was a Saturday, and the short family shopping trip was a chance to do something together, given that Joel was home for the weekend. As they pulled up to their home, Warren Marshall's pickup truck was in the driveway.

"I thought Sharon wasn't visiting this weekend?" said Sue.

"She's not supposed to," shrieked Jennifer, who was nonetheless thrilled with the unexpected visit.

They pulled up to the side of the truck and Jennifer looked toward the front door of the house, but Sharon wasn't there. Neither was Warren.

"Maybe they went for a walk," said Sue.

They grabbed their shopping bags, opened the front door, and were startled to see Warren curled up on the living room sofa, apparently sleeping. Off to the side, sitting in the Queen Anne chair, was Sharon. She was looking down at the floor and crying, rubbing her hands together.

Before anyone could say anything, Warren opened his eyes and casually picked himself up off the sofa.

"My damn back. We came to visit and I had to sit down. The garage door was open, so we let ourselves in your house."

Jennifer called out to Sharon to follow her upstairs. Warren remained seated on the sofa, talking about his back and inability to obtain medical help.

"Those damned doctors won't help me. I'm in such pain. I can't work; I can't get anything done!"

Warren spewed on for several minutes about his back and his overall misfortune, then finally stood up but continued his diatribe.

Joel was furious, but kept his anger in check. Given the Fishers' fondness for Sharon, they didn't want to say anything harsh to her father. Warren finally stopped complaining about his back and said he'd return later in the afternoon to pick up Sharon. He walked out the front door and drove away.

Neither Joel nor Sue had a clue as to how Warren and Sharon had entered the house without a key. The garage door was closed and the house alarm was on, or so Joel thought.

The Fishers walked through the entire house and were satisfied that nothing was missing. Perhaps Warren was telling the truth, that he needed to lie down to relieve his aching back. Whatever the reason, they were convinced that there was something wrong with Warren Marshall.

CHAPTER 4

Sharon Marshall took the SAT again in June 1985 and this time scored a 1230, more than good enough for acceptance into most colleges. Add in her sterling grades, and Sharon could practically choose the college of her choice.

Yet only one school was on her list—Georgia Tech.

Her lofty grades and participation in numerous extracurricular activities, including the Future Business Leaders, Science Club, Math and Computer clubs, ROTC, the ROTC Drill Team, and the Cadet Honor Society, earned her one important honor: inclusion in the *Who's Who Among American High School Students of 1985*.

It was a successful year for Sharon, who even found time for a boyfriend.

His name was Jason Anderson, a fellow junior at Forest Park. Jason was a big, strapping, blond-haired boy who played on the varsity football team. A poor student with a penchant for getting into trouble, teachers and students at Forest Park didn't quite understand the match between the brilliant, beautiful, college-bound girl and the trouble-prone jock.

Sharon's relationship with Jason diminished the time spent with Jennifer, though the two would still talk on the phone once or twice a week, usually discussing details of Sharon's dates. But the stories Sharon told Jennifer varied from what the students at Forest Park High School were hearing.

Word had spread quickly how Sharon and Jason were always accompanied by Sharon's father. Jason didn't seem to mind at first, especially after Sharon explained that her father was a lonely widower and she hated to leave him by himself. Still, students couldn't help but talk about the strange situation, how Warren would follow the couple to the movies or to the diner.

Luckily, Warren didn't accompany Sharon to her junior prom, though she almost got tossed off the committee in the weeks preceding the event. Sharon would bolt from committee meetings at 4 P.M. to be home in time to complete her house chores, but to remain on the committee and earn the class credit, she had to put in the same time and effort as the other students.

Mrs. Worley, the teacher advisor, pulled Sharon aside one afternoon and said as much.

"You don't understand. I have to be home. My father is not well and needs my help," explained Sharon. "There's nothing I can do."

Mrs. Worley gave in, but regretted her decision the night of the junior prom, when Sharon somehow managed to sneak outside to Jason's car in the parking lot. When they walked through the front door fifteen minutes later, they brushed by Mrs. Worley. Sharon's purple, ankle length dress was crumpled, her hair in disarray. Jason's tuxedo shirt was untucked and hanging outside his black pants.

Mrs. Worley looked on disapprovingly. She was surprised

at Sharon, but there was little she could do other than shake her head and whisper under her breath, "teenagers."

Sharon's relationship with Jason ended a month later and by mid-summer, she was spending more time with Jennifer and the Fisher family. Heading into her senior year, Sharon was focused on one goal—acceptance to Georgia Tech.

Jennifer entered her sophomore year in total lockdown. She'd had a disappointing freshman year, continuing to struggle with her studies, and her parents had had enough. She was barred from hanging out at the mall or Stone Mountain Lake. They even limited Sharon's visits.

The two friends continued to talk on the phone. While Sharon was upbeat and supportive, especially after completing her application to Georgia Tech, Jennifer fell into a depression that carried through the fall. She was trying to find her place in the world; Sharon prepared for a life filled with so much promise.

The phone rang in the Fisher home late one afternoon in March of 1986, and when Jennifer picked it up and said hello, all she could hear was screaming.

"I got it! I got it! I got into Georgia Tech!"

It was Sharon. She had just arrived home from school and waiting for her in the mail was the acceptance letter from Georgia Tech University.

"I'm going to Tech! I'm going to Tech! Can you believe it!" screamed Sharon. "And Jenny, I got a scholarship! A full scholarship!"

Jennifer squealed back into the phone, "Aaaaaahhhhhhh!" rejoicing along to the great news.

It was something Sharon had talked about since they'd first met at the student council camp two summers ago, and now she had made it happen. Sharon wasn't just happy, she was delirious. All the hard work, the studying, and the extracurricular activities paid off. She was going to stay home in Atlanta, attend Georgia Tech University, study to become an aerospace engineer, and eventually work for NASA.

It was a beautiful dream that was bearing fruit.

But something was wrong. As they spoke, Jennifer sensed a sudden change in Sharon's demeanor.

"What's the matter? You just told me this great news," said Jennifer.

Sharon paused.

"It's Daddy. He doesn't know yet. I'm not sure when he finds out he'll let me go."

"Are you kidding? This is your dream. How could he not let you go?"

Sharon explained, as she had so many times before, that her father had health issues. If it wasn't a bad back it was his neck, or his arthritis.

"Jenny, I clean for him, cook for him. He'd be lost without me. If I don't take care of him, who will?" said Sharon. "We don't have anybody else."

Sharon didn't have any aunts and uncles or cousins or grandparents, at least not that she knew of. Jennifer always thought it was sad that a young girl grew up missing a family, especially her mother. But Sharon appeared to be comfortable with her father. They had managed to get along fine, even if Warren was a little weird. And now Sharon had earned a full scholarship to Georgia Tech.

"Your dad is going to be so proud of you!" said Jennifer.

"Being proud of me and letting me go to college are two different things, Jenny," said Sharon.

Later that night, as Jennifer was getting ready for bed, the phone rang. It was Sharon, who spoke in a barely recognizable whisper.

"Jenny, I told Daddy. He's letting me go to college."

CHAPTER 5

The full-page ad placed in the 1986 Forest Park High School yearbook spoke of unfulfilled promise and reminded all of a dream that, for the short term, had died.

The ad, which featured a black-and-white photo of Sharon, drew attention for its seductive nature—Sharon posing demurely, her shirt collar up and buttons open. Underneath in large type was SHARON MARSHALL and below was *Look out, Georgia Tech! Hello future Air Force General and aeronautical engineering career. Dad.*

The ad was placed eight weeks earlier, just before teachers and students noticed a change in Sharon's physical appearance. She was gaining weight, particularly in her face and midsection. When questioned, she'd say she couldn't take her hands off junk food, from cakes to potato chips and ice cream. But it was obvious something was seriously wrong, and the quiet talk among the teachers was that Sharon must be pregnant.

Several teachers pulled Sharon aside and quietly asked her about her condition, even asking point blank if she were pregnant. Each time she denied it. But by May, it was clear that Sharon was carrying a baby, and it was decided that the ruse had to end.

Sharon was called into the guidance office and there, unable to hide the physical truth, she broke down and cried, admitting that yes, she was pregnant and was due in early July.

The father, she said, was her new boyfriend, a student named Curtis Flournoy.

Sharon was devastated. Warren became enraged when he learned about the pregnancy and insisted she give up her scholarship to Georgia Tech. Sharon's mood darkened in the weeks before graduation, her father having barred her from receiving her diploma with her graduating class. Depressed, Sharon ran away with Curtis, heading west to Alabama. It didn't take Warren long to find them at a motel just across the state line. He burst into their room, his entrance startling the teenage lovers. Warren remained calm and gently pulled Sharon up by the arm. No need to discuss this now, he said. They'd all get a good night's sleep and talk in the morning before returning to Atlanta. But there would be no discussion. Curtis found a note tucked underneath his door. It was from Warren, and it said that he was not the father of the baby. He was warned to leave Sharon alone. Curtis ran outside and knocked on the Marshalls' door, but there was no answer. The motel clerk said they'd left in the middle of the night.

The summer began for Jennifer Fisher as it ended the previous year, in total lockdown. She struggled with her grades again and fell in and out of periods of depression, especially after her parents learned she was experimenting with marijuana. Not even Sharon was allowed to visit, and the two friends grew somewhat distant. Jennifer was in a bad way, and weeks had passed since she'd last spoken to her friend. It was mid-June when Sharon reached out, and when she did, she was crying. She had some news to share.

"You need to sit down."

"Why?"

"I'm pregnant."

Jennifer was shocked, numb.

"Who was it? Your new boyfriend?" she said.

"Yeah, it was that guy I was seeing," said Sharon.

Jennifer never knew anyone her age who was pregnant and was at a loss for words, even with a friend as close as Sharon.

"Are you going to get an abortion?" asked Jennifer.

"No, absolutely not. That's not even an option. We're leaving soon, going to move away. The weather is really killing my dad's back, and he needs a better climate."

"Move?" said Jennifer. "What about college? What about your scholarship?"

Sharon took a deep breath.

"I'm going to have to hold off on college for now. I could start in a year. We'll see. My dad is pretty upset and I need to give him time to chill out."

Jennifer had dealt with her own problems the past year or so, but nothing as life changing or dramatic as this. Trying to process it all was difficult. Sharon said they were leaving soon but wanted to visit Stone Mountain.

"Jenny, can I see you? I want to come by before I leave," said Sharon.

Warren pulled up to the Fisher home the following Saturday morning, dropped off his daughter, then quickly sped away, not bothering to say hello.

Sharon walked inside, shoulders slouched, chin to her chest. She was embarrassed and didn't quite know what to say to the Fishers, who had treated her like their own daughter over the past three years.

Sue Fisher was crestfallen when she learned the news and embraced Sharon warmly, tears flowing down Sharon's cheeks. Jennifer cried with her friend, and the three women walked into the kitchen to talk. It was clear after several minutes of conversation that this wasn't the Sharon Marshall the Fishers had come to know and love. Sharon was stressed, that much was obvious. That magnetic glow she exuded was gone, stripped away as she spoke about her predicament. And there was more news.

"I think we're going to Arizona," said Sharon, staring at the floor. "The dry weather will help my father's arthritis, and it's pretty inexpensive to live there."

Sue and Jennifer exchanged wide-eyed glances.

"And I was thinking that maybe next year I'll go to Arizona State. They mailed me a brochure. It looks nice," said Sharon.

Sue could only sit and watch as Sharon's life unraveled before her eyes. She wanted to grab her, shake her, hug her, yell at her. Sharon was like a daughter, and Sue wanted to deal with this like a mother. But she resisted. Warren Marshall may not have been a prize, but he was Sharon's father, and Sue would never interfere. It wasn't her place. She pulled Sharon into her chest and held her tightly.

"Whatever you need from us, you know we'll be there for you," said Sue.

She kissed Sharon on the forehead, then walked out of the kitchen, leaving Jennifer and Sharon alone to say good-bye.

Sharon looked up toward Jennifer, a slight smile brightening her face.

"Want to feel the baby?"

Sharon pulled her shirt up and over her protruding belly, then took Jennifer's right hand and guided it to a spot above and to the right of her belly button.

"Feel that?" said Sharon.

Jennifer giggled with every movement. But it felt so strange. This was a moment they were supposed to share when they were older, when they graduated college and were married. Jennifer felt a profound sadness.

The beeping from Warren's truck outside sounded an end to the brief visit, and the two friends walked toward the front door. Sue and Joel were there and each said good-bye, giving Sharon a kiss and a hug and reassuring her that if she needed anything, she should call them.

Sharon then turned to Jennifer, and the two friends embraced, holding each other tightly.

"Don't forget to write me with your new address and phone number," said Jennifer.

"I won't forget," said Sharon. "I'll write you every week. I love you, Jenny."

"I love you too, Sharon."

Warren beeped his horn again, and Sharon slowly walked out of the Fisher home and got into her father's truck. The Fishers watched as Sharon and Warren drove down their block and out of view.

The envelope that arrived in mid-July was postmarked "Mesa, Arizona," and was addressed to Jennifer Fisher.

Inside was an eight-page letter from Sharon that began, "Dear Jenny."

Sharon had had her baby, a boy, and Jennifer cried when she read the details about the birth of Sharon's son—the painful and long labor, the birth, how much he weighed, and the wealthy family that adopted him. Warren had found the couple. They were two doctors from Texas who lived in a huge house. The baby would even have his own personal nanny. Sharon described the few minutes she'd had with her son, how she'd touched his hands and feet and fingers and toes. He was a beautiful boy, and she was crushed when the nurses took him away. It was so hard to give him up, she wrote, but she felt good that he was going to have a good life.

Jennifer cried right through the final page, where Sharon asked if she could visit.

She arrived two weeks later, having taken a Greyhound bus cross-country. Jennifer and her mother greeted Sharon as she walked off the bus, and they were thrilled to see that it was the Sharon of old.

She had regained her glow and on the ride to the Fisher home was her bubbly, happy self. The week that followed was the happiest Jennifer had felt in a long time. They visited some of their old haunts, including the mall and the beach, guzzled Moosehead beer, and late one afternoon even decided to become blood sisters. They tiptoed into the kitchen, took a steak knife and poked at their fingers, but drew no blood. They laughed as they tried pricking the middle of their hands. Jennifer drew blood first, then Sharon. They held their hands palms up, with the warm blood trickling over their fingers, and pressed them together.

"You know we're now soul sisters," said Sharon.

Jennifer couldn't help but giggle holding Sharon's wet, warm hand.

"That's right, we're sisters," said Jennifer.

It was shortly after dinner, when the last dirty dish was washed and put away, that Sharon asked Sue if they could talk. She had something on her mind, and it was important.

They sat down in the living room, and Sharon looked directly into Sue's eyes.

"Do you think I can stay here and live with you?"

Sharon explained that she didn't like Arizona, her life wasn't good there, and she wanted to remain in Atlanta, a familiar city.

Most of all, she wanted to be with the Fisher family.

Sue listened, but told Sharon she didn't think it would be possible. It wasn't that the Fishers didn't want Sharon. They loved her. Instead Sue explained that it would be up to her father to decide.

Sharon said no, arguing that it was her decision, and pleaded with Sue to change her mind.

Sue sensed a change in Sharon, a desperation. She asked if something was wrong, if there were other reasons why she wanted to leave her father. Sharon said no.

"I'd really like to stay here," she said, her voice cracking with emotion.

"Why don't you ask your father. If he approves, then we'd be happy for you to stay with us."

Sharon shook her head.

"No, that's not a good idea."

Sue turned to Joel, who had walked into the room, and explained that Sharon wanted to live with the Fishers. Joel didn't like Warren Marshall, but agreed with his wife. They could not, and would not, take responsibility for a young woman who had a parent.

Sharon decided to end the conversation as abruptly as it began.

"You know what, I was thinking, I have to go home. I keep my dad's books and he's lost without me. I don't know what I was thinking. As a matter of fact, I should call him."

Sharon walked over to the den, picked up the phone, and called her father. A minute later she pulled out her pocket calculator and began adding and subtracting numbers given to her over the phone. She then turned toward the Fishers and whispered, "See, he really can't do anything without me."

As their conversation continued, Sharon told Warren she was boarding a bus the following morning for the return trip home. Joel interjected, suggesting that he put her on a plane.

"I don't think you should be traveling on a bus alone," he said.

Warren said no, but Joel insisted.

The drive to the airport the next day was relatively quiet. Sharon remained mum, staring outside the car. As happy as she had been when she'd arrived the week before, she was equally sad, which was disconcerting to Jennifer. She'd always known her friend to be upbeat, happy. But the events of the last month had changed all that, and Sharon was sullen. Her hopes and dreams had faded, and her future was uncertain.

When they entered the terminal, Sharon began to cry like a baby. It was clear she didn't want to go, and Sue Fisher fought to keep her emotions from taking over, reminding herself that Sharon was not her daughter, and unless Sharon told her something otherwise, it wasn't her place to interfere.

"Sharon, are you sure there isn't anything you want to tell me?" asked Sue.

Sharon said no, wiping away her tears. Jennifer prodded her to tell them what was really wrong, but she knew that wasn't Sharon's way. During the three years they had known each other and become best friends, Sharon would divulge intimate details of boyfriends or talk about her once bright future, but she'd never let anyone really get inside. The Fishers surmised that Warren had something to do with that. He had been, and was, a demanding and controlling presence in Sharon's life.

Sharon tried hard to smile as she thanked Joel and Sue for their love and hospitality. She then turned to Jennifer.

"I'm going to miss you, Jenny. Please don't forget me."

"Forget you? Sharon, we're best friends. We'll always be close."

Sharon wiped her cheeks.

"That's right, Jenny. We'll always be close. Remember, we're sisters."

CHAPTER 6

Tulsa, Oklahoma
April 1990

Dim lights highlighted the single dancer gyrating against a silver pole at the Passions gentlemen's club. Several dozen metal folding chairs, the kind used at church Bingo parties, surrounded the stage and were half-filled with scrubby men lunging with paper money in hand.

Dank and seamy, Passions reeked of muck and beer. Half a dozen men encircled two pool tables in the rear near the main entrance while several others sat on wooden stools along the mirrored bar on the right—some watching the entertainment, others too drunk to do anything but sit and stare into the neon beer signs that flickered above the bar.

The throbbing music that accompanied the dancer came to an end, and she walked off the stage to a smattering of applause, with some men leaning over to place even more bills in her G-string. Others reached for her breasts, but she smacked their hands away.

"Oh, c'mon. Just a little touch, Connie."

"You guys know the rules," she said.

Shapely and bleached blonde, Connie was a nineteen-year-old college student named Karen Parsley when she answered the ad for "Exotic Dancers" during the summer of 1988. Connie had never danced in public before, much less without any clothes on, but overcame any lingering doubts and apprehension after her first night when she left the club with 175 dollars. It was more than she ever earned working a full week at TJ Maxx.

Connie made even more after learning the subtleties required to maximize earnings, such as hustling for tips by delivering drinks to customers or providing a private show.

Dancers could earn as much as two thousand dollars, or more, per week at Passions. The work wasn't easy; the hours were tough and the dancing physically draining. And there was the clientele, which ranged from lonely business executives to beer-swilling blue-collar workers to deranged perverts who remained in the shadows until the club closed early in the morning, when the dancers were escorted to their cars by the club's burly bouncers. New women passed through Passions each week and, despite the money, only a hardy few remained, like Connie, and Lavernia Watkins, a crooked-toothed brunette known as "Bambi," and June Bolles, who took the name "Desiree."

Connie worked a manageable three-nights-a-week schedule, kept her day job to maintain health benefits, and filled her free time with her studies. She figured that as long as the money kept coming in, working as a stripper in a dive like Passions wasn't the worst thing in the world.

Walking off the stage and through a door beneath a Private sign, Connie wiped the heavy perspiration from her brow as black eye makeup dripped down her cheeks. She was attractive, but like many of the women who danced at Passions, Connie had a hard look that suggested she had more life experience than her age would indicate.

She stood there naked, picking the bills from her waist, mostly ones and fives, when J.R. Buck, the club's owner, interrupted her. Fortyish, J.R.'s real name was Clyde Caster Buck, Jr. Short and stocky with light brown hair, J.R. wasn't much of a businessman, given the letters from creditors and the bounced checks that filled the drawers in his desk. But his employees were always paid on time and he seemed to watch out for the girls, which was more attention than most of them received outside the club.

Something was wrong, and J.R. couldn't mask his concern.

"You have a call. It's Clarence Hughes. He said there's been an accident. Tonya's in the hospital. He's in Oklahoma City. Take it in my office."

Connie reached into the dressing room, grabbed her robe, and flung it around her back as she ran to J.R.'s office, where she picked up the phone.

"Clarence? What happened! What did you do to her?"

"I didn't do nothing!" said Clarence. "She went out for some baby food last night and got hit by a car. She's out, unconscious, in a coma. Thought I'd call and tell you. We need her money. Don't come visit, doctors won't allow it. I'll come there and pick it up. Probably on Tuesday."

"Why is she in Oklahoma City?"

"She had a doctor's appointment. A gynecologist."

"Where's Michael?"

"He's with me. He's fine."

"What hospital is she in?"

"Presbyterian. Oklahoma City. But like I said, she's in bad shape and doctors don't want no visitors. I got to go. I'll be by for her money on Tuesday."

Connie placed the phone down and sat in J.R.'s chair as several dancers and other employees gathered in the doorway.

"Tonya's in the hospital. She got hit by a car last night. I don't know what happened, but Clarence said it was some sort of accident," said Connie. "First night she ever takes off, and she ends up in the hospital? Bullshit. He tried to kill her."

Oklahoma City was 120 miles to the west—southwest on I-44, and Connie enlisted Kevin Brown to accompany her to Presbyterian Hospital. Kevin was a college student and a Passions customer who knew Tonya well.

When they arrived two hours later, Connie went directly to the information desk, asked for Tonya Hughes's room number, and then took the elevator to the third floor, leaving Kevin in the lobby. She found the room, saw the ridiculous No Visitors sign taped to the door, then poked her head inside. Tonya was alone, lying on her back, faint noises coming from the medical equipment monitoring her condition.

Connie opened the door all the way and slowly walked up to Tonya's bed, stopping by her side. Tonya looked like she always did, like a pretty blond angel. Her face was unmarked, as were her arms. Connie was confused. Clarence said she was hit by a car, but she appeared to be in perfect condition. There were no scratches on her face, no broken bones, no scrapes from the road. She looked as if she were sleeping.

Connie leaned over and whispered, "Hey, Tonya, it's Connie. I came to take care of you. Kevin is here. You're gonna be all right now."

Tonya Dawn Hughes had arrived at Passions in the fall. Blonde with blue eyes, Tonya initially drew attention for her odd figure, which suggested far too much time with an inexperienced, or incompetent, plastic surgeon. Her breasts were almost comical, the implants round and hard. They looked unnatural, like two oranges that squirted milk. Her hips and thighs were too full for her short body, resembling a woman who had just given birth.

What Tonya lacked physically, she made up with her passionate dancing, and she was immediately hired. Originally from Alabama, she said she'd learned her trade at a club in Tampa, Florida. Her maiden name was Tadlock—Tonya Dawn Tadlock. She lived in a piss-poor trailer park on the other side of Tulsa with her husband, Clarence, and two-year-old son, Michael. Tonya worked a demanding seven-days-a-week schedule, never missing a day except for Thanksgiving and Christmas, when the club was closed.

Following her arrival, Tonya attracted a small following. She often performed as a young teen, appearing on stage wearing a low-cut school sweater, pleated skirt, bobby socks, and high-heeled shoes. Her music of choice was "Locomotion," the 1962 classic by Little Eva.

Tonya rarely drank alcohol and eschewed the various drugs that pervaded the club, such as speed, cocaine, and marijuana, which drew her closer to Connie, who also avoided drugs. They were also close in age. Tonya was a year younger, and unlike the other girls, she and Connie were devoid of tattoos.

Connie also admired Tonya's intelligence. She was smart and liked to read between sets. Books, magazines—it didn't matter. She usually brought something to read. There were even nights when she'd walk into the club with a crochet set under her arm. She was making a sweater for her son. Tonya explained that the reading and sewing calmed her painfully ailing stomach. She often complained of some unknown medical problem and was never without large jars of Rolaids, which she popped into her mouth like candy.

It was clear to all at Passions that Tonya's problems centered on her volatile husband, Clarence. He was twice her age, maybe more, with thin gray hair that hung to his neck. Of medium size, Clarence was about as nondescript as one could get. His unremarkable features led many to question Tonya's attraction to him, though it was clear that Clarence was obsessed with his young wife. He controlled her every move, driving her to work daily and often picking her up late at night. He was creepy, calling the club nearly every hour throughout the evening to monitor Tonya's whereabouts. Most unsettling to all was his demand that Tonya bring home a minimum of two hundred dollars each night.

Tonya obeyed her husband and hustled for every dime, either by dancing or mingling with customers at the bar. When she'd fall short, she'd be in a nervous tizzy, knowing that Clarence was waiting in the parking lot. Connie and the other dancers would offer to make up the difference, but Tonya would decline. She'd meet her husband, turn over every penny, and bear the brunt of his anger. She'd return the next day with fresh bruises on her body.

Tonya's plight drew empathy from her coworkers at Passions. She was overworked, and at times while sitting at the bar entertaining a customer she would close her eyes and fall asleep on his lap. She'd awaken with a tap on her shoulder from Connie or one of the other girls.

"Tonya, c'mon. You have to dance."

Tonya would stumble toward the stage, regain her wits, then lose herself and her clothes to the music while the men in the club followed her every fluid move.

Tonya's situation angered Connie and some of the other girls, who tried unsuccessfully to convince her to leave her husband, to take her son, and simply leave town. Tonya guarded her privacy, and Connie was really the only girl who could talk to her. Tonya said she feared Clarence, and always trembled when discussing her situation. She said that she had tried to run away twice before, a long time ago, but he had tracked her down both times and said if she ever tried it a third time he'd kill her. Tonya knew her husband well and believed him. Her black-and-blue marks served as reminders of his resolve.

"Things are not as they seem with me," she once said to J.R. Buck.

Compounding Tonya's problems was Clarence's relationship with local law enforcement. He was a member of the Tulsa Fraternal Order of Police and had a good friend, a sheriff's deputy, who lived in the same trailer park. Clarence also had several guns in the house, including a shotgun. With his police connections and weapons, Tonya believed there was no place for her or Michael to hide.

There were times when Clarence pulled into the parking lot to drop Tonya off and they were met by Connie or one of the other dancers, who would yell out to Clarence that Tonya should leave his sorry ass.

"If she ever left me, I'd kill the bitch," would be Clarence's standard response.

Given Tonya's reluctance to take matters into her own hands, Connie decided she would help her friend out of her predicament.

Tonya would have a boyfriend.

She was first paired up with Chris Matheney, a Passions bouncer who'd drive her home on nights when her husband remained home. Like everyone else in the club, Matheney noticed the bruises on her body. He figured the fresh black-and-blue circular welts from her shoulders down to her ankles were the result of Tonya's new relationship.

"He found out, didn't he?" said Matheney.

"No, no," said Tonya calmly. "It's OK, really. Don't worry about it."

Her disposition changed dramatically when Matheney said he was going to confront Clarence.

"This guy needs an ass-kicking," he said.

"He'll kill you!" shrieked Tonya. "He has connections everywhere. You don't understand. Just let it go."

Matheney liked Tonya, but the added baggage of

Clarence was too much, and their relationship fizzled. A month later she turned to Kevin Brown, a college student and frequent Passions customer.

Kevin was drawn to Tonya the first night he saw her on-stage. He bought her a soda after her set and learned she was married but appeared desperately unhappy. Kevin became a regular at Passions and soon heard all the awful stories concerning Tonya, particularly the one where Clarence hit her in the head with a soda bottle because she didn't prepare dinner in a timely fashion.

Tonya and Kevin dated, sneaking out of the club for late-night dinners while Clarence remained in the parking lot. On nights when Clarence didn't drive Tonya to work, he'd call the club and Connie would answer the phone, telling him that his wife was busy with a customer, which technically was the truth. Only this customer was now her boyfriend.

As their relationship evolved into something serious, Kevin offered to take Tonya and her son out of state. Kevin had friends, family, and the money to get Tonya out of Oklahoma safely.

Tonya initially declined, fearing for Kevin as she did for Chris Matheney, herself, and especially her son, Michael.

"I want to leave. I've thought about it every day for the past year. And I'm ready to leave. But you don't know this man. He has connections. He'll kill you, me, and Michael," she said. "I need to be sure that we're safe."

Michael was the only true joy in Tonya's sad life. He turned two years old on April 21, could count to ten, and recite part of the alphabet, from A to H. Several mornings each week, Tonya, Clarence, and Michael would visit Connie at TJ Maxx on their way to breakfast at the Country Buffet, which was next door. It was clear to Connie that the bond between mother and son was deep. Tonya was openly affectionate with her son, holding his hand, kissing him on the cheek, and always smiling when she spoke to him. By contrast, Michael appeared to have little interest in his father. He spurned his awkward offers to hold his hand, instead turning to his mother for comfort, holding his arms out to her to pick him up, then burying his head in her chest and wrapping his arms around her neck.

Connie knew that Tonya led a difficult life, but she couldn't do much for her. Tonya was a private person, revealing little about herself or her past. All anyone really knew was that she was a young, married mother from Alabama with a psychotic husband. But then, no one pried since most of the dancers at Passion's had histories they wanted long buried, lives they didn't want to remember, or changed completely.

Tonya Dawn Hughes was no different.

So it came as a great surprise to Connie and several others at Passions when they learned of Tonya's plan to leave her husband. Kevin had finally convinced Tonya that she could escape without notice, and in the weeks before the accident everyone at Passions noticed a subtle change in her demeanor. She wasn't just "going through the motions," as she had since she'd arrived in the fall. She was energized, as if she had a purpose. She smiled easier, talked more, and gave everyone at Passions a brief glimpse at what all believed was the real Tonya. And they liked what they saw. There was even a brief conversation about going to college and becoming a nurse. The sudden turnaround was noteworthy, if only because everyone knew Tonya was intelligent, but no one believed that she'd ever leave her controlling husband.

Tonya didn't reveal how she would leave her tormentor. But Connie could see a newfound determination in Tonya's eyes. She was serious, and she was scared.

"If he finds out, he'll kill me and Michael," said Tonya. "But I can't stand him and can't stand being around him. I'm going to get away."

CHAPTER 7

Connie pulled a chair to the side of Tonya's bed and sat there, softly caressing her forehead and whispering into her ear when a nurse walked in to check her vital signs. Startled, Connie stood up and said she was a friend who drove down from Tulsa.

As Connie spoke, Tonya's head moved, following Connie's voice.

"Oh my God, she's responding to you," said the nurse.

Tonya raised her right arm and appeared to be reaching for Connie, who grabbed her hand and held it tight.

"I'm going to get a doctor," said the nurse.

Tonya was still in a coma but appeared to be slowly emerging from her unconscious state. Kevin was allowed to visit and when he spoke, Tonya moved her head in his direction.

Recognizing her friends was good news, and the medical staff was pleased with her progress. Given the significant blow she had received on the back of the head, doctors initially had their doubts that she would recover. They had other doubts, too, and they centered on her husband, Clarence.

He had displayed little emotion when he arrived that first morning, and his bizarre No Visitors sign startled the nursing staff. Of more concern was the mysterious theft of Tonya's personal effects, including her clothes. All were missing. Perhaps most disconcerting were Tonya's injuries. When Connie questioned Tonya's condition and the lack of visible marks and bruises, the doctor pulled her aside.

"This was no car accident," he said.

"I knew it," said Connie.

Connie was quick to share her suspicions concerning Clarence and the violent nature of Tonya's relationship with her husband, whom she was planning to leave.

Kevin had told Connie just that morning the details of her bold plan, and Kevin was going to help.

"What changed her mind? We've been telling her to run for months," said Connie.

"Something happened over the past month," said Kevin. "She wouldn't tell me, but she started talking about a new life, of going to college."

Connie was surprised to hear that Tonya had finally wised up. But then, it didn't make much sense. Tonya was doing something she never did; she was making plans. She was talking about a future.

The medical staff took Connie aside and suggested she visit with the Oklahoma City Police Department. They also made it clear that it was time to go. Clarence was clear in his demands that Tonya receive no visitors. Connie remained in Oklahoma City, taking a room at a nearby hotel. Considering Tonya's response to Connie, the medical staff welcomed her visits and would call her whenever Clarence left the hospital.

Connie was sure that Clarence had something to do with

Tonya's injuries, and only hoped that when Tonya awoke, she'd tell the medical staff, her friends, and the police what had really happened early Thursday morning. Tonya's condition gradually improved enough that Connie left Oklahoma City on Sunday morning and by midafternoon was at Passions relaying the good news. Though she had yet to regain consciousness, doctors were sure she'd come out.

"Maybe by midweek," said Connie.

A few hours later, she received a call from Clarence. He was still in Oklahoma City, and he was irate.

"Who told you to go to visit her in that hospital!" he screamed. "I told you she can't have no visitors! Those bitches at the hospital will all be fired. No one is allowed in that room. No one!"

Connie held her composure. She explained that Tonya was her friend and no one, not even her husband, was going to keep her away. She said nothing about visiting the police, something she figured she'd do once Tonya recovered. Clarence's anger quickly subsided as he changed the subject. He needed money and asked Connie if she wanted to buy some furniture.

"I'm moving to here and need to sell everything in the trailer in Tulsa. You interested?"

"Moving? What for?"

"To be near Tonya."

"What about Michael?"

"Never mind Michael. I'm his daddy and I'll take care of him. I'll call you on Friday. If you want the furniture let me know then."

Connie called the hospital and told them that Clarence was clearing out and suggested they keep an eye on Tonya. He must have tried to kill her once, she reasoned, and what's to stop him from trying again? Connie decided to head back to Oklahoma City the next day and gave the hospital her home and work numbers in the event of an emergency.

Early the following morning the phone rang. It was the hospital. Tonya's condition had suddenly worsened. She was on life support and not expected to live through the day.

Tonya was going to die, and if Connie wanted to say good-bye, she had to leave now.

When Connie arrived at Presbyterian Hospital early in the afternoon she ran up to Tonya's room. The No Visitors sign was gone, and Tonya's bed was empty. A nurse pulled her aside and told her that Tonya had been pronounced dead. With the exception of two nurses and a doctor, no one was with Tonya at the end. Not even her husband, who was given advance notice in the morning, but said he wouldn't be there. Instead he barked out orders to have her organs donated and her body immediately cremated. There would be no funeral or service of any kind.

"Cremated?" said Connie between her tears. "She didn't want to be cremated. I know. We talked about this stuff. We both wanted to be buried. And we have to have a service. How can that bastard not have a service?"

Connie was led downstairs and into a room where Tonya was lying on a gurney, covered by a white sheet from head to toe. The nurse pulled the sheet to reveal Tonya's face. She looked the same, as if she were sleeping. Connie exploded in tears. Her friend was gone.

"What happened?" said Connie to the nurse. "She was coming along. She was supposed to come out of it."

"We don't know," said the nurse. "Her husband visited with her last night and this morning her vitals were falling. There was nothing we could do. She never came out of her coma."

An orderly walked in and said it was time to move the

body. Connie kissed Tonya's forehead and said good-bye. The gurney was rolled away and the Oklahoma Organ Sharing Network facilitated delivery of Tonya's organs to various individuals. Her heart was given to a sixty-six-year-old Arizona woman who returned to her husband and grown children following the transplant operation. Tonya's liver went to a thirty-nine-year-old New York woman who was married with two sons and was a registered nurse. One kidney went to a twenty-four-year-old man from Texas, married with one child. The other kidney was transplanted into a fourteen-year-old girl from Oklahoma who had been on dialysis for one year. Two blind Oklahoma residents were given Tonya's corneas, and an assortment of individuals benefited from donated bone.

Connie was led to the lobby and drew sympathy from the medical staff, which had been leery of Clarence Hughes from the beginning. Connie asked about a wake and a funeral, and the hospital agreed to move Tonya's remains to Tulsa, so long as a check to cover the transportation expense arrived by the end of the business day, and her husband gave permission.

Connie called J.R. Buck, who readily agreed to front the money to transport the body. She then called Clarence, and told him that having a funeral was the right thing to do. Connie explained that the employees at Passions would pay for the funeral, and that Tonya deserved a decent burial.

"You're going to pay for a funeral?" said Clarence, who resisted, but finally relented, stipulating there would be no open casket during the wake. Connie relayed the news to the medical staff, which agreed with the decision for a closed casket.

Before leaving, the nurses told Connie of one last problem, and it had to do with Michael. He wasn't talking or crying. He was dirty and smelled of urine. It was gently suggested that Connie visit social services.

CHAPTER 8

On Tuesday, May 1, Eleanor Johnson of the Oklahoma Department of Human Services drove to 6306 N. Meridian, Apt. #103, Oklahoma City, Clarence Hughes's new address. He had called DHS that morning and requested placement of his son in voluntary foster care. Clarence said his wife had just died and that he needed someone to care for his two-year-old son for a week. Clarence was on the telephone when Ms. Johnson arrived. He had emptied his trailer in Tulsa, and boxes littered the living room. Ms. Johnson waited patiently for Clarence to finish his call, watching as Michael crawled into his father's lap and gave him a hug. Clarence placed the phone down and told his guest that his wife was to be buried on Friday, May 4. He'd pick up Michael on Monday, May 7.

Michael was taken to Choctaw, some twenty miles west of Oklahoma City, where he would live with a temporary foster family. Upon his arrival, Michael was led by the hand to the front porch, where he stopped. He couldn't lift himself over the first step and began to cry, emitting the same intense, guttural animal sounds he did on the ride over. The social worker lifted him by the arm and walked him inside the house. Standing in the foyer, Michael dropped to his knees and slammed his head down on the hard floor, over and over.

Ernest and Merle Bean had served as foster parents to more than sixty children over six years but had never received a boy in such a distressed emotional state.

The Beans lived at 17580 Bode Road in a comfortable neighborhood dotted with attractive homes all separated by tall trees. Choctaw was a quiet, rural area, surrounded by open fields. Merle was a homemaker and Ernest an amiable, self-employed air-conditioning and heating technician who once worked for Sears. Deeply religious, with four children of their own, the Beans believed it was God's will and their Christian duty to open their modest home to so many troubled children. When the call came in that morning concerning temporary housing for a two-year-old boy named Michael Hughes, the Beans said fine, bring him over. It would only be for a short while, perhaps a week, said a Department of Human Services supervisor. Michael's mother had died the day before—killed in a car accident, and his father was busy with arrangements and other personal business.

Michael wouldn't stop crying. He was lying on the foyer floor and appeared to be in utter agony. The Beans felt for the little boy, but his screaming and banging was disturbing the other children under their care. Merle had never turned down a child before, but she was quick to call DHS.

"Don't ask me to keep this boy," she said.

After Tonya's organs were harvested on April 30, Dr. Charles Engel at Presbyterian Hospital transfered her body to the Oklahoma City office of the Chief Medical Examiner, where Dr. Larry Balding began his autopsy at 10:30 A.M. on May 1.

Balding's examination revealed numerous older bruises over much of the body, with fresh abrasions on her lower left back, a swollen left ankle, and a previously undetected fracture of the right fibula between the knee and ankle. Tonya's remaining organs, including tongue, stomach, intestines, lungs, and pancreas, were normal. Balding also noted that Tonya had had several pregnancies and multiple medical procedures, including the breast implants and implants in her buttocks.

Most severe was the damage to Tonya's head. The brain was swollen and filled with blood throughout the dura, the cavity between the skull and the brain tissue. The severe impact to the back of her head, which caused the large hematoma just above the neck, rocked her brain forward, causing damage to the left occipital lobe and cerebellum and a distinct softening of the brain matter. There was no evidence of natural disease.

Balding determined the probable cause of death was "Closed Head Injury," the result of a "violent, unusual, or unnatural" death.

Under "Manner of Death," Balding checked "Homicide."

Connie returned to Oklahoma City on May 2, visiting first the police and then DHS. The police, privately aware of the coroner's report, seemingly ignored her, explaining that Tonya's death was ruled a hit-and-run accident and there was nothing they could do. Connie left in a huff, then met with social workers from DHS, only to learn that Michael Hughes was already placed in their temporary care. They told her that Clarence had placed Michael with DHS the day before. Connie suggested that Clarence learned his wife was going to leave him and killed her, and that she feared for Michael's safety under Clarence's care. DHS workers said they would investigate. The following day Connie received a call. It was Clarence again, and he was furious.

"How could you do this to me!" he screamed. "They're not gonna give me Michael!"

The juvenile bureau of the district attorney's office had filed an application alleging that Michael was a deprived child and that he should be made a ward of the court, which could ultimately result in termination of Clarence's parental rights. For the moment, Michael would not be returned to Clarence as planned. Profoundly pleased with the news, Connie didn't let on to Clarence, saying only that social services approached her, asked a few questions, and that she didn't give them much.

"That's my son. He needs his daddy. You better help me get him back," said Clarence.

Connie suggested they meet with social services the day after the funeral to straighten things out, but she had no intention of helping Clarence. Tonya's funeral was to be held on Friday, and Connie's only intention was to get through the solemn event without incident.

The closed wooden casket was surrounded by bouquets of flowers, mostly red and white carnations or roses, all from friends and coworkers at Passions.

Pews on the right side of the Ninde Garden Chapel were filled with an equally colorful collection of individuals, including strippers, prostitutes, and bouncers. J.R. Buck, Bambi, Desiree, Tammy, Kevin, Chris, and Connie sat up front. Several regular customers were also there, including Dr. Ray, a smallish man who had showered Tonya with money.

The left side of the chapel, reserved for Tonya's family, was empty.

It was Friday, May 4, and the service was to begin at 2 P.M. Connie prepared a small program card. "In Remembrance, Tonya Dawn Hughes, September Nineteenth, Nineteen Hundred Sixty-seven, April Thirtieth, Nineteen Hundred Ninety." Printed on the inside was the Twenty-third Psalm, which begins with "The Lord is my shepherd, I shall not want."

It was shortly before 2 P.M. when Clarence arrived. He snarled his way into the chapel, wearing dark glasses, a blue suit, his thin hair pinned back in a short ponytail and dyed a macabre burgundy, the coloring still wet and running down the back of his neck. Clarence was accompanied by two burly men in suits, both Tulsa sheriff's deputies, one of whom lived next door to Clarence. Fire burned in his eyes as he walked down the center aisle, stopping at the first pew and looking down at Connie.

"Bodyguards," he said, pointing to his two companions.

The Reverend M. Miles Henry began the service, giving way to Clarence, who had something to say. He positioned himself in front of Tonya's casket and told the assembled friends that they didn't really know his wife.

"She had secrets that will never be revealed, and it would be best for all of you to just let things be," he said. "Bury her and let things be. Do you hear me! Let things be!"

His voice raised, Clarence morphed from a grieving husband to a tent-revival preacher spewing fire and brimstone, raising his hands and his voice as he accused all those present of sins before God, of living a sinner's lifestyle that would surely damn them all to Hell.

Connie sat there, smoldering, wanting to pounce on Clarence and tear him apart. She looked over toward his bodyguards, who kept their eyes away from Clarence and on

Connie and the others. One of the bodyguards exposed his gun kept inside his suit jacket near his chest. It was surreal. Clarence looked and sounded like a sacred preacher, his arms flailing and his garish silver belt buckle, with the word *Painter*, reflecting the lights inside the church.

Connie knew he was a murderer.

After twenty minutes, Clarence directed his attention toward Connie. He seethed over Michael, and he blamed but one person.

"All of you didn't really know her, and you don't know me, yet you're taking my son away! How dare you! How dare you!"

Clarence returned to his seat, satisfied that he had infuriated everyone in attendance. The reverend paused for several minutes, then delivered his remarks, which were decidedly in Clarence's favor.

The service concluded, and Clarence placed a photo on top of the casket. It was a picture of a man, probably around thirty years old, and a girl, around five years old, sitting in his lap. Connie didn't know what to make of it, and didn't want to ask. Perhaps it was Tonya's father.

The mourners exited the church, preparing to go to the Park Grove Cemetery. Clarence would not attend the burial, but stood on the chapel steps, his neck still red with dye, reminding everyone what he'd said.

"Let it go," said Clarence. "Just let it go."

Flanked by his two bodyguards, Clarence looked away from the mourners and toward the street as more than a dozen police cars swarmed in front of the chapel, followed by a black hearse. Clarence walked down the steps of the chapel to the lead police car, opened the back door and climbed inside.

Connie, J.R., and the others stood there, unsure of what was unfolding, but hoping that the police would finally arrest Clarence for the murder of his wife.

Fifteen minutes later Clarence emerged from the car, shook hands with a police officer, then walked away, his bodyguards behind him. The police seized Tonya's coffin. The burial would be postponed as the investigation into her death continued.

The two life insurance policies in the name of Tonya Dawn Hughes totaled $80,000, and designated Clarence Marcus Hughes as the beneficiary. The policies were new, having been purchased just months before, and Clarence told the clerk on the phone he had no idea he'd be calling so soon.

"A terrible tragedy, just a terrible tragedy," said Clarence.

Nonetheless, Clarence called just hours after the funeral to inquire how to begin the process of collecting on the policies, one of which was for fifty thousand dollars, the other for thirty thousand dollars.

The clerk asked Clarence for his Social Security number, then asked him to sit tight. He returned to the phone a few minutes later, asking again for Clarence's Social Security number.

"There seems to be a problem with the number you gave me. It doesn't exist," said the clerk.

Clarence apologized, saying he mixed up his numbers, and gave him another number. The clerk asked Clarence to hold on, then returned a few minutes later.

"Sir, we seem to have a problem here."

"What number did I give you?" said Clarence. "Oh, no. I'm so confused. I buried my wife today. I'm sure you can understand."

Clarence gave the clerk a third nine-digit number, then waited nervously, remaining on the phone a full five minutes before the clerk returned.

"Everything is in order," he said quickly.

Clarence noticed a slight change in his voice.

After hanging up the phone, Clarence packed his bags and drove out of Tulsa, heading east.

He knew that the final Social Security number given to the clerk was not for a Clarence Hughes—but for a Franklin Delano Floyd. He also knew that when the clerk saw the name, he would no doubt notice that Floyd was a federal fugitive, on the run from authorities since 1973 for parole violation and attempted kidnapping.

The insurance company notified the police, who contacted the U.S. Marshals office. It didn't take long, following conversations with the Oklahoma City Police Department, to realize that Floyd was probably armed and considered dangerous. Police strongly believed, based on the coroner's report, that Floyd, a.k.a. Clarence Hughes, killed his wife—ostensibly to collect her insurance money—and were gathering evidence in the hopes of bringing charges forward. Clarence could not identify the gynecologist in Oklahoma City that Tonya was scheduled to visit. They also learned that Tonya obtained her Oklahoma driver's license using a phony birth certificate.

When U.S. Marshals arrived at Clarence Hughes's apartment, he was already gone. When they searched Hughes's history, he had none. He was a ghost. So investigators turned their attention to Franklin Delano Floyd.

CHAPTER 9

Franklin Delano Floyd was born June 17, 1943, in Barnesville, Georgia, the youngest of five children. His older brother, Billy, was born in 1933, followed by Dorothy in 1934, Shirley in 1937, and sister Tommye—spelled with a "ye"—in 1939.

His father, Thomas H. Floyd, was born in Georgia and labored in a cotton mill. He came into this world on April 10, 1912. Unassuming and friendly when he was sober, his demeanor became decidedly darker once he started drinking the clear and potent moonshine he made in the woods near his house. He abused his wife and his children, who would remember the nights when they'd hide under their beds when their father returned home from a night of drinking, belt in hand.

Thomas succumbed to liver and kidney failure and died in June of 1944 at age thirty-two, leaving his wife Della, age twenty-nine, to support and care for the large family. Della had little money and was forced to move into her mother's small second-floor apartment over a grocery store in Barnesville. The arrangement lasted fifteen months, proving too difficult for all concerned, especially Della's parents who asked her to leave. With nowhere to go and no means to raise her children, Della contacted the Lamar County Department of Public Welfare. Social workers there suggested she place her children in the Georgia Baptist Children's Home in Hapeville.

Opened in 1872 in downtown Atlanta to care for twenty-two children orphaned by the Civil War, the children's home was funded by the Georgia Baptist Convention Cooperative Program. A charter was approved in 1888, and the children were moved from Atlanta to the first campus in Hapeville in 1899. By 1932, the home subsisted on funds solicited from churches and the public.

A strict criteria determined admittance to the home, which was reserved only for children orphaned "by death or by circumstances." As far as the home administrators were concerned, all children under its care were orphans, with the goal to make Christian men and women out of them.

On January 5, 1946, Della Floyd completed her application and a week later, January 11, received word that the Board of Directors charged with overseeing the home unanimously voted to admit the Floyd children. Conditions for acceptance included Della's understanding that she was severing her parental rights to her children, and visitation would be limited to one visit on a Saturday every three months, which was an exception to the rules. Children with a living parent were generally limited to two visits per year.

Desperate, Della sat down her two oldest children, Billy, thirteen, and Dorothy, eleven, and explained that she had no choice, that she couldn't feed or clothe them. She loved them dearly, but had to do this.

"You're going to a place that will give you good opportunities," said their grandmother.

On January 21, 1946, a woman wearing a long black dress and black shoes arrived for the children. They said good-bye to their mother, and upon their arrival at the home they were placed together in quarantine. Franklin, the youngest, was only two years old at the time and during that first night crawled into bed with his older siblings. An attendant came into the room and pried a crying Franklin away, placing him in a separate room with younger children, where he would remain apart from his brothers and sisters.

The Floyd children detested their new home, which for them resembled an asylum for mentally ill children. The attendants, or matrons, were often cruel and punished children for the slightest infraction of the rules. Discipline consisted of beatings over a piano bench. Once, a girl in the midst of completing her homework reported that Dorothy, who was playing jacks, was bothering her. The matron took out a belt, lifted up Dorothy's skirt, bent her over the piano bench, and struck her several times. Male matrons dispensed punishment to the boys, while females would discipline the girls. The matrons were usually husband-and-wife teams inexperienced at overseeing children and unable to find stable postwar employment.

The daily routine at the orphanage was simple yet demanding. Children were awakened at 6:30 A.M. for breakfast, which consisted of either biscuits or pancakes and syrup. They were ushered away for schoolwork until noon, when they always ate peanut butter and jelly sandwiches for lunch. The children were sent to the neighboring fields to pick and plant fruit and vegetables, which ended up on their dinner table. Green beans, butter beans, and corn served as the main dinner fare, with bread and milk. Rarely, if ever, would meat be served to the children. Matrons enjoyed fried chicken on Sundays.

The day ended at dusk.

All the Floyd children were eventually separated and placed with children in their respective age groups. Girls lived in cottages, ten to a room on one side of the property, while boys were herded into separate cottages, ten or more to a room.

Clothing—always used and donated—was issued based on need.

Children attended church every Wednesday night and Sunday morning, and occasionally on Saturday night. For Christmas each child received a fruit-and-candy basket, courtesy of local donations.

During the summer, when school was out, the children worked in the fields.

Life at the home was strict and often unbearable, but the children were relatively healthy, attended school, and visited church every week. It was only a few weeks after their arrival that Della wrote to the home requesting permission to visit but was denied. By the summer of 1946 she wrote again asking to see her children and was told she could be accommodated in September, but not to expect to visit again until 1947. The children now belonged to the home, and though encouraged to remain in contact with their mother, the children were treated as if they had no mother. In response to yet another request to visit, the home advised Della to "leave her children alone." Della would visit once or twice a year, but continued to write seeking more visitation.

The home's denial letters always ended with, "They are well and happy, and are doing fine in every way."

In reality, the children had their problems, particularly Franklin.

Considered to be smart as a whip, Franklin was a sensitive boy. Handsome, his mannerisms were seen as feminine, and other boys in his cottage would pick on him daily. Often the bickering would escalate into fighting. When he was six years old, Franklin claimed he was raped by a group of boys who tracked him down near a tree in the field and violated him with a broom handle. Franklin would become a discipline problem and for the next ten years would commit various offenses, from stealing chocolate bars from the commissary and fighting to continuous attempts to run away. On one occasion, his hand was placed in a pot of hot water after he was caught masturbating. Another time he was whipped. His school grades fluctuated, rising to satisfactory in the seventh grade. The following year, in eighth grade, he failed every class.

Franklin wasn't the only boy experiencing problems at the home. There were numerous instances of boys being whipped for various infractions. On one occasion, in 1951, a male matron attempted to whip one boy and was attacked by a group of boys. Several workmen passing by spared the matron serious injury. The harsh discipline at the home eventually made its way into the Georgia juvenile courts in 1965, which suggested that punishment such as whipping with a leather strap constituted brutality, forcing the home to review its policies.

One by one through the 1950s the Floyd children left the Hapeville orphanage, usually on their eighteenth birthday. The older brother, Billy, was the first to leave. He joined the army and served in Korea, then returned to Georgia and married. His wife, Betty, thought he was as mean as a snake and too stupid to turn a radio dial.

Franklin was the last to go, practically expelled from the home in 1959 after he ran away yet again, broke into a house, and stole food. The home called his sister Dorothy and said he would not be prosecuted if she would be willing to take him in. Dorothy was living in South Carolina, married to a military man, and had two young sons. Dorothy agreed and Franklin was released, to the relief of the home staff. John C. Warr, the home's general manager, wrote that "We have done our best for Franklin, but I do not think he has ever been really happy here."

Franklin stayed only a few weeks with Dorothy before her husband, who considered Franklin dangerous, kicked him out. He was taken in by Judge Purdy, a local domestic relations judge, for five months before leaving for Indianapolis, Indiana, in search of his mother. He found her there, working as a prostitute. Two weeks later Franklin left for California after convincing his mother to sign papers for him to join the U.S. Army. He enlisted on July 11, 1959, and served in Missouri and Oklahoma for six months before he was thrown out in December after Army officials learned he had forged his enlistment papers and was underage.

Franklin returned to Indianapolis to live with his mother, but she was gone. He drifted to Philadelphia, New York, Miami, Atlanta, New Orleans, and finally Los Angeles. Broke and destitute, he was arrested in February 1960 after breaking into a Sears store, where he attempted to open a gun case and triggered a burglar alarm. Police arrived and there was an exchange of gunfire. Franklin was shot in the stomach. He survived following surgery and was placed in the Youth Institution at Preston, California, from June 1960 until August 1961.

On November 1, 1961, he was taken into custody for violating his parole, having left the state with another youth, James Marvin, for a camping trip to Alaska. Franklin underwent psychiatric testing and was released in January 1962.

In May 1962, he returned to Hapeville, Georgia, and lived near the very orphanage he detested. It wasn't long after his arrival that he stood accused of a heinous crime—kidnapping and raping a four-year-old girl.

In June 1962, Franklin walked into a bowling alley and abducted the girl, taking her outside to neighboring woods. A physical examination determined that the girl had been sexually molested, with semen stains and bite marks on and around her vagina. On July 31, he was convicted in Fulton County Superior Court of child molestation and sentenced to ten to twenty years. The kidnapping charge was dropped. His proclamation of innocence for child molestation was ignored and he was incarcerated at the Reidsville state prison.

On November 1, 1962, he was sent to Milledgeville State Hospital for psychiatric testing. Four months later he escaped while being escorted to an eye examination. Franklin stole a car and drove it to Macon, where he bought a pellet pistol and on March 15 robbed the Citizens and Southern Bank of $6,810.28. He was captured later that day and confessed to robbing the bank, but explained he needed the money to appeal his conviction on the child molestation charge.

On July 12, 1963, Franklin was sentenced to fifteen years for the bank robbery and sent to the Federal Reformatory at Chillicothe, Ohio. Two months later he attempted to escape with two other inmates, hot-wiring a prison fire truck and crashing it through a fence near the rear gate. The truck was damaged from the crash, and the inmates were captured. Franklin pled guilty to attempted escape and destruction of government property. He was sentenced in October to an additional five years in prison, to run concurrent with his bank robbery conviction, and was transferred to the federal penitentiary at Lewisburg, Pennsylvania.

Franklin had a difficult time at Lewisburg, a maximum-security prison that housed far too many violent criminals, most from the Washington, D.C., area. Targeted by more aggressive inmates for his immaturity, youth, and conviction for molesting a child, Franklin was regularly raped and beaten. Pedophiles were considered the lowest form of life in prison, and given that many of the inmates were abused as children, they showed no mercy with Franklin. The abuse was so severe that Franklin climbed the roof of a prison building and threatened to jump. He was talked down by prison personnel and taken to the prison hospital ward for psychiatric evaluation. Following his release from the hospital, he was returned to the general population, where he was repeatedly raped and beaten and disciplined for a variety of offenses, including insolence, running in the corridor, threatening an officer, fighting, and leaving a detail without permission.

Unstable and unable to cope with the harsh and violent environment at Lewisburg, Franklin was transferred in June 1964 to the Medical Center of Federal Prisoners in Springfield, Missouri, for another psychiatric observation.

In February 1965, he was transferred to the federal penitentiary at Marion, Illinois.

Marion was a new, maximum-security facility designed to replace the famed federal prison at Alcatraz, which closed in 1963. As during his tenure at Lewisburg, Franklin fared poorly at Marion. He eventually submitted to a "daddy" for protection to stay out of harm's way. He was still subject to performing sexually, but the beatings stopped, allowing Franklin to discover and nourish an interest in law. He also studied for and received his GED.

The newly found serenity also prompted contact and reconnection with the Georgia Baptist Children's Home. Franklin wrote frequently to the general manager, John C. Warr.

Franklin's letters were often long and eloquent, acknowledging his troubled past, his sorrow for any pain inflicted on his "friends" at the home, and hope that his life would one day follow a good and decent path. In 1966, Franklin even sent Warr a Christmas card. While Warr replied with several letters of his own, encouraging Franklin to continue with his studies, he held a decidedly different opinion of Franklin in letters to prison officials. In one missive, Warr was clear in explaining that Franklin Floyd was a deeply troubled man who gave "us lots of trouble."

"He has a keen mind, but in my experience, he is so emotionally unstable. I hope he will behave himself," wrote Warr.

In February 1968, Floyd was transferred to the Reidsville State Prison to complete his federal bank robbery sentence and serve the balance of his Georgia state conviction concurrently for the 1962 attack on the four-year-old girl. Reidsville was one hundred miles to the east of Atlanta and was no different than the tough federal system. Convicted child molesters were subhuman, and once again Floyd felt the wrath of his fellow convicts.

Too weak and cowardly to defend himself, Franklin befriended David Dial, a career criminal serving four years for a drug charge. Dial was well over six feet tall and 240 pounds. His physical presence and nasty disposition struck fear in much of the prison population. Dial took a liking to Franklin and offered him protection. Together they passed the countless hours of boredom that comes with prison time playing chess and talking, though it was Franklin who did most of the talking. He denied molesting the four-year-old girl and bitterly complained about his lot in life, particularly the treatment he received growing up at the children's home.

Dial would nod his head in agreement.

"Southern Christians are some of the most sadistic people around," said Dial. "They'd beat you to death in the name of Jesus."

In November 1971, Franklin was paroled from his state

sentence as part of a mandatory release program and sent to the federal penitentiary in Atlanta to serve his remaining sentence for the 1962 escape attempt from the federal prison at Chillicothe, Ohio.

The United States Penitentiary in Atlanta served as the birthplace of a revolution in prison life. Inmates there supported a new "religion" called the Church of the New Song, or CONS. They fought for and won legal recognition as an official "church," which provided, within its bylaws, that worshipers be served "communion," or Harvey's Bristol Cream and steak, on Sundays.

Given the revolutionary rhetoric and raw emotions of the late 1960s and early 1970s, jailhouse lawyers and others with a penchant for rabble-rousing were drawn to the new church, including Franklin Floyd. CONS offered new friendships and associations. Inmates, unaware of his child-molesting conviction, now simply called him Floyd.

A year later Floyd was paroled from his federal sentence. He was sent to a halfway house in November 1972, and released in January 1973. He remained in the Atlanta area but was arrested on January 27 for attempting to kidnap a woman by sticking his finger in her back near a gas station and demanding she take him into her car. After driving off, Floyd slapped the woman, called her a bitch, and grabbed at her clothes. The woman screamed, stopped the car, and managed to escape. Floyd was taken into custody on February 2, 1973. He called his friend David Dial, who had been released, and he posted the three thousand dollar bond.

Floyd failed to appear for his trial on June 11 and federal authorities issued a warrant for his arrest as a parole violator.

No records existed of Floyd's whereabouts from June 1973 until his arrival in Tulsa the summer of 1989, leaving a sixteen-year mystery for police to solve.

CHAPTER 10

Michael Hughes's first five days with Ernest and Merle Bean were disastrous. He cried every day, made grunting and growling noises, would not talk, would not sleep, and continually banged his head against the floor. On the sixth day, the screaming subsided, as did the crying. He still wouldn't talk, but he began to pay attention to some of the other children in the house and, for short moments, watched cartoons on television.

On May 3, the Beans received a call from DHS informing them that a formal complaint had been filed alleging that Michael was mistreated under his father's care. Michael was to remain with DHS until the matter was investigated.

Social worker Toni Sanders interviewed Joe Dunn, the Hughes's landlord in Tulsa. Dunn said he had known the Hughes for approximately seven months. They claimed to have come from Alabama, where Clarence worked as a painter, and were in the process of purchasing their rented mobile home and the surrounding property when Tonya died. Dunn said he had been in the Hughes's home several times, had never seen any evidence of neglect toward Michael, nor had he ever seen any signs of drugs or alcohol. If anything, said Dunn, Clarence was always bragging about his son, telling people how smart he was.

Kevin Brown told Sanders that he was in love with Tonya Hughes and was planning to help her leave Tulsa with her son. A recent change in her attitude summoned the courage to begin talking about divorce and the start of a new life. Kevin wanted to be part of that life. Tonya was deathly afraid of her husband, and for good reason. She told Kevin that Clarence had terrible secrets, the kind that could put someone in jail for life. Kevin had wanted to hear more, but Tonya had ended the discussion.

In the end, all that Kevin really knew about Tonya was that her parents were killed in a car accident when she was a child and that she had no other living relatives. Tonya had known her husband, Clarence, her entire life. He lived down the road from where she grew up in Alabama. They had a child together, and married in New Orleans before landing in Tulsa.

On May 10, DHS notified the Beans that Michael's father had disappeared, and that DHS was moving ahead through the courts to terminate Clarence's parental status. Michael was to be placed in permanent foster care.

Merle wasted no time in telling them what they should do with Michael.

"Leave him with me," she said.

Despite his severe emotional state, Merle felt great empathy and became attached to the cute boy. Merle loved children, and she figured even the toughest cases were no less deserving of a loving and caring home.

While loving Michael was one thing, caring for him would require infinite patience. He was still in diapers, wasn't potty trained, and didn't drink milk. When he first arrived, his bottle was filled with half water, half Pepsi Cola.

Merle quickly changed his diet, filling his bottle with milk and giving him regular meals. Clarence had told the social worker that Michael didn't like peanut butter, but when one of the other children in the Bean home made himself a peanut butter and jelly sandwich, Michael motioned toward the light brown jar. Merle spread some on a slice of white bread, and Michael was hooked. Soon he'd be eating peanut butter regularly and anything and everything Merle could put on his plate.

Michael slowly adapted to life with Merle, Ernest, and their large family. On occasion, he would smile at some of the other children in the home, especially the Beans' children. But there were constant reminders that all was not well with the boy. On trips outside the home, Michael would violently rock in his car seat, sending the full-size Chevy Van from side to side. When he was tired of rocking, he'd slam his body and head against the back of the car seat. He could barely walk and couldn't talk, making only grunting noises. His attention span lasted but three or four minutes. It would take three months for the crying to fully subside, and a full year before he'd utter a single word.

A week after the funeral service, Tonya Dawn Hughes was finally put to rest. Her friends at Passions collected money to transfer her body to the Park Grove Cemetery. No one called Clarence, who had seemed to drop out of sight anyway. Connie and the others were still fuming over Clarence's behavior the week before. They had been embarrassed in their heartfelt attempt at saying good-bye to someone they loved, but really knew nothing about.

Tonya danced at Passions for nine months yet confided in

no one. Though friendly, she spoke at length to but a few people, among them Connie and Bambi. Following the burial, where it was decided that Clarence would not be told the location of Tonya's final resting place, Connie and Bambi began to discuss locating Tonya's family.

Tonya had told different stories to different people. To some she said her parents were killed in a car accident when she was a child. To others she said she was estranged from her family. Connie decided to get to the bottom of it all, figuring that if Tonya did have relatives somewhere, they should know that she was dead.

Connie turned to J.R. Buck to begin the search. He reviewed her employment application, and saw Tonya's maiden name was Tadlock and that she was from Alabama, or so she said. J.R. figured he'd start there and called operator assistance, asking for any phone numbers related to the name Tadlock. There were several, and J.R. began dialing. Twenty minutes later, a woman answered the phone, and J.R. introduced himself as the owner of a dance club in Oklahoma.

"Did you know a Tonya Dawn Tadlock?" said J.R.

"Yes, I did," said the woman. "I'm her mother."

J.R. paused a moment. He'd never delivered bad news before, especially telling someone that his or her child was dead.

"Ma'am. I have some pretty bad news for you. Tonya is dead. She was killed in a car accident last week."

"Excuse me?" said the woman.

"I'm calling to tell you that your daughter, Tonya, is dead."

"Sir, I don't know what you're pulling or if you're just mistaken, but my daughter's been dead for twenty years. She died when she was a child, only eighteen months old, from pneumonia. She's buried in a cemetery near me. Her name is on the gravestone. Tonya Dawn Tadlock."

CHAPTER 11

Amid the steady drone of crickets hidden in the summer darkness, deputy U.S. marshals quietly surrounded the trailer home on Baron Chapel Road in Augusta, Georgia, their guns drawn. It was 3:30 A.M. Deputy U.S. marshal Thomas Brady gave the sign for the Richmond County dispatch to call inside the trailer, wake up its occupants, and inform them that they were surrounded and should come out with their hands on their heads.

Only one individual emerged.

Franklin Delano Floyd was handcuffed and placed in a waiting car, arrested on a felony fugitive warrant. Authorities received a tip that he had been living in Augusta for six weeks after fleeing from Oklahoma City, and working odd jobs, usually the kind of jobs people don't ask questions about, such as carpentry or painting.

When he was arrested, he was using the name Trenton B. Davis, and had used other aliases, including Preston Morgan, Whistle Britches Floyd, Kingfish Floyd, and Clarence

Marcus Hughes, some of which he said were names he took from tombstones. Once he acknowledged his real name, he preferred to be called Floyd.

Floyd was arraigned and taken to the Augusta–Richmond County Joint Law Enforcement Center. From there, he enlisted the assistance of his old friend David Dial who lived nearby. With the exception of one phone call from Floyd as he was leaving Tampa, Florida, during the summer of 1989, the two men had been out of touch since 1973, their last contact a postcard to Dial from Freedom Village, Illinois, near Chicago, after Floyd jumped parole.

Floyd asked Dial to go to the trailer where he was arrested and retrieve his property. Floyd was transferred to the federal correctional facility in Atlanta, where he called the Oklahoma Department of Human Services and informed the agency that he had been arrested as a federal fugitive, having been on the run for seventeen years. He said he was going to serve his time and turn his life around and asked DHS to care for Michael until his release, at which time he planned to regain custody of his son.

Floyd then called Mack Martin, a well-known and respected criminal attorney in Oklahoma City. He had contacted Martin before, just prior to Tonya's funeral, to represent him before the Oklahoma County Juvenile Court in matters relating to allegations that Michael Hughes was an alleged deprived child, allegations made by Connie.

Martin agreed to represent Floyd, who was now on the phone a month later explaining he had been arrested on a fugitive warrant, was going to serve time in prison, but did not under any circumstances want to lose custody of his son.

Martin relayed Floyd's wishes at a hearing before the juvenile court on August 23, 1990. Representatives from DHS argued that Floyd placed Michael in temporary foster care following the death of his mother, and then abandoned the boy when he failed to pick him up as agreed on May 7. Michael was beginning to adjust to life with his foster parents, who in turn had inquired about adoption. Martin argued that Floyd wrote his son every week, in care of DHS, and was planning to take a parenting class in prison with the ultimate goal of regaining custody when he completed his sentence. DHS officials agreed that upon Floyd's release, he would regain custody of his son and were prepared to discuss services to address Floyd's ability to provide a safe, loving home for Michael.

The court recognized Floyd as Michael's father and a review hearing was scheduled for February 1991.

The news did not sit well with the Beans. Floyd was a convicted felon and a pedophile, and Michael was still an emotional mess. Only God and Michael's dead mother knew why Michael was in such bad shape. While the crying subsided, he still couldn't talk. He was two years old, still in diapers, and prone to sudden emotional outbursts.

The Beans regularly kept DHS informed as to Michael's condition and were instructed to take him to counseling. Upon examination the counselor determined there was nothing wrong with Michael, that he was a perfect boy in every way.

Merle wanted to check the counselor's credentials.

Following several more unproductive visits Merle suggested to the counselor that he place Michael in a situation where he would be denied. Clarence left instructions never to say no to Michael.

"He's a perfect boy?" said Merle. "Put Michael in a negative situation."

Merle left the room, and a half hour later the counselor appeared.

"We'll have to change our evaluation," she said.

Floyd continued to write to Michael from his cell at the

federal prison in Atlanta, though the letters never reached the boy, instead remaining with DHS. Michael was now under evaluation, and the testing revealed that he was 50 percent delayed in most areas, including speech and learning abilities, and, once he started school, would qualify for special education programming.

In December 1990, Floyd was transferred from Atlanta to the federal prison at El Reno, near Oklahoma City. Upon his transfer, Floyd sought and was granted visitation with Michael.

Oklahoma City police continued their investigation into the death of Tonya Dawn Hughes, and they had but one suspect, Franklin Delano Floyd. They knew of his history of violence toward his wife and had a motive, the eighty thousand dollars of insurance policies. But the police could not find that one bit of elusive evidence directly linking Floyd to the crime. Paint chips recovered at the scene of the accident indicated the car that hit Tonya was red. Floyd's car was blue.

Particularly frustrating for police was the victim: Tonya Dawn Tadlock Hughes had no background, and thanks to J.R. Buck, they knew it wasn't the victim's real name.

Floyd would only say he met Tonya in Chicago, that they had a child together in Alabama in 1988, married in New Orleans in 1989, and ended up in Tulsa. He offered little else, which left police frustrated in their unsuccessful attempts to learn more about the mysterious woman.

Michael Hughes was scheduled to see his father for the first time in eight months in January 1991. Floyd was an inmate at the El Reno prison, and Merle and Ernest Bean drove

Michael to Midwest City, where they were to deliver Michael to a social worker. When they arrived, Merle opened the back door, but Michael wouldn't leave his car seat. Merle reached in to grab hold of him, but Michael resisted. He then put his arms around Merle and held on tight. Ernest had to pry Michael's fingers from Merle's coat. They placed him in the back of the social worker's car, but Michael wouldn't let them close the door, so Merle held Michael in with one hand and closed the door with the other.

Floyd was ecstatic that he would be receiving a visit from his son, and proudly spoke of Michael to anyone who would listen. The visit was supervised by a DHS social worker and lasted one hour. When Michael finally arrived, the boy was cautious and noncommunicative.

"Come here to your daddy," said Floyd, picking him up and holding him tight. Floyd played with him, told him how much he loved him, and guaranteed that one day soon he and his daddy would be together again.

The review hearing on February 7, 1991, paved the way for Floyd to regain custody of Michael. Floyd agreed to complete parenting classes at a local college, and the court also ordered that Michael be circumcised, per Floyd's wishes. On a last note before the hearing ended, the court also ordered a paternity test.

Floyd received another visit from Michael later that month, but on March 20, 1991, Floyd was admitted to the hospital complaining of pain in the chest, arm, and leg and an inability to sleep. Doctors prescribed a halter monitor, which is worn for twenty-four hours and measures heart activity, but Floyd declined. He also refused to allow blood to be drawn for testing. An electrocardiogram test proved normal. On two occasions Floyd cursed the staff, and a psychiatric evaluation was ordered. Floyd had a long history of prescription drug use, most recently Ativan, an antidepressant. The attending psychiatrist believed that Floyd was manipulative and suffered from nervousness and panic attacks. Floyd spent twenty days in the hospital and was discharged on April 9.

The monthly supervised visits with Michael at the El Reno prison continued through the year. Another juvenile hearing was held on January 9, 1992. Attorney Mack Martin produced a certificate showing that Floyd completed his parental classes and also produced a marriage certificate, proving Floyd and Tonya Hughes were married in 1989.

The court noted that the paternity test, ordered a year before, had never been completed, and the judge again ordered the test, along with an AIDS test for Michael. In addition, Floyd was ordered to pay 150 dollars per month to DHS for child support.

Floyd agreed to the child support payments but balked at the paternity test.

"I want you to object to the paternity test. I'm the father," he told Martin.

Floyd resisted the paternity test, and in his continuing bid to prove to the court he was a worthy parent, he solicited a Positive Behavior Memorandum from Cecil Nichols, a case manager at El Reno. Nichols wrote a glowing memo, commenting on Floyd's polite and cordial behavior and work ethic.

"Mr. Floyd has experienced several emotional difficulties while being incarcerated at FCI El Reno. He has had to deal with the death of his wife, the placement of his only child in the Department of Human Services, and being the recipient of a new criminal charge. Mr. Floyd has risen above all these difficulties with a maturity that is extraordinary. He has handled each difficulty in a very knowledgeable and businesslike manner. I have come to respect Mr. Floyd for the turmoil and tribulations he has been through during his life and hope his future will work out in a way that he is able to make a positive contribution toward society and provide his son with the guidance and upbringing he desires."

By July, Floyd was ordered to comply with the paternity test, and blood was drawn.

In September, as the monthly visits with Floyd continued, Michael was enrolled in a special class for developmentally and emotionally delayed children at the Choctaw Elementary School. He had made progress in his two years with the Bean family, who provided a loving and nurturing environment. Now four years old, he was finally potty trained, and his vocabulary was improving. His first real word was directed toward Merle, and it was *momma*. Several days later he began calling Ernest *daddy*.

But Michael continued to exhibit strange behavior, having become phobic over dirty hands, which caused him to go berserk, off the wall. Choctaw school officials said they would work with Michael.

The Beans were troubled by Michael's monthly visits to the El Reno prison, though they had no choice but to prepare Michael, who was picked up at home by a DHS social worker, driven an hour away to El Reno, then returned later in the day. For six months, Michael resisted the visits and, as in his first trip, had to be physically removed from the Beans' minivan. The visits eventually became a matter of routine and Michael was less resistant, though following his time with Floyd, Michael would become sullen and withdrawn.

The Beans relayed their concerns to DHS officials, complaining that the visits were hurting the boy. But DHS officials were receiving decidedly different opinions from their caseworkers. In one report, a caseworker observed two visits at the prison and did not see "any signs of distress" in Michael.

"Michael was very willing to play with his father and asked to play specific card games," reported the caseworker.

Michael also displayed affection to his father, frequently sitting in Floyd's lap. In DHS interviews with Floyd, he expressed a willingness to do "anything the court says" to retain custody of his son upon his release. Floyd was obsessed with his son, and fully expected to have custody the second he was released from prison.

The results from the paternity test were mailed to DHS in the fall, and DHS attorneys immediately went to court to request a signed order terminating Franklin Delano Floyd's rights as Michael Hughes's father.

Testing revealed that Floyd was not Michael's biological father.

Floyd was irate, claiming the testing was flawed and that he was, indeed, Michael's father. In December 1992, the state trial court agreed with the findings of the paternity test and terminated Floyd's visitation and all contact and rights to Michael Hughes.

Floyd was also ordered to stop paying child support.

Floyd's attorney challenged the ruling, claiming the court erred by failing to conduct an evidentiary hearing, which would have given Floyd opportunity to challenge the paternity test. Floyd also argued that regardless of the paternity test he had a common-law relationship with Tonya and a two-year statute of limitations for any challenge to Floyd's claim as Michael's father had expired.

Floyd, through attorney Mack Martin, took his case to the Oklahoma Supreme Court.

The Beans put adoption proceedings in motion.

CHAPTER 12

When Franklin Delano Floyd was released from the Federal
Correctional Facility at El Reno on March 30, 1993, after
serving thirty-three months, his first order of business was
to visit his parole officer.

Generally a parolee would return to the district from
which he had been sentenced, which in Floyd's case was
Tulsa. But since Michael was in foster care in Choctaw,
Floyd argued that his continuing litigation demanded his
presence in Oklahoma City. He requested and was accepted
for parole supervision in Oklahoma City.

Waiting for him was United States Probation Officer
Gary Homan. A short, round man with a friendly disposition, Homan was a native Sooner who began his career as a
correctional officer at El Reno in 1975. He worked his way
up the ranks, was promoted to the education department,
then as a counselor and case manager. In 1986, he was appointed to serve as a U.S. Probation Officer for the Western
District of Oklahoma, where he supervised federal inmates

on parole. In 1991, he received a promotion to specialist over dangerous offenders, including gang members and sexual predators.

Upon his arrival, Floyd was overly cooperative, signed all the necessary documents, and relayed that he understood the terms of his supervision, which included finding a job and a place of residence. Floyd said he had great plans and would work as a paint contractor.

"Nothing doing," said Homan. "You're not going to be self-employed. You'll get a job and will bring me your pay stub."

Homan wasn't big on treatment. He had worked with convicts and ex-cons for eighteen years and concluded that in most cases the die had been cast. To Homan, Floyd was nothing more than a pedophile and convicted felon, and nothing was going to change that. Homan was also puzzled and concerned by the sixteen-year gap in Floyd's file, with no reported activity from 1973 to 1989.

What did he do? Where was he? Homan had questions but no answers. Homan also knew that Floyd was flush with cash, the proceeds from the $80,000 insurance policies. With no charges against him, Floyd eventually collected, and used the money to hire Mack Martin.

"I want to see you here in my office every week, and every Wednesday night at the halfway house," said Homan.

Wednesday was special offenders night at the Oklahoma Halfway House, where Homan conducted weekly group therapy sessions. Pedophiles, rapists, and bank robbers— twelve in all, and all with multiproblems—gathered to discuss life on the outside, their progress, and, if they had one, their futures.

They were Homan's Dirty Dozen.

Floyd had no trouble discussing his sorry life. He was a natural talker and, during the hour-long sessions, he talked about his childhood at the Baptist Home, his prison years at Lewisburg and Marion in the 1960s, and how he gave in to sexual predators to stay alive.

Floyd's problems were no worse or better than some of those shared by the other members of the group, but it was clear after two sessions that there was something seriously wrong with Floyd, who stood out even among a group of ex-cons.

Floyd talked about his family, saying his mother was a prostitute living in Indiana, and he talked about his dead wife, Tonya, saying he believed that organized crime figures killed her. Most often, though, Floyd talked about Michael, his anger over losing the boy setting him off on a tirade. One minute he was a bizarre character, flailing his arms and raising his voice as if he were preaching at a church, screaming about the injustice of the world. The next minute he was Mr. Milquetoast, a regular guy who could be anyone's next-door neighbor. Floyd connected with no one at the sessions, and he soon became an outcast, even in a group as sordid as Homan's Dirty Dozen.

Joining Homan at group sessions was William Schmid, a veteran psychologist and vice-president of Hillcrest Behavioral Medical Center, which was contracted to provide psychological services for the Oklahoma Halfway House.

Schmid served as co-leader for the group discussions but also met with Floyd individually at his Hillcrest office. Initial testing indicated that Floyd was antisocial, a nondescript man who could be easily ignored if not spoken to. But once engaged, it was clear to all he was dangerous. Floyd was also highly intelligent, and during his weekly meetings with Homan and Schmid, he talked about his pending appeal to the Oklahoma Supreme Court. The paternity test and decision to terminate his parental rights were a severe blow to Floyd, who was so depressed during one meeting he threatened to kill himself. Homan once asked Floyd for the identity of Michael's real father, and whether his wife was having affairs. Homan, like the various police agencies investigating Tonya Hughes, knew nothing about her, only what Floyd would offer, which wasn't much.

In July 1993, the Oklahoma Supreme Court reversed the decision of the trial court to terminate Floyd's parental rights to Michael. The court ruled that Floyd's rights were violated when the trial court refused to hold an evidentiary hearing to allow Floyd to contest the paternity test. Visitation was restored, though the date for the hearing had yet to be determined.

Believing he was now on the road to regaining custody of Michael, Floyd charged that Merle and Ernest Bean were abusing Michael. Floyd presented no evidence, yet claimed that Michael alleged the Beans were "mean" and tried to choke him. The Beans denied the charges, yet were helpless, even when Floyd sought a court order preventing the Beans from giving Michael a haircut.

As the matter of parentage was to be decided by the courts, Floyd called Mack Martin fifteen to twenty times a day to discuss the case.

In the spring of 1994, five-year-old Michael visited with Floyd in Martin's downtown office. Martin excused himself, leaving them alone for twenty minutes. When Michael returned to Choctaw, he went to bed with his shoes and socks on. Merle asked him to take them off, but Michael said he couldn't, that Floyd said not to.

Merle took off the shoes, and inside a sock was a photo of Floyd.

"He said it was our secret," said Michael.

* * *

Floyd gave up his odd jobs with various painting crews to accept a single position as a maintenance man at the Lyrewood
Pointe Apartments in Oklahoma City, a shabby, low-rent
complex. Floyd believed that the steady, forty-hours-per-
week schedule, along with the regular paycheck, would influ-
ence the court in his battle for Michael. Floyd was also given
a residence at the complex, which in his mind provided even
more stability for Michael. Prior to Floyd's hiring, Gary
Homan informed the apartment manager of his criminal past,
including the rape conviction from 1962.

With a steady income, an apartment to call home, and a
glowing recommendation from his supervisor, who described
Floyd as a "model employee," Floyd sought psychiatric testing, ostensibly to prove he was a qualified parent and to seek
approval for an increase in visits from one to two per month.
Dr. Bruce Pickins, who supervised Floyd's monthly visits
with Michael, recommended the additional visit as a means
toward working for reunification, but was overridden.

To help his cause, Floyd turned to Dr. Eleanor Jessen, a
clinical psychologist referred by Dr. Schmid, his group
counselor. Floyd underwent testing on May 28, May 30, and
June 1.

Jessen's three-page report commented on Floyd's nervousness and defensive nature, which included a compul-
sion to explain his situation. By the third session he felt
more comfortable, and the defensiveness melted away. Floyd
spoke freely and was cooperative. Jessen noted that Floyd's
years at the orphanage and in prison had taken their toll.
His self-esteem was damaged, although not morbidly so,
and he was easily depressed. Jessen also noted that Floyd
could be "expansive and can get pumped up with his own

sense of competence, a common defense against the pains of disappointment in self."

Jessen determined that Floyd was "not criminal in character—not antisocial." She recommended that "reunification of Mr. Floyd and Michael should be actively pursued and should be brought about as soon as possible."

Carrie Box spent the Fourth of July holiday at a friend's house, and at the end of the day decided to race her boyfriend to their home at the Lyrewood Pointe Apartments. Box, in her mid-twenties, would run the few blocks home while her boyfriend would run to their car, and try to beat her to the front door. Box won the race, and upon entering her apartment saw a man standing in her bedroom, rummaging through her dresser drawers.

He held a pair of Box's panties in one hand, close to his nose, and a knife in the other hand. He saw her standing there, ran toward her, and knocked her to the floor. As Box tried to fight him off, her arms made contact with the knife, producing deep gashes. The man punched her in the eye, then reached for her panties, saying, "Your boyfriend paid me to do this."

Box continued to fight, fearing for her life. Her boyfriend arrived and tried to pin the man down, but he managed to run out the door. The boyfriend followed, tracked him down, and held him until police arrived.

Gary Homan returned from a festive Fourth of July holiday to learn that Franklin Floyd had been arrested and charged with aggravated assault for his attack on Carrie Box.

Floyd's position as maintenance man required that he have master keys to all the apartments, and Floyd used his key to let himself into Box's apartment. Police found a pair of panties in his back pocket.

Homan knew, despite Floyd's talk to the contrary, that he was dangerous. Homan now believed that Floyd was pure evil, even after listening to Floyd scream during a meeting at the county jail.

"It's a bum rap. I was framed," yelled Floyd.

Homan had heard enough.

"I'm going to hang you out to dry."

Homan returned to his office and told his bosses that under no circumstances was Floyd to be freed on bail, and parole officials had to find some creative loophole to keep him there. His parole could not be revoked until the assault charge was adjudicated, and that was not going to happen anytime soon. Mack Martin made an appearance before the Oklahoma County district judge, and to Homan's disbelief Floyd was released on seven thousand dollars bail.

Floyd returned to the Oklahoma Halfway House, and his activity was dramatically curtailed. Floyd was fired from the apartment complex and found a job as a painter. He was allowed to leave the home in the morning to go to work, but ordered to return at the end of his day.

On the heels of his arrest, the state court scheduled the evidentiary hearing for September 23, and would deliver its decision on Floyd's bid to regain custody of Michael.

Floyd knew that if he was found guilty of the assault charge he'd have no chance at ever receiving custody of Michael. Desperate and obsessed with the boy he called his own, Floyd decided to take matters into his own hands.

CHAPTER 13

With the start of a new school year, six-year-old Michael
Hughes woke up each morning at 7 A.M., dressed, ate
breakfast, washed his hands, and brushed his teeth. Then,
under the watchful eye of his foster mother, Michael would
leave the house, walk down the driveway to the street, turn
to the right, and walk to the corner, where a yellow school
bus would pick him up at precisely 8:20 A.M.

Michael was a first-grade student at the Indian Meridian
Elementary School in Choctaw, which was two miles down
the road from the Bean home. When he cheerfully left for
school the morning of September 12, 1994, he was far different from the emotionally disturbed basket case the Beans
had received four years earlier.

Michael's speech had improved tenfold, and his crying
spells were long gone, as was his bed-wetting. No one
called him Pookie, a name from his distant, troubled past.
He was simply Michael, and he had gained a normalcy in
his life, having responded to the loving and nourishing

environment Merle and Ernest provided. Michael had grown into a handsome boy, with a mop of brown hair and big, brown eyes. He smiled easily, laughed loudly, and enjoyed being a member of the Bean family. He fished with Ernest and sang "Dear Mr. Jesus" at church on Sunday with his foster family.

Legally, though, Michael continued to be a ward of the state as the Beans' efforts to adopt him were stymied by the courts, which were still wrestling with Franklin Floyd's petitions to be recognized as Michael's father.

That prospect, however slim, worried the Beans. They had always been leery of Floyd, whom they believed was nothing more than a predator. His arrest in July simply confirmed what they already knew while recent events in August heightened their awareness, and deep fear, of Floyd.

Early one morning they were awakened by the incessant barking of their dog, which noticed something in the backyard. Ernest investigated and followed as the dog led him two hundred feet into the woods, where they found a fresh campsite.

That same week Merle thought she saw Floyd driving by her home in a pickup truck. She quickly called DHS.

"He's looking to get Michael," said Merle. "I'm telling you he's going to take him."

The Beans remained protective and kept Michael within eyesight. They avoided any mention of Floyd in Michael's presence, even when the youngster began to articulate events from his past. He said he had dreams, and remembered being in a dark place, maybe a closet, for long periods of time. He was scared and he would cry out for his mother. But she was gone. It was Floyd who'd eventually come to his aid.

Merle relayed the story to a DHS staff member, who suggested that Michael was recalling real events, theorizing that Floyd locked Michael in a bedroom or even a closet whenever he would leave the house, perhaps when he drove Tonya to work.

They were distant, disturbing memories, but they seemed real nonetheless. Merle comforted Michael, holding him in her arms, lightly kissing his head, and gently telling him to forget those bad dreams.

"You're with people who love you, Michael," said Merle.

Michael nuzzled into Merle's embrace, comforted in knowing he was safe and secure.

Nearly five hundred students were enrolled at the Indian Meridian Elementary School, all of them in grades kindergarten through third. Of the thirty teachers on staff, eight taught first grade.

Classes were already under way on Monday, September 12, when Franklin Floyd entered the school at 9 A.M. and walked uneasily to the office of Principal James Davis.

Floyd was disheveled and wore a rumpled dark gray suit and a brown felt hat with a narrow brim. His salt-and-pepper hair matched his mustache. The door to the office was open and Floyd walked in, only to see Davis sitting behind his desk conversing with Gary Berland, the intermediate school principal.

Davis did not recognize Floyd but he said his meeting would be over in a minute and politely asked him to wait outside. Floyd stood in the hall, next to the doorway, and when Davis concluded his meeting, he motioned for Floyd to come in. The two men shook hands and Davis closed the door. Davis, fifty-four, was a big man at six-feet-four and 215 pounds. He sat in his chair behind a desk topped with papers. Floyd sat opposite Davis.

"This is something that's hard for me to do," said Floyd.

"I've been grieving for four years, and I'm ready to die. I want you to help me get my son."

Floyd reached into his front pants pocket and pulled out what appeared to be a gun, exposing the brown handle and trigger. Davis had no doubt it was a gun, probably a .25 or .32 caliber automatic.

"If you won't help me, you won't live because I don't want to live. It's like what happens at the post office. People get killed because they don't care. That's me. I don't care."

Startled, Davis tried his best to remain calm. He didn't want to do or say anything that could place any of the five hundred young students or faculty in danger.

"Who is your son?" said Davis.

"Michael Hughes. He's in the first grade. I don't know what room he's in."

"Well, we'll have to check the list," said Davis, who reached down to open a drawer.

"No!" said Floyd, jumping up from his seat, the gun remaining in his pocket, only the handle exposed. "Tell me the names of the first-grade teachers."

Davis explained that he had to get the folder from a drawer, which he did, slowly. He pulled out a folder and began naming the teachers, one by one. He was stopped when he said "Houter."

"That's the one," said Floyd. "Now we're going to her room and you're going to call Michael out, and then we're going to go outside to your car. All I want is a ten-minute head start and then I'll let you go. Understand?"

Davis nodded, rose from this chair and the two men walked out into the hallway, with Davis leading the way. They stopped at room 814. Floyd remained to the side of the doorway and out of view as Davis took a deep breath, opened the door, and poked his head into the classroom.

"I need to see Michael Hughes for a moment, please. And have him bring his bag."

The teacher motioned for Michael to get up from his chair, take his Aladdin backpack, and walk to the doorway, where Davis took his hand and led him out.

Michael wore a blue T-shirt with red sleeves and red-and-blue shorts. His black, high-top sneakers bore the word *hoop* in white. He walked into the hall and smiled at Floyd, exposing two new front bottom teeth, both slightly crooked. Floyd motioned for Davis to walk down the hallway toward the school entrance.

"I want you to tell the people in the office that you'll be right back," said Floyd.

Davis stopped in front of the school offices, opened the door, and told a secretary that he'd be back soon. Floyd followed Davis outside, directing him to the school parking lot.

"Where's your car?" said Floyd.

"Over there. It's the white truck."

Davis drove a pickup truck, a new 1994 Ford F150 XLT with a white camper shell that covered the back. The front license tag read "Fish Oklahoma" while the rear license read QCN305.

Michael had remained quiet, unsure of what was happening. Floyd told Davis to open the car door.

"I appreciate you cooperating with me," said Floyd.

"I don't have much choice," said Davis, who opened his side first, then sat in the driver's seat.

Floyd walked around to the passenger side and opened the door for Michael, who climbed in and sat in the middle, with Floyd sitting next to the passenger window. In Floyd's hands were handcuffs, duct tape, and the pistol, which was now in full view. It was small and chrome-plated. Davis drove out of the parking lot onto Indian Meridian Road and was directed toward a field about a mile and a half away, where they parked the truck behind several bales of hay.

"Michael, we're going to go find your dog. You stay here, ok?" said Floyd, who turned to Davis. "Leave the radio on."

The two men left Michael sitting in the truck and walked about twenty yards into woods where Davis saw a green sleeping bag, cooler, and quilt. They continued another twenty yards beyond the campsite, where Floyd told Davis to stop next to a tree.

"I'm going to handcuff you to this tree and tape your mouth shut," said Floyd, who kept his gun pointed toward Davis's back.

He ordered Davis to squat down, lean his back against the tree with his arms extended behind him. Floyd handcuffed one wrist, then the other, with the tree between Davis's arms. He took out his roll of duct tape and covered Davis's mouth.

"I'll call someone after two hours and tell them where you are, understand?"

Davis nodded, but grimaced in pain. Floyd left a key for the handcuffs on the other side of the tree then walked away, but returned a few minutes later. He peeled the tape from Davis's mouth.

"How do I get into the camper?" said Floyd.

"What?" said Davis.

"The camper. I can't get into the back of the truck. How do I open it?" said Floyd.

Davis gave him instructions, then asked Floyd to loosen the handcuffs.

"They're hurting," said Davis.

Floyd retaped his mouth, then took off.

Davis was uncomfortable: a middle-aged man forced into a squatting position, his hands behind his back wrapped around a tree, and handcuffed. Davis knew he couldn't remain in the squatting position much longer, so he pressed his back against the tree and tried to shimmy his arms and body upward. It took him nearly a half hour to raise himself into a standing position, sweat pouring down his face and neck. The struggle knocked his glasses off his face and loosened the duct tape over his mouth, allowing him to call out for help. It would be two hours before someone would answer his call.

The Oklahoma City field office of the Federal Bureau of Investigation was usually busy on any given day, given its share of bank robberies, drug investigations, and occasional kidnappings. Mid-level in size when compared to the FBI's fifty-six field offices throughout the country, the 120 special agents assigned to Oklahoma City were no less experienced.

They occupied the top floors of a sixteen-story building several miles north of the downtown area. The Violent Crimes Major Offender squad worked out of a corner of the top floor, the twelve agents assigned to the squad among the most respected in this bureau. Each squad had its own supervisor and primary relief supervisor, after which came a senior agent who was given the task of coordinating specific investigations. When it came to kidnappings, that role fell on the shoulders of Special Agent Joe Fitzpatrick.

Originally from Carbondale, Illinois, Fitzpatrick was recruited by the FBI in 1970, persuaded to leave his job as vice president of an Arkansas bank for the more noble pursuit of law enforcement. His first assignment upon leaving the academy at Quantico, Virginia, was in Minneapolis, which was followed by a transfer to the Milwaukee field office. In 1975, after gaining some seniority, he voluntarily transferred to Oklahoma City, where he would remain for the next twenty-three years.

Fitzpatrick was of medium size with a strong, compact physique, the result of regular visits to the Y and a steady diet of tennis. He had dark hair with silver streaks throughout, and was soft-spoken almost to a whisper, exhibiting a simple quietness in tone and demeanor that belied a ferocious tenacity.

During his nearly two decades in Oklahoma City, Fitzpatrick developed a sterling reputation as an experienced agent, who during his career took some of the toughest assignments the bureau had to offer. He worked undercover in the late 1970s, growing his hair down to his shoulders and a beard that covered his neck. During a shooting involving bank robbery suspects and Oklahoma state troopers, Fitzpatrick flew in on a Huey helicopter, his wild hair blowing around his head.

Later he served with the bureau's SWAT team and then took the assignment with the Violent Crimes Major Offender Squad. It was a prestigious assignment, the kind of work where agents seeking the excitement of kicking down doors and investigating high-profile crimes would find great satisfaction. Fitzpatrick served as the bank robbery coordinator and then as the agent in charge of kidnappings.

He was an icon to the younger, less-experienced agents and was as easygoing as they came. Married, with three children, he enjoyed the peaceful solitude of fly-fishing along the red clay banks that rimmed every lake and fishing hole in Oklahoma and the competition from a good game of tennis.

Tragedy struck Fitzpatrick in the mid-1980s when his youngest son collapsed during a high school tennis match and died, the result of a rare heart defect. The loss was devastating, and Fitzpatrick would never be the same. His closest friends and colleagues noticed the quiet man becoming even more withdrawn. But he managed to maintain a per-

sonal record of closing every case assigned, a record that had
remained intact when he picked up the phone on September
12, 1994, and spoke with the Choctaw deputy chief of police, Billy Carter.

A brief discussion over jurisdiction ended when Fitzpatrick learned that the suspected kidnapper was a convicted felon considered armed and dangerous. He had a
two-hour head start and was probably heading out of state.
Fitzpatrick sent two agents to Choctaw to gather more information and, by late afternoon, was on the phone with Assistant U.S. Attorney Mark Yancey, seeking a federal
warrant for the arrest of Franklin Delano Floyd.

After learning the details, Yancey agreed that Floyd was
probably heading out of state, but with no proof or evidence
of flight, it would be difficult at best convincing a judge to
issue a warrant for kidnapping. Instead, Yancey said he
would appear before the judge in the morning seeking a
warrant for felony use of a firearm during a kidnapping. In
the meantime, he gave Fitzpatrick authorization to make a
warrantless arrest in the event Floyd was captured overnight.

With jurisdiction in hand, Fitzpatrick followed standard
FBI procedure. A teletype was issued with all the pertinent
information on the alleged perpetrator and victim, including their names, ages, and addresses. The notice was the first
of several teletypes sent to FBI bureaus throughout the
country. Communications were prioritized within three different categories. Notices labeled "routine" required other
agencies to respond within twenty-four hours while "priority" classifications required a response within one hour. Bureaus were to drop everything when they received an
"immediate" teletype.

Michael Hughes's kidnapping was classified "immediate" and after consulting with his superiors, Fitzpatrick was
given a free hand to reign in the bureau's vast resources.

More agents rushed to Choctaw to interview Principal Davis, other school personnel, and Merle and Ernest Bean, as well as coordinate efforts with Chief John Whetsel and Deputy Chief Carter of the Choctaw Police Department. Gary Homan, who had spent eighteen months with Floyd as his parole officer, was called in to explain what he knew about his habits, his personality, his friends, and his recent demeanor. Dr. Schmid and DHS caseworkers were also interviewed.

An APB, or All Points Bulletin, was issued to police agencies throughout the region on the white Ford pickup truck while agents were assigned to visit Floyd's last known addresses in Oklahoma City and Tulsa. Finally, a standard indices check of Floyd's prison and arrest records—updated following his capture in Georgia in 1990—revealed he used several different aliases while living in other cities, including Louisville, Atlanta, Phoenix, and Tampa. Fitzpatrick noted, with great interest, that Floyd was also a suspect in the 1990 death of his wife, a homicide still under investigation by the Oklahoma City police and Tulsa police.

With agents scurrying around Oklahoma into the night, Fitzpatrick remained at his desk quarterbacking the bureau's efforts. He read each and every file found on Floyd, and within twenty-four hours, Fitzpatrick had a working knowledge of the man he was chasing, having followed his history from his 1962 arrest and his time in prison, to his release in 1972. He disappeared, resurfacing in 1989 in Tulsa.

Fitzpatrick read about the tragic death of Tonya, Floyd's subsequent capture for parole violation, his sentencing, and his legal battle for Michael.

Floyd wasn't Michael's biological father, that much was sure, and the boy apparently flourished during his four years with his foster family. Michael had been given a rare chance, an opportunity to live a normal, healthy life. But Floyd returned, and Fitzpatrick worried for the boy.

Consultations with FBI behaviorists and profilers devised two scenarios: Either Michael was in immediate and extreme danger, or Floyd had a relationship with the boy and wouldn't hurt him in the short term. All agreed with the latter but acknowledged that the longer Floyd remained on the loose and given the pressure that would be placed on him by the FBI, the less of a chance Michael Hughes had of returning home alive.

At best, Fitzpatrick figured that Michael had a week, maybe ten days, before becoming a liability, which gave Fitzpatrick a self-imposed deadline of September 22 to find the boy alive.

Fitzpatrick had already called home, informing his wife that she wouldn't be seeing him anytime soon, and he spent what would become many sleepless nights reviewing new information that was streaming into his office from his own agents and field offices around the country.

Some of the information came from the Oklahoma City and Tulsa police investigations into the murder of Tonya Hughes. Still other details came from names disclosed in interviews with Floyd following his arrest in 1990, along with records and phone numbers found in Floyd's apartment at the halfway house.

The revelations were disturbing.

Floyd assumed several identities after his flight from Georgia in 1973. The first was Trenton B. Davis, a name he used while living in Oklahoma City from 1975 to 1978 where he worked as a maintenance man for the Oklahoma City school district.

Floyd, a.k.a. Davis, left Oklahoma City in 1978, appearing in Louisville, Kentucky, in 1980, where he found work as a painter and went by the name of Warren Marshall. He remained there until 1982, disappeared again before emerging in Atlanta in 1982, Phoenix in 1987, and Tampa in 1988, in each location using the name Warren Marshall.

He was in Tulsa in 1989 under the name Clarence Hughes and married to his young wife, Tonya Dawn Hughes. Fitzpatrick knew that wasn't her real name, which added another bizarre element to the investigation. She was a stripper who was apparently planning to leave her abusive husband when she was killed. Floyd cashed in on her death, receiving an eighty-thousand-dollar life insurance payment. He went to jail to serve out his parole violation and the gun charge, yet fought to keep Michael, who wasn't his biological son.

It was clear, given Floyd's 1962 arrest, that he was a pedophile, and Fitzpatrick believed he didn't have to question Floyd's interest in his "son," which added another level of urgency to the search.

Fitzpatrick was noticeably disturbed; he talked less, and seemed to always be in deep thought. During the first few days of the search, it was clear to other agents in the field office that Fitzpatrick was emotionally involved, a common trait for Fitzpatrick, who always fell easily. But his superiors knew his emotions served as the main motivation for his success. Fitzpatrick cared, yet never crossed the line and lost his objectivity.

Searching for a six-year-old boy who had only recently been given a new lease on life would test Fitzpatrick in ways he had never been tested before.

The other agents in the VCMO squad dropped whatever they were doing and worked the case during the initial days of the investigation, while agents from other squads were pulled in to lend a helping hand. Fitzpatrick dispatched agents to the Oklahoma City school district offices to review Floyd's personnel records as Trenton Davis and track down and interview anyone who may have known him.

Field offices throughout the country, with special attention paid to Louisville, Atlanta, Tampa, and Phoenix, were sent new communiqués seeking any information to help with the investigation.

Fitzpatrick had tremendous resources at his disposal, and he used them all. Agents sent to search Floyd's room at the Oklahoma Halfway House found personal belongings kept in a locked garage behind the building. Of particular interest were photos. Some of the pictures were of Michael, others of his mother, Tonya. Fitzpatrick reviewed each one, and took particular interest in Tonya. She was posing seductively, wearing a tiger-striped outfit. She was attractive, but Fitzpatrick couldn't help but notice that she looked young, perhaps even an adolescent in one particular photo. If Fitzpatrick had to guess, she could have been as young as fourteen. Floyd had claimed after his arrest in 1990 that he had met her in Chicago. Fitzpatrick didn't buy it. No one knew her real name, and the truth concerning her real identity began to gnaw at him. It was yet another question that couldn't be answered in a case that was bulging with too many unknowns.

As the hours turned to days, then a full week, Floyd and Michael had all but disappeared. All of Fitzpatrick's training and experience told him that time was running out for the boy, and he desperately needed some sort of break or clue.

He found one on the seventh day of the search when an agent rushed into the field office and hurried to Fitzpatrick's desk with a photo in his hand. The agent had just interviewed Jim Ennis, a former Oklahoma school district employee who worked with Floyd in the 1970s. During the interview, Ennis produced a color, wallet-sized photo of a man posing for a picture with a girl in his lap. The man was wearing a dark suit and blue tie. Ennis said he knew the man as Trenton Davis, and the pretty little girl with blond hair in the pretty blue dress was his daughter, Suzanne.

Ennis said Davis had given him the photo years ago, when they worked together. Floyd was proud of the picture, a "family" photo of a single dad and his young daughter. The photo, and Davis, had long been forgotten after Floyd dropped out of sight in 1978. It was just a few weeks ago when "Davis" suddenly reappeared. He looked older, grayer, and seemed disturbed, far more so than when they had been friends. He said he came back to reclaim the old photo. Ennis said he didn't have it, that he had lost it long ago.

After Davis had left, Ennis rummaged through his picture box. Lo and behold, there it was. When the FBI showed up at Ennis's door, and he learned that Trenton Davis was really Franklin Delano Floyd, he knew exactly where to find that photo.

Ennis had placed it in the agent's hand and watched his jaw drop. The agent knew right away what he had and raced back to the field office. He was now standing in front of Joe Fitzpatrick, taking deep breaths, with excitement in his eyes and a slight smile of satisfaction apparent at the corners of his mouth. Fitzpatrick studied the photo, his eyes focused on the girl sitting on Floyd's lap. She couldn't have been more than five years old, maybe six. She was unsmiling, and looked to be unhappy. Floyd was much younger, with black hair, a crooked mouth and deep, dark eyes. Fitzpatrick placed the photo down on his desk and compared it to other photos of Floyd, his wife, Tonya, and Michael. Fitzpatrick's eyes darted back and forth, and he shuffled Tonya's photos next to the portrait photo. His heart beat fast and his palms sweated as he realized that the girl in both photos were one in the same.

"Oh my God!" shouted Fitzpatrick. "He kidnapped her too!

CHAPTER 14

Dallas, Texas, police officer Amilio Ayala was working regular patrol duty on Saturday, October 22, 1994, when he pulled up to the massive Wonder Bread factory on Denton Street. The facility took up four square blocks and employed more than five hundred people who baked and distributed bread and other products twenty-four hours a day. Three parking lots surrounded the facility, one in the front used by supervisors and office personnel, another in the back reserved for employees, and another on the side used by mechanics. The employee parking lot in the back was adjacent to Love Field airport, and a DART, or Dallas Area Rapid Transit station, was down the street.

Ayala, assigned to the Northwest bicycle patrol, was scheduled to help with security for the annual Wonder Bread open house. He unlocked his bike from the back of the patrol car and was pulling it down when he was approached by several factory workers.

A white Ford pickup truck had been parked for several

weeks in the employee lot, and they believed it was stolen. They took Ayala to the truck, a Ford F150, the back of which was parked against the building. The Oklahoma license on the back read QCN305. Ayala peered inside the driver's window and saw the radio was still in place and the steering column untouched.

Ayala called in the plate number to central command, asking if it was hot. The response was quick: The truck was stolen out of Oklahoma City. The perpetrator was believed to be Franklin Delano Floyd, who was wanted for kidnapping. He was considered armed and extremely dangerous and in the company of a six-year-old boy.

Ayala roped off the car and waited for backup to arrive.

Word that the truck had been found in Dallas traveled immediately to the Oklahoma City FBI field office, and Joe Fitzpatrick called Mark Yancey at the U.S. Attorney's office, asking for and receiving an additional arrest warrant, this one for kidnapping.

Floyd had traveled out of state, and finding the truck was the first real clue in the now six-week search for Floyd and Michael. Fitzpatrick rarely left his office, continuing his grueling all-day and all-night, seven-days-a-week schedule, catching much needed sleep whenever he could. The news about the truck produced a newfound sense of urgency. All involved in the investigation were tired and frustrated. Promising leads that sent agents to cities throughout the country turned up new information about Floyd, but not Floyd himself.

If one thing was clear, Floyd was not stupid. During his years as a fugitive, he had proved resourceful. He remained in a few select states, subsisting with the help of a network of former inmates who helped him with birth certificates, driver's licenses, and, if needed, food and money. The help went way back, starting with David Dial, Floyd's old friend from prison.

Dial provided room and board after Floyd's release from the halfway house in 1973. Floyd got a job prepping rental cars for Avis at the Atlanta airport but quickly got into trouble. It was Dial who bailed Floyd out of jail after his arrest for attacking a woman at a drive-in restaurant. Floyd fled prior to his trial and Dial claimed he didn't hear from him for seventeen years. The FBI didn't believe him. Dial had been in and out of jail for thirty years and had no love for law enforcement. Floyd was his friend. So when Dial was asked what he knew about the girl traveling with Floyd, he said that Floyd told him her mother was a crack addict and he just took the girl, who was four years old, to keep her out of that environment.

"I believe him, too. She was never on any milk carton, was she? No," said Dial.

The story didn't move Dial's interviewers, who knew that it was Dial who provided shelter when Floyd bolted Oklahoma after Tonya's death. Floyd used the name Daniel Pittman and even had an I.D. that read Pittman.

"Franklin was real good with I.D.s," said Dial, who took great satisfaction in the FBI's inability to find his friend. "You know he learned that in prison, which is pretty funny, ain't it? Prison is a good teacher. If you ain't a criminal when you get in, you will be when you get out."

When Fitzpatrick read the notes from the David Dial interview, he felt a sudden urge to jump on a plane and fly to Georgia himself. Dial knew more than he was saying, a lot more—especially when it came to the mystery of Tonya.

Fitzpatrick had sent notices to field offices throughout the country, and the information that began to arrive daily at a steady pace helped fill in some of the blanks in the Floyd timeline.

After Floyd, using the name Trenton Davis, resurfaced in 1975 in Oklahoma City, he enrolled Tonya, then known as Suzanne, in the public school system. She was said to be bright, and could read, spell, add, and subtract by the age of five, or whatever her real age was when she entered the first grade.

The pair fled in 1978 following a babysitter's allegations that Floyd was sexually abusing his daughter. No charges were filed and they disappeared for two years, eventually ending up in Louisville in 1980 with new identities, Warren and Sharon Marshall. Floyd worked as a painter and joined the local Kiwanis club and a Baptist church. He and Sharon attended church together regularly every Sunday. Sharon performed exceptionally well in school but two years later they abruptly left Louisville for Atlanta. They kept their identities, Warren and Sharon Marshall, and lived in north Atlanta, where Sharon was enrolled as a freshman at Northside High School.

But she didn't finish the school year, transferring to Baldwin High School in May 1983. It wasn't lost on Fitzpatrick that Reidsville State Prison was in Milledgeville, about one hundred miles east of Atlanta and the same prison where Floyd served time from 1967 to 1971. Fitzpatrick did not believe in coincidences. He knew Floyd returned to Milledgeville for a reason—just what, he didn't know. Fitzpatrick's interest was further piqued when he saw that Sharon was pulled out of Baldwin High School just four months later, in September, right after the start of a new school year. They moved back to Atlanta, and Sharon enrolled at Riverdale High School, where she remained from September 1983 to January 1984 before transferring to Forest Park High School, where she remained until her graduation in June 1986.

They later turned up in Phoenix, Arizona, where Sharon

took a job as a hostess at the Marriott Hotel restaurant near the airport. There she met Greg Higgs.

Fitzpatrick obtained copies of Floyd's phone records dating back to when he arrived in Tulsa, and noticed among the names a call to Greg Higgs in Phoenix in May 1990, just days after Sharon's death.

Fitzpatrick reached Higgs, and learned that he was Michael's biological father. He was twenty years old and working as a waiter in 1986, having arrived from Seattle a year earlier to attend college. Tall and thin with dark hair and sharp features, Higgs rented an apartment nearby and worked at the restaurant after school to make ends meet.

When the new hostess arrived at the Marriott, she created a stir among the men who worked there, including Higgs. Sharon was friendly and outgoing and talked to everyone, from the busboys to the maître d'. She was attractive and easy to like, and rode a purple scooter to and from work. Higgs was smitten and eventually worked up the courage to talk to her a day after she arrived. Sharon made it easy, smiling and engaging in conversation, even asking about *his* interests and goals in life.

Sharon said she planned on studying aerospace engineering at Arizona State.

Higgs got up his nerve and asked her out for a date. She smiled and said, "Yes."

Higgs thought that was too easy.

They decided to go "float" the Salt River, sitting in inner tubes as the lazy river carried them downstream.

Higgs drove to Sharon's house, which was in a trailer park on the outskirts of Phoenix. Sharon was waiting by the front door. As soon as Higgs arrived she called out to her father, who emerged from the back of the trailer.

He introduced himself as Warren, eyed Higgs from head

to toe, and made it clear he wanted his daughter home by midnight.

"And don't let my daughter drown," he said as he walked into the house.

Higgs and Sharon spent the afternoon in the water and under a sun that produced 110 degree heat. As they floated down the river, Sharon told Higgs that she was from Georgia and her mom had died when she was young. She had planned on going to Georgia Tech, but her father's health was poor, so they moved to Arizona hoping the low humidity would help his back. Sharon talked about her good marks in high school, and said that she was a lieutenant colonel in the ROTC.

Being from Georgia explained the slight southern twang, thought Higgs.

Following their "float" they stopped for cheeseburgers and French fries before Higgs drove Sharon home, hours ahead of the deadline set by her father.

"He just looks out for me," said Sharon, explaining why her father appeared to be so strict.

Higgs didn't mind. He kissed her and asked for another date. Sharon smiled, said, "Yes," and then "good night."

Over the next three months, their relationship blossomed into something more serious. Higgs occasionally saw Warren, usually when he picked Sharon up from work. Only once did he see Warren inside the restaurant, roughly a week after Sharon struck up a conversation with several businessmen. They had stopped for a bite to eat between flights, engaged Sharon in conversation, and became smitten with the young hostess who was working to save money for college. So impressed were the businessmen, they offered to pay her tuition.

Sharon was taken aback, thanked the men, and then said

she wanted them to meet her father. They told her they'd be traveling through again in a week. When they arrived, waiting for them was Warren, who dismissed any conversation about college and awkwardly tried to convince them to invest in a house painting business. It sounded like a scam to Higgs, who remained quiet.

When it was all over and the men had left, Sharon seemed down. They had withdrawn their offer and wished Sharon well.

"What was that all about?" asked Higgs.

Sharon wouldn't say, offering only that her father was trying to get his feet back on the ground. She walked away abruptly, ending the conversation.

The next day Sharon returned to her cheerful self again, and remained that way for two months, when she surprised Higgs with a note.

It had been left with another hostess, who waited a day to give it to Higgs. Sharon had left Arizona. She had apparently come into the restaurant, picked up her last paycheck, and was gone. The letter didn't say much other than that Sharon and her father had to leave.

Two months later Higgs received a letter in the mail postmarked Texas. It was from Sharon and began, "Dear Greg." Sharon explained that her leaving wasn't his fault, that the relationship had been working well. But her father's health was deteriorating and they had to move.

Higgs didn't understand why they'd moved to Texas. It was just as hot as Arizona, and far more humid. The envelope had no return address, so Higgs couldn't write back. He thought he had seen the last of Sharon Marshall.

Eight months later, in the spring of 1987, Higgs walked into work and to his surprise saw Sharon standing at her old station.

She reentered his life as suddenly as she had left it, explaining that she and her father had just returned to Arizona after traveling to Texas and several other states, none of which she identified. Her father couldn't acclimate to the weather, as his back illness flared up every other day.

"Don't hate me," she said, looking Higgs in the eyes.

"I don't," said Higgs, who was actually pleased to see his old girlfriend.

He had dated several other girls during the prior year, none of whom matched Sharon's beauty or intelligence.

They quickly became a couple again, though Higgs made it a point to avoid Sharon's father at all costs. Their relationship continued through the fall of 1987, when Higgs arrived at work one day to learn that Sharon had once again quit her job and, just like the last time, disappeared.

He never saw Sharon again.

Higgs told Fitzpatrick he never knew Sharon was pregnant, and only learned he had a son when he received that call from Floyd in May 1990, who had assumed his previous identity of Warren Marshall.

Warren told him that Sharon was dead, killed in a car accident just days earlier, and that Higgs was the father of her two-year-old son, Michael.

"Sharon was working as a topless dancer in Arizona and we left because she didn't want to screw things up for you. She thought if you knew you had a kid you'd stop going to school," said Warren. "We went to Puerto Rico for a year. Now she's dead, and I need to know if you'll take the boy."

Higgs was stunned. He also didn't flinch, saying he'd take Michael. Warren said he'd get back to him in a day or so, but never called. That was the last Higgs ever heard from Warren Marshall.

After leaving Phoenix in 1987, the Marshalls' trail took them to Florida, where they lived in the Tampa area until

1989. They ended up in Tulsa, but stopped first in New Orleans to marry.

It was a bizarre tale, one that Fitzpatrick had a difficult time comprehending much less explaining: Floyd kidnapped a toddler, raised her as his daughter, eventually married her, killed her, then kidnapped her son. It was tragic, sad, unbelievable, and diabolical. It made him boil. The hardened special agent allowed his emotions to transport him to the edge of that forbidden border, where cool objectivity blurred into compulsive rage.

Fitzpatrick sat at his desk and took a deep breath, regaining his composure and senses. He knew that Franklin Floyd had already ruined one young life.

Fitzpatrick didn't want him to destroy another.

Flushing Floyd out of wherever he was hiding was proving difficult, so Fitzpatrick devised a plan. It was a long shot. Floyd's movements had a familiar pattern, and always ended with him living in either Oklahoma, Kentucky, Georgia, Arizona, or Florida, "safe grounds," particularly the Atlanta area, which seemed to hold a special attraction for Floyd. Fitzpatrick notified the state department of transportation offices in each of those states to be on the lookout for driver's license applications under the names Franklin Floyd, Trenton Davis, Clarence Hughes, or Warren Marshall.

Two weeks later, on November 9, Fitzpatrick received a call from a clerk at the Florida Department of Transportation. A man named Warren Marshall sought to renew his Florida driver's license.

He was in Louisville, Kentucky.

CHAPTER 15

Joe Fitzpatrick boarded a plane and arrived in Louisville, Kentucky, late in the afternoon on November 9, 1994. Agents from the FBI's Louisville field office greeted him, then directed him to a waiting car, where he was briefed.

Floyd was working as a salesman at a used car lot, JD Byrider Sales, on Preston Highway. He was expecting his driver's license from the Florida Department of Transportation to arrive the next morning via Federal Express.

The plan was simple. An FBI agent impersonating a Federal Express driver would pull up to the used car lot and deliver Floyd's package, preferably outside, where Floyd would be arrested.

Fitzpatrick still held out slight hope that Michael was alive, and he cautioned the team that it was in their best interest that Floyd's arrest go smoothly.

Fitzpatrick, six agents from the Louisville field office, and a contingent of local police surrounded the car lot, closing off each escape route though remaining out of sight. At

9:45 A.M. the Federal Express truck arrived. An FBI agent, wearing a purple Federal Express uniform, walked into the parking lot, and Fitzpatrick watched from an unmarked car as a man who matched Floyd's description walked out of the office to meet the driver.

When the agent handed over the package, Floyd was quickly surrounded by seven FBI agents, guns drawn.

Floyd was startled but remained calm.

"What's going on?" he said.

"I have a copy of a warrant issued out of Oklahoma for kidnapping for Franklin Floyd," said Fitzpatrick.

"You have the wrong person," said Floyd.

Fitzpatrick coolly pulled a laminated fingerprint card out of his jacket pocket and held it up in front of Floyd.

"We'll know soon," he said.

Floyd didn't waste another second.

"I'm Franklin Floyd," he said, giving himself up with no resistance.

Fitzpatrick read Floyd his rights, handcuffed him, and then asked him the question he'd been waiting to ask for nearly two months.

"Where's Michael?"

"He's fine," said Floyd. "He's not here, but he's fine."

Floyd was led to the back of an unmarked car while agents searched through his green duffel bag and wallet.

The bag produced a single bus ticket from Atlanta to Louisville, dated September 30, and a map of Atlanta torn from an atlas. Inside the wallet were three photos: one of Sharon when she was a teenager, another of Michael as an infant lying naked in his crib, and a third of an unidentified woman. She appeared to have dark hair down to the shoulders and full cheeks and lips. The photo was old, though the woman's features were clear.

Also found inside the wallet was an address book with

current addresses and phone numbers for his sister, Dorothy Leonard; his old prison friend, David Dial; another woman, Rebecca Barr; and the name and current address of the woman Floyd was convicted of raping in 1962 when she was only four years old.

"What's this all about?" said Fitzpatrick, startled by the discovery.

Floyd said nothing. Fitzpatrick sat beside him in the car as agent Mack Bond drove them to the Louisville field office, followed by a contingent of police and unmarked FBI cars. Once inside the FBI field office Floyd remained handcuffed and was taken to a small room, where he sat down at a rectangular table. Bond closed the door, and Fitzpatrick pulled out the photo of the girl known as Suzanne Davis in 1975, sitting on the lap of a much younger Franklin Floyd.

"That don't bother me," said Floyd.

"Well, where did you get her?" said Fitzpatrick.

"Get? Get? I didn't 'get' her," said Floyd, annoyed at the suggestion.

"Well, we know she's not a relative of yours," said Fitzpatrick. "Where did she come from?"

Floyd paused.

"I was living in Indianapolis in 1974 and was seeing a woman, a prostitute. Her name was Linda Williams. She was a drug user. I wanted to marry her but she said no. She had a little girl, and I couldn't leave her there. Just wasn't right. Was a bad environment, so she came with me," he said, relaying the story clearly and succinctly.

"So Williams is her last name?"

"I didn't say that," said Floyd. "I told you who her momma was. I didn't say her name, and I'm not gonna tell you."

"But her name was Suzanne Davis when you lived in Oklahoma City, right?"

"Yeah."

"Where did you go after that?"

"Just around. Don't really remember," said Floyd, shrugging his shoulders.

Fitzpatrick continued, not bothering to look at his notes, spitting out facts from memory.

"And later you moved to Louisville in 1980, where her name was Sharon Marshall, and your name was Warren Marshall?"

"Yes."

"And Sharon is Michael's mother, right?"

"Yep."

"Can you tell me his date of birth?"

"April 21, 1988. Born at Tampa Hospital."

The interview continued, and Floyd was alternatively talkative and combative, answering most questions but dodging others. He rationalized his life as the result of one misfortune after another and blamed others for the way it turned out. He claimed to have used more than forty aliases during his flight from justice, delighting in the fact that he was never caught.

"You people were so stupid. I could still be running if I didn't love my son so much," he said.

"Where did you get the names?" said Fitzpatrick.

"Took 'em off tombstones. Was real easy. I'd move from city to city, without saying so much as good-bye," said Floyd, leaning over the table toward Fitzpatrick. "Let me tell ya'. That's the only way you can be a successful fugitive, is to move around. You people couldn't catch me."

Fitzpatrick looked Floyd dead in the eye.

"Mr. Floyd, you were not a fugitive from the FBI. If you were, believe me when I say this, we would have found you long ago."

Floyd fell back into his seat as the interview continued, the questions centering on Floyd's seventeen years as a fugitive.

"I was a painter, you know, and a damn good one," he said proudly. "I'd always go to a new town, do a good job to get referrals. And you know what, I'd always get work from Jewish people. I'd always take the mezuzah off the side of the door. Other guys would just paint over it. Not me. I was real careful. They loved me."

Floyd boasted how he befriended doctors and lawyers, and how he'd join various organizations—from the Kiwanis club to the Fraternal Order of Police—to help him maintain his cover. The second he thought someone was on to him, he said he'd pack his bags, grab "Sharon," and bolt to the next city.

"And her name was Sharon," said Floyd. "That's what I always liked to call her."

That was fine with Fitzpatrick, who had heard enough about Floyd's talents for evading the law and wanted to hear more about the girl he stole long ago.

"Oh, Sharon was smart as a pistol," said Floyd. "She was a pleasure, but you see, she ruined her life. She got pregnant. I told her, 'Sharon, how could you do this to yourself? How could you soil yourself with those boys?' She was such a good girl, it was a shame."

"What happened to that baby?" said Fitzpatrick.

"Which one?"

"The first one, when she was in high school."

"Can't tell ya," said Floyd, who wouldn't identify the baby's gender but said the child was born in Atlanta and adopted.

"We found a nice home for it before we went to Phoenix."

"That's where Sharon met Greg Higgs?"

"Yeah, Greg Higgs," said Floyd, his face twisted with disgust. "He didn't care about her. He just took her wholesomeness and used her. He got her pregnant but wasn't going to take care of her, so we left."

"You seemed to leave a home whenever Sharon found some other attachment," said Fitzpatrick.

"What the hell does that mean?" said Floyd. "I took care of that girl. I couldn't leave her with someone like Greg Higgs! Aren't you a daddy? Don't you understand that?"

Fitzpatrick didn't want to answer the questions, so he looked down to his folder and flipped a couple of pages.

"After Phoenix you went to Tampa?"

"Right, Tampa. That's where Michael was born. It was a beautiful sight, watching him come into this world. That's what no one understands about all this. I was *there*. I took care of him when he was sick. I was his *father*."

Floyd's demeanor changed when the interview turned to Michael. He sat there, handcuffed, acting as if he were the victim and his actions the result of a grave injustice. Fitzpatrick didn't want to hear it. He was sick of Floyd. He had chased him for two months, and he knew everything about his sordid and sorry history. If one thing was certain, in Fitzpatrick's eyes, Floyd was not a victim.

Fitzpatrick decided to change the subject away from Michael and back to Sharon, but Floyd was angry. And as proud as he was of Sharon just moments earlier, he now spewed venom.

"She was a whore. A fucking whore. She ruined her life and that's where she belonged. With all those sodomites. I hated that life she chose for herself. She did drugs. It was a tragedy. She got pregnant again after Michael. But I didn't care. You see, I wasn't attached to her anymore. I raised her, and she was a good girl who went to church, but she became a whore and a drug addict. I only cared about Michael."

"What happened to that other baby, after Michael?"

"It was a girl. She was adopted by a nice family in New Orleans."

"That's where you married Sharon, right? Why?"

"To give Michael a name. It was a marriage of convenience."

"Did you ever have sex with Sharon?"

"Hell, no. Don't even ask me a question like that. Do it again and I ain't saying another word."

Fitzpatrick paused and fumbled through his files to give Floyd a chance take a breath and relax his tone. After a few minutes, the questions started again.

"So you left Tampa for Oklahoma in 1989. Where did you get those names, Clarence Marcus Hughes and Tonya Dawn Tadlock?"

"From tombstones. Like I said, I got all my names from tombstones."

"And what about Michael, what was his real name?"

"Michael Gregory Marshall."

Fitzpatrick paused again, going through his notebook.

"Mr. Floyd, let me ask you about David Dial. You knew him, correct?"

"We were friends in prison. I helped him with his legal defense. I became a lawyer in jail. Not a real lawyer, but I studied the law. I knew lots of guys in jail who were smart like me and studied the law. I saw him again after Sharon died. Stayed with him for a few days but the son of a bitch slapped me around and I had to leave."

"Did you ever see him again?"

"No."

"OK, Mr. Floyd, let's talk about September twelve, nineteen ninety-four. You were at the Indian Meridian School, correct?"

"I was there. I was being chased by people in the Mafia. They were following me because Tonya took money from them. A lot of money. I know where it's buried, so they were following me around. I didn't take Michael. I left my car there because it wouldn't start. It was the Mafia guys who took him."

"So why leave Oklahoma City and violate your parole?"

"Because I was being followed by these people."

"You know this doesn't make any sense."

"I don't give a damn what you think. I'm telling you what happened."

Floyd said after leaving Oklahoma City, he traveled to Kansas City, Dallas, Atlanta, and then Louisville.

"Why did you go to Atlanta?"

"For psychological reasons."

"You want to explain?"

"No."

"Why did you go to Louisville?"

"I like it there. I used to live there."

While Floyd talked, agents from the Louisville field office searched his apartment and interviewed his neighbors and coworkers. Everyone had seen Floyd since his arrival in October. No one saw Michael.

The interview finally concluded, but Floyd offered nothing about Michael's whereabouts. He was led out of the room while Fitzpatrick and Bond remained inside.

"That bus ticket was dated September thirtieth, one way, from Atlanta to Louisville, for one passenger. Whatever happened to Michael happened in Atlanta," said Fitzpatrick.

Fitzpatrick returned to Oklahoma City while Floyd was taken to a federal holding cell in Indiana to begin extradition proceedings for his eventual return to Oklahoma to stand trial for the kidnapping of Michael Hughes.

Fitzpatrick wanted to add the murder of Michael Anthony Hughes to the list of charges.

CHAPTER 16

It was 6 P.M. on November 15, and Jennifer Fisher Tanner was washing dinner dishes in her San Diego, California, home when she received a phone call from her mother, Sue.

She said she had some news.

"We found Sharon."

"Oh my God!" Jennifer shrieked, bouncing up and down on her kitchen floor with delight. "Where is she! How can we find her!"

It had been six long years since Jennifer last spoke to her friend, losing contact in 1988. Jennifer had since spent countless hours trying to find her, and now her mother was on the phone with the news Jennifer hoped she would one day hear.

But Jennifer's questions were met by silence on the other end of the line.

"Mom? What's wrong?"

"Jenny, Sharon is dead."

"Dead? Mom, what are you talking about?"

"She's dead, Jenny," said Sue. "You better sit down. It gets worse. She was on the news. You're going to have to call the FBI. It appears that Warren was not her father. His real name was Floyd. Franklin Floyd."

Jennifer stood rigid. Her profound happiness transformed in a second into confusion and shock.

"What do you mean?" she said, holding one hand on the phone and the other to her head, not sure that any of this was making sense.

"Jenny, Sharon was kidnapped when she was a little girl."

Jennifer was nauseous. She fell to the floor, screaming "No! No! No!" and clutching her chest, her heart bouncing inside, tears rolling off her cheeks.

Her husband, Zach, walked into the kitchen.

"Jenny? Jenny? What's the matter?" said Zach, trying to lift his stricken wife off the floor.

Jennifer shook her head. She couldn't talk and couldn't breathe, the air having been pressed out of her lungs by the startling news. She waved him away, then sat for ten minutes trying to collect herself while her mother waited patiently on the other end of the line.

Jennifer recovered enough to produce a low, slow drawl, her voice cracking.

"Mom, when did she die?"

"According to the news, about four years ago. She was hit by a car. They think Warren did it."

"Oh my God. How did she get on the news?"

"Jenny, there's still more. This is hard. Remember her little boy? When Sharon died he went into foster care. Warren took him. They found Warren in Kentucky, but the boy is gone and they don't know who Sharon is. They don't know anything. The FBI has a hotline for anyone who knew her. You need to call them immediately."

Jennifer was numb, her body in agony.

"FBI? Give me the number."

Sue said she'd send Jennifer the newspaper clippings and record the television news.

"Jenny, are you ok? Have Zach make you some hot tea. Call me if you need to talk."

Sue hung up, and Jennifer slowly lifted herself off the floor, the phone still in her hand. Zach walked over to her, grabbed the phone, and then asked her what was wrong.

Jennifer shook her head back and forth.

"Sharon is dead."

"Sharon? Your friend from high school? What happened?" said Zach.

Jennifer stared at the FBI hotline number she'd scribbled on a piece of paper, still trying to comprehend the awful news.

The two friends had remained in touch after Sharon's teary-eyed departure from Atlanta in 1986, writing letters and calling every few months. They were more like pep talks with Sharon urging Jennifer to lay off the marijuana and to pick up her grades.

"Jenny, you have to get your act together! You have to go to college!"

Jennifer would learn about Sharon's romance with Greg Higgs and her job at the Phoenix hotel. And she remembered the Christmas card, wishing the entire Fisher family a happy holiday from "The Marshalls."

During the summer of 1987 Sharon called to report that she had broken up with Greg, saying he was too "clingy." Later, in the fall, Sharon called again. She said she was in South Carolina, only Jennifer knew there was something terribly wrong.

"Jenny, I need you to come see me."

Sharon sounded awful.

"Sharon, are you all right?"

"No, Jenny. I need you to come up. My daddy will call your parents about coming up for a week or two."

"Sharon, you know I would, but can't. It's impossible for me to get away. My parents would never go for it."

Jennifer knew that was a half-truth. Her parents would never let her visit alone, but Jennifer would never put herself in a position like that again, alone with Warren. She remembered the one night she stayed with the Marshalls, when Warren barged into Sharon's room. His face was cherry red as he fell into a crouched position, holding a handgun with both hands, his arms extended, screaming, *"I told you girls to get to bed!"*

He pointed the gun at Jennifer, then at Sharon. Jennifer thought he was going to pull the trigger. Instead Warren started laughing, as if it was some kind of joke. Sharon stood there, half naked, trembling. Jennifer thought she was going to pass out.

The next morning Sharon had made breakfast, scrambled eggs and toast, and no one mentioned the incident until Warren left the house.

"Jenny, I'm sorry about last night," said Sharon. "Are you all right? My dad gets like that every now and then. He's just kidding around, you know. He always threatens me with a gun."

Jennifer wished her mother would come quickly and get her out of there. She never told her parents about that night. She knew she couldn't if she wanted to remain friends with Sharon Marshall.

The memory was still fresh as Sharon begged her friend to visit with her in South Carolina. "Jenny, I need you. I really need you."

Sharon spoke with a strangeness Jennifer had never heard before; there was something in her voice that suggested Sharon *didn't* really want Jennifer to visit but was being forced to make the request. She could hear Sharon saying, "I want you to come" but could see Sharon's head shaking back and forth, *"No, don't come!"*

Sharon was crying, and Jennifer could hear the phone being yanked out of Sharon's hand.

"What kind of friend are you if you can't come up and visit her?"

It was Warren. He asked to talk to her parents, but Jennifer said they weren't home.

"Mr. Marshall, I can't come up. It's impossible. I'm sorry," said Jennifer, who heard a click, then a dial tone.

Months would pass before Jennifer heard from Sharon again. It was in May 1988, when a card arrived congratulating Jennifer on her graduation from high school. Sharon didn't know it, but Jennifer earned a B average her senior year and acceptance to Georgia Southern University. It was a major accomplishment, one achieved with the help of Sharon, whose encouraging voice remained somewhere in the back of Jennifer's head, imploring her to finish school on a positive note.

The envelope was postmarked "Tampa, Florida," but had no return address. On the cover of the card were dancing animals, rabbits and cats and dogs holding pom-poms and wearing blue sweaters that spelled out "Way To Go." Inside Sharon had written: *"I hope all the festivities of graduation flow smoothly. They'll be moments you'll cherish and never forget. I'm sorry that I can't be there to share them. Good Luck in all your plans and goals!!! Love ya, Sharon."*

Several weeks later, in June 1988, Jennifer received a two-page letter from Sharon.

Dear Jenny,

How are you? I am fine. Long time, no hear, huh? You may think it was because I was mad about you not coming up. I got over that a while ago. But, I wasn't hurt at the time. No, life's just been so busy with work and everything.

You'll notice by the return address that I'm in Tampa now. We moved not long after we talked last. There wasn't enough work in S.C. to support us. We saw ourselves going broke. We heard there was some good work going on here and tadah! It's an OK town. There's not much that I'm interested in here, but it'll do for now.

I work at a bar again cocktailing. It's good money. Daddy recently retired from painting permanently. He fell off a ladder a couple of weeks ago and was told to stop his profession. He figures he'll get into some kind of sales work. Life's been pretty decent financially anyway. We have a truck and an AMC now. It's a great little car!

I met some nice guys here. The nicest would have to be Steve. He's from California and is the carpenter for Van Halen. I'm not lying! When the Monsters of Rock Tour came through, a bunch of the roadies came in the club. We (a couple of girls and me) partied with them the whole week they were here. I met Metallica and Sammy Hagar. Steve and I promised to keep in touch and meet again someday. I pretty much just look but don't touch.

Plans? I'm moving back west in a couple of weeks. Can't stand the humidity. I'm not sure exactly where yet, but I promise to tell you when I get there.

Questions. Family? Writing me? School and graduation? College? Summer plans? Love life? Work? Car? Etc.

I'm going to go now. I've been writing this letter three days now. I'll get free time to write more later.

Love ya, Sharon

Jennifer was relieved to see that that Sharon seemed all right, much better than when she received that strange phone call from South Carolina.

There would only be two more contacts with Sharon, both on the phone. One would come in the fall. Sharon was still in Florida, and she had some news. She had a six-month-old son, whom she had named Michael.

"Sharon! Why didn't you tell me before?" said Jennifer.

"I don't know. Maybe I was embarrassed. Imagine me, pregnant again? But I love this boy. I was worried that Daddy wouldn't let me keep him. Michael cries a lot and is kind of whiny. Daddy gets frustrated with him when I'm away. He's usually crying when I come home so I usually just pick him up and take him into another room to calm him down. But things are OK," said Sharon.

She said she was still waitressing at some club, making decent money. Life, on the whole, was good.

"Is that what you want, cocktailing?" said Jennifer.

"Well, the outfits are kind of skimpy, but it's not that bad," said Sharon.

Jennifer couldn't help but notice the irony; her brilliant friend with a promising future was now the mother of an infant son and waitressing tables while Jennifer had straightened her life out and was going to college. It was, thought Jennifer, so sad.

Even sadder was that Jennifer knew she wasn't talking to the Sharon of old. Something was missing. Sharon's voice and tone were matter-of-fact, unemotional. Jennifer had first heard it a year earlier during that strange call from South Carolina. The Sharon of old was always so upbeat and bursting with energy.

Now she sounded as if she had given up.

Their last contact was in the form of another phone call several months later, and Jennifer remembered her surprise when Sharon talked about breast implants.

"Daddy always thought I should look a little bigger," she said.

The two friends talked for another ten minutes. Sharon was pleased to hear that Jennifer was doing well in college, but there was a tinge of sadness to her voice. Jennifer knew that Sharon should have been in school, finishing up her degree at Georgia Tech, going to football games and frat parties, and planning what everyone thought would be a promising future.

"Jenny, I've got to go," said Sharon. "I love you."

It was the last time Jennifer ever heard from Sharon.

Jennifer spent years searching for her friend. Countless Internet searches, visits to the local library, calls to operator information in Arizona, Georgia, and Florida, states she knew where Sharon had lived, and even a letter to Sharon's last known address, which was in Tampa, proved fruitless.

Jennifer had desperately wanted Sharon to attend her graduation ceremonies from the University of Georgia, which she had transferred to in 1990. And she saw Sharon as the perfect choice to serve as her maid of honor at her wedding in 1992 to Zachary Tanner, a Navy man who was stationed in San Diego.

But Sharon was gone.

Jennifer remained in her kitchen for thirty minutes, standing in the same spot and staring at the FBI hotline number before reaching over, picking up the phone, and dialing.

"Hi, there was a story in Atlanta about a little boy that was missing. His mother was my best friend."

CHAPTER 17

The reports that arrived from the Louisville and Atlanta FBI field offices were incomplete, and Joe Fitzpatrick was frustrated. Louisville agents were able to account for all of Floyd's time in Kentucky after his arrival on September 30. But the Atlanta file was thin, with few clues—aside from the truck he left in Dallas—as to Floyd's whereabouts from September 12 to September 21, 1994.

Thanks to the efforts of the Louisville field office back-tracking Floyd's activities, Fitzpatrick knew that Floyd was in Atlanta on September 21, when he checked himself into Grady Memorial Hospital for psychiatric observation. Floyd spent eight days at Grady, where he was treated for some undefined but deeply troubling event in his life. Floyd explained that his wife and son had died, and the grief was unbearable. But he gave no details, and doctors were suspicious. He remained at the hospital until September 29, when he checked himself out and took a cab to the Travelers Aid office.

Travelers Aid was a United Way–sponsored agency that helped single individuals short on money return to their homes from Atlanta. They provided meal tickets to a local Burger King and discount Greyhound bus tickets. Caseworker Wilber Purvis received a call that morning from the Louisville Travelers Aid office that a Warren Marshall, a patient at Grady Memorial Hospital, was stranded in Atlanta and needed assistance returning home.

Floyd, a.k.a. Marshall, had called the Walnut Street Baptist Church, where he was a member when he lived in Louisville from 1979 to 1981. The church called Travelers Aid, and Floyd arrived at the Atlanta office at 11 A.M. He told Purvis he had been in Atlanta for two years searching for his daughter, who had run away from home. Unable to locate her, Floyd said, he became depressed and checked himself into the psychiatric ward at Grady. Floyd was calm, but spoke only when spoken to. Purvis tried to get more information on his daughter, and also asked about any relatives. Floyd said he didn't have any.

Purvis gave Floyd a voucher to purchase the bus ticket, worth $36.75, and a $3.50 voucher for Burger King, which was inside the bus terminal. Floyd, maintaining his Warren Marshall identity, arrived in Louisville the next day.

Agents from the Louisville field office backtracked the bus ticket found in Floyd's duffel bag to the Travelers Aid office in Atlanta, then to Grady Memorial. All who came in contact with Floyd said he traveled alone. Fitzpatrick believed that Michael made it to Atlanta, but since investigators were unable to account for Floyd's activities the week before he checked into the hospital, he was sure that whatever happed to Michael occurred during that "lost" week. The hospital stay was a chance for Floyd to "decompress" following Michael's death.

He arrived in Louisville on September 30 and stayed two

nights at the St. Vincent de Paul men's homeless shelter before renting an apartment at the Victorian house, an old apartment complex.

Within days after his arrival he secured a job as a painter with a small contracting company called Art Works. Admired for his painting prowess, Floyd was assigned finishing work. But his persona was deemed peculiar, if not creepy. During the introduction to his foreman, William Leonard, Floyd said, "My name is Warren and my wife is a whore in Las Vegas."

A week later, while working in a house attic, Floyd told another worker, Greg Panther, that he had kidnapped a five-year-old boy in Atlanta and that his wife was a prostitute. A shaken Panther relayed the story to Leonard.

Tenants at the Victorian house originally tried to help Floyd, giving him clothing and food. But they were soon struck by his behavior.

Terry Evans, a neighbor who lived below Floyd, wondered if he ever slept. The neighbor could hear him walking in his apartment all hours of the night. Floyd never spoke about a lost son, but complained to Evans that he had a daughter who was a prostitute. Tenants were also curious when Floyd ordered a Florida driver's license, borrowing money and a telephone to make the call, insisting he didn't want a Kentucky license.

Floyd eventually stopped talking to Evans after he refused Floyd's request to watch a movie on his TV.

Floyd wanted to watch *The Fugitive*.

Floyd was eventually let go from the painting crew and found another job selling used cars at JD Byrider Sales.

Fitzpatrick went back to the Atlanta report and zeroed in on September 20. It was the day before he checked himself into Grady Memorial. A woman placed a "car for sale" ad in the classified section of the *Atlanta Journal-Constitution* and received a call from a man who wanted to see the car. The man asked the woman if she could drive to meet him, and she agreed. The man got into the car, drove it for a few minutes, and then attacked the woman. She escaped, but the man drove off with the car, which was reported stolen. The assailant matched the description of Franklin Floyd.

Fitzpatrick knew they had to find that car, a responsibility that rested with the Atlanta field office and Special Agent William Bray. A twenty-year veteran of the FBI, his last five years in the Atlanta office, Bray was the Atlanta agent assigned to the Franklin Floyd case. Following Floyd's arrest, Bray reached out to Rebecca "Becky" Barr.

Barr's phone number was found inside Floyd's address book, and it was discovered later that they had known each other since their days at the children's home. Barr claimed that she had no previous contact with Floyd, which was met with disbelief by Bray, who asked Barr to cooperate to help find Michael.

Floyd was in Jeffersonville, Indiana, awaiting a transfer to Oklahoma City and continuing to stifle investigators, offering no information on Michael's whereabouts.

Barr agreed to cooperate with the FBI, making contact with Floyd over the phone to see if he'd tell her what happened to Michael and where investigators would find his remains.

"How do I make contact?" said Barr, concerned that Floyd wouldn't tell her anything if he found out she was sharing information with the FBI.

It was decided that Barr would call the prison and leave a message for Floyd to call her, which he did. The call came in collect, and Floyd used Barr as a sounding board. Did she know anything? Had she been contacted by the FBI? What was she telling them?

Barr said not to worry, that she wouldn't say or do anything to hurt her old friend. Floyd called Barr often, and she incurred a $364 phone bill, which the FBI agreed to pay to Barr, in cash.

Following subsequent conversations with Floyd, Barr agreed that Michael was probably dead and suggested possible burial sites, including a cemetery in Poterdale, Georgia, where Floyd's father was buried. She also suggested several streams and creeks, which were searched but provided no clues.

After several weeks the Rebecca Barr exercise was going nowhere, and the information coming from Floyd was confusing and repetitive. Bray told Barr he'd no longer reimburse her calls and started thinking of another way to get to Floyd. He didn't have to think long.

Floyd decided to call Bray from jail, and suggested that the FBI insert newspaper ads, specifically written by Floyd, which would serve to inform the "people" who had Michael to give him up. Floyd mailed his instructions to Bray, who in turn consulted with Joe Fitzpatrick in Oklahoma City. They decided to turn over the instructions to Floyd's newly appointed public defender, Susan Otto, which infuriated Floyd, who quickly called Becky Barr screaming that the FBI would find Michael dead.

"They're going to pull him out of a creek," said Floyd.

The offices of the United States Attorney for the Western District of Oklahoma were on the sixth floor of the Oklahoma Tower, a sparkling building in downtown Oklahoma City, just blocks away from the federal court building and the Alfred P. Murrah Federal Building.

Assistant U.S. Attorneys Mark Yancey and Edward Kumiega were assigned the task of prosecuting Franklin Delano Floyd for kidnapping, possession of a firearm, and several other offenses relating to the abduction of Michael Hughes.

Both Yancey and Kumiega were highly skilled and competent attorneys. Yancey, thirty-five, joined the U.S. Attorney's office in 1990 and had developed a solid reputation as a capable prosecutor. Originally from Tampa, Florida, Yancey was as clean-cut as they come—he looked like an evening television newscaster. Of medium size, he was handsome and well groomed, his white shirts neatly pressed and starched, his dark hair parted on the side and perfectly combed. His face appeared to be polished, his skin shining. A 1982 graduate of Florida State University, Yancey went straight to law school, studying at Samford Law in Alabama and graduating in 1986. His career took a decidedly unexpected detour when he was recruited by the FBI. His first and only assignment upon his graduation from the FBI academy was working with the U.S. Attorney's office. After four years he was offered a position as a government prosecutor in Oklahoma City.

Yancey had been on top of the Michael Hughes kidnapping from day one, facilitating the initial arrest warrant on a firearm charge, and later adding the federal kidnapping charge after the stolen truck was recovered in Dallas. Yancey spoke in direct, forceful tones, and never let his guard down.

By contrast Ed Kumiega, thirty-eight, was far more low-key, a straight shooter from Jersey City, New Jersey, who found his way to Oklahoma by studying law at the University of Tulsa. After graduating in 1980, Kumiega had a choice between returning back east or taking a job as an assistant DA with the Washita County, Oklahoma, district attorney's office.

He took the Washita job, where his legal skills quickly earned him a promotion to first assistant DA. By March 1990, he was working for the U.S. Attorney's office.

Kumiega had been driving along I-40 back in September when he heard the news on the radio about the Michael Hughes's kidnapping. He though it was sad and tragic, but figured it would be a state case.

He learned later that night he was wrong.

Kumiega walked with a distinct limp, which he carried from birth, wore wrinkled shirts, and had an office that looked more like a repository for loose papers. Like Yancey, Kumiega had a keen legal mind. It was decided early on that Kumiega, with his lengthier experience, would be the lead prosecutor for the government on a case that wasn't as cut and dried as it appeared to be.

Despite the overwhelming evidence that Floyd kidnapped Michael at gunpoint, there was a very real legal issue here, one that caused great concern for the young prosecutors: Was Floyd within his legal and parental rights as Michael's father to take him from the Indian Meridian Elementary School? If so, he would be exempt from federal kidnapping charges, which carried up to a life sentence. While the state courts said Floyd was not Michael's father, basing their opinion on the fact that Floyd gave up custody of Michael to DHS and was not the biological father, Kumiega and Yancey weren't so sure the federal court would agree.

Floyd had previously argued that while he was not Michael's biological father, he could be loosely defined as a parent because he acted as Michael's male parenting figure for two years prior to the death of Michael's mother.

The question consuming Kumiega and Yancey was, does the word *parent* include a person who is not biologically related? Congress never defined the word *parent* in its statute, 18 *USC* section 1201, the federal criminal code involving kidnapping. If the statutory exemption was limited to biological parents, Floyd could not prevail. But according to various interpretations of the word *parent*, including the definition in the *Oxford English Dictionary*, a parent was defined as a person who has borne a child, whether a father or mother, or a person who "holds the position or exercises the functions of a parent: a protector, a guardian."

Floyd claimed the latter. He had presented himself as Michael's father for two years and, in concept, cared for and supported him. Kumiega and Yancey found themselves in a legal quandary, knowing they'd have to answer for the court the definition of a parent.

Floyd had been charged with kidnapping, interstate transportation of a stolen vehicle, and possession of a firearm during a kidnapping and carjacking. The kidnapping charge was by far the most serious, but if Floyd could successfully argue to the federal court that he was Michael's father, the prosecutors realized that the kidnapping charge could be dismissed. Though not fatal to the government's case—the firearm charge carried a twenty-year term—getting Floyd on kidnapping would put him away for good.

It was cutting-edge law, and the young lawyers were unsure—and worried—how this would play out.

The first order of business for Kumiega and Yancey was the actual indictment and presentment of evidence before a federal grand jury. Compared to state courts, the federal court system moved at warp speed, and the indictment and trial could happen within six months. The case of the *United States of America* versus *Franklin Delano Floyd* was considered a "Rocket Docket," and Kumiega and Yancey knew they had their work cut out for them and cleared their calendars.

This was a full government investigation, and they were given the necessary resources to successfully prosecute the case. In addition to obtaining all the FBI files and Floyd's prison records, they scheduled interviews with everyone and anyone connected to the case, with full power and authority to fly anyone to Oklahoma City.

They subpoenaed David Dial and forced him to travel from his home in Georgia to testify before the grand jury. Dial had just been released from prison on yet another drug charge, and his large frame and unsettling demeanor spooked everyone. Still, his testimony convinced all that Floyd was dangerous.

Kumiega and Yancey worked seven days a week, often late into the evening, even stopping for a beer or two at a local pub late at night to continue their strategy sessions. They'd return home, get little sleep, then pick up again early the next morning.

They developed a strong and decided opinion of Franklin Floyd, the FBI files providing complete information about his childhood, arrest, and prison record, and fairly accurate estimates of his whereabouts during the fugitive years from 1975 through 1989.

They surmised that Michael was dead, but had no idea as to his whereabouts. They wanted to find his remains and determine the cause of death, but that proved extremely difficult. Interviews with witnesses from Kentucky and Georgia suggested several scenarios. One witness, a prisoner who befriended Floyd at the Oklahoma County jail, claimed Floyd admitted throwing Michael off a bridge. Floyd even added that he could hear "the little bastard's" screams as he fell to the river below, which he hit with a sickening thud.

Another witness said Floyd admitted he killed the boy and placed him in a drainpipe being prepared for the 1996 Atlanta Olympic Games.

The FBI and local police searched lakes, streams, and riverbeds throughout the Atlanta area, but found nothing.

The most disturbing, and believable, story came from Floyd's sister, Dorothy Leonard.

She called Joe Fitzpatrick following a telephone conversation with her brother, who had called collect from the Oklahoma County Jail.

"I'm sorry to bother you, but I just spoke to Franklin and he told me how he killed that little boy," said Dorothy.

"What happened?" said Fitzpatrick.

"He called me, collect, and he was angry. He said that I told the police he molested my children, and that it was lies. He kept talking, and said he killed Michael. He drowned him."

Dorothy paused. She found it difficult to repeat the story.

"Go ahead, Mrs. Leonard. Take your time," said Fitzpatrick.

Dorothy took a deep breath, exhaled, and continued.

"I was sitting on my couch talking to him on the phone, and he said he had taken Michael places to have a good time. But he said Michael was crying all the time, that he wanted to go home, and said he 'couldn't shut the brat up.' He said they had a motel room and when they went there he wanted to give Michael a bath and told him to take off his clothes. Franklin turned on the water and kept it running when Michael got in the bath. Franklin told him to lie on his stomach. But Michael turned around and saw Franklin taking his clothes off. Michael started to question him, asking Franklin why he was taking his clothes off too. Franklin told me he said they were going to play games together, and got into the tub with Michael, who was hollering for him to get out."

Fitzpatrick was transfixed, taking in every word, writing furiously on a yellow pad.

"Franklin said he stayed in the tub, then started asking Michael if he loved him. He told me he said, 'Michael, do you love me?' Michael said 'No.' Franklin was upset, and pushed Michael's head in the water, then let him come up for air. He asked him again if he loved him, and Michael said 'No' again, so Franklin put him under again. It happened a third time, with Michael saying 'No.' I know Franklin. He must have been so mad at that poor little boy he just held his head under the water until he stopped moving."

"Did Franklin tell you that, that he held Michael under

the water and drowned him?" said Fitzpatrick, his throat tightening.

"Yes, that's what he said. But then he said he took his body and, these are his words, 'discarded the little son of a bitch.' Mr. Fitzpatrick, I'm shaking. Franklin said he put him in the trunk of a car and got rid of him. This was too much for me. I started screaming. My husband had to come in and bring me around. I had to hang up the phone."

Dorothy was crying, but Fitzpatrick wanted to hear more.

"Mrs. Leonard, did he say where he put Michael's body?"

"No, sir."

Fitzpatrick thought about that conversation long and hard and, in the end, believed Dorothy Leonard.

The story gained more credence on January 14, 1995, when FBI agents in Atlanta recovered the Dodge Shadow Floyd allegedly stole the day before checking himself into Grady Memorial Hospital on September 21. The car was found in a parking lot and cadaver dogs alerted police to the trunk area, where they picked up a high level of distress from scents usually emitted by a dead body. Fitzpatrick believed that Floyd killed Michael, perhaps in the motel, placed his body in the trunk, and either buried it or tossed it into a stream before abandoning the car in the parking lot. Floyd then checked himself into the hospital for a week, before taking a bus to Louisville.

The news was distressing, but expected.

Kumiega, Yancey, and Fitzpatrick all knew Michael was gone. Now they just wanted to see Floyd put away for life.

On January 18, 1995, a federal grand jury returned a seven-count indictment against Franklin Delano Floyd. Included among the charges were kidnapping, carrying a firearm, and stealing a car by force and driving it to another state. If convicted on all counts, Floyd faced life in prison, and would die behind bars.

The trial was scheduled for March 29, 1995, before Judge Wayne E. Alley, and Kumiega and Yancey had little more than two months to complete their preparations, which included additional interviews with potential witnesses and formulating a coherent strategy.

As the lead attorney, or "first chair," Kumiega had ultimate authority on tactical decision making. But he and Yancey agreed on virtually everything. They enjoyed an easy and constructive rapport, often challenging each other intellectually while remaining huddled in their downtown offices well into the night, ordering dinner in and reading through hundreds of reports.

They knew they would have to focus on proving the kidnapping charges since none of the evidence alluding to the murder of Michael Hughes was admissible. Judge Alley did not want to turn this into a murder trial. It was a kidnapping case, period.

By the time the grand jury handed up the indictment, there was little the two attorneys didn't know about Franklin Floyd.

Sharon was another matter. She was, simply, an enigma. With no positive identification and little information coming from the various cities where she and Floyd had lived, it was difficult for Kumiega and Yancey to formulate any opinion other than that she was a stripper and, allegedly, a prostitute while working in Tulsa. She also apparently danced nude in Florida when they lived in Tampa.

There was some information circulating that Sharon was something of a student during her high school years in Georgia, but the report from the FBI's Atlanta field office was devoid of any useful background information. The prosecutors decided they would have to learn more about Sharon Marshall and reached out to the one person who knew her best.

CHAPTER 18

The biting cold and howling wind outside the Will Rogers Airport was a bitter change for Jennifer Fisher Tanner, who just hours earlier had left her home under the golden sun of southern California.

Leaving her young son and flying to the country's mid-section in the middle of January was not something Jennifer would have opted for. But she did just that, flying to Oklahoma City, courtesy of the Federal Bureau of Investigation after receiving a call from Joe Fitzpatrick.

They first spoke the day after she called the FBI hotline in November. He asked a few questions and quickly determined that Jennifer was genuine. He suggested they meet and talk. Jennifer agreed and waited for his call. Two months later, she stepped off the plane and walked outside to a waiting car that would take her downtown to meet with Fitzpatrick, Ed Kumiega, and Mark Yancey.

The tragic news about Sharon and her son, and the

shocking revelations about Floyd, had devastated Jennifer and her family.

They talked by phone nearly every day, asking over and over, *"Why didn't we see anything?"* They suffered through rolling waves of guilt and sadness and, above all, overwhelming heartbreak. They were also confused, unable to understand why Sharon never said anything.

Sharon loved being at the Fisher home. Jennifer was her best friend and she embraced Sue and Joel. They were her family. They were her friends. The Fishers could have, and would have, protected Sharon, taken her in and called the police. If only she'd told them something. Even during that last visit in 1986, when Sharon asked if she could stay. Why didn't she say why? they asked. She was telling us something, but just couldn't tell us exactly what was wrong. If she'd only said *something*.

Remembering that day at the airport, the Fishers now felt as if they had sent Sharon back to the devil, and the guilt was overwhelming.

Jennifer was understandably nervous when she arrived for her meeting, the events of the past two months taking a severe emotional toll. She had been admitted to the Balboa Naval Hospital for observation. She spoke with the base chaplain and told him that her best friend had died and her boy was gone. Jennifer could see that even the chaplain was startled by the horrible story, and he suggested that Jennifer begin intense weekly therapy sessions. Doctors also prescribed anxiety medicine, which helped, but it didn't stop those moments when Jennifer would cry uncontrollably.

Yancey explained that they still did not know the real identity of her friend, but they would use the name "Sharon" since it appeared to be the name she used throughout most of her life. He began with an overview of what they knew: that

Sharon had apparently been kidnapped at a young age and traveled with Floyd, a convicted pedophile who claimed to be her father. As each unbelievable detail was explained to Jennifer, she could only close her eyes and shake her head, thinking, *This couldn't have happened to my friend.*

"Did she ever tell you or give you any indication that Floyd was not her real father?" said Yancey.

"No. Sharon rarely talked about her father or her past. It was just something she wouldn't discuss. I just figured it was too painful for Sharon to discuss because it reminded her of her mother, so I let it go. And my parents weren't the kind of people to push or pry. It just wasn't anything we ever questioned," said Jennifer.

"What did you and your family think of Floyd? Was there a lot of contact with him?"

"We all thought he was weird, but never suspected anything like this. He'd drop Sharon off at my house and ramble on about things to my parents. He always complained he had a bad back and tried to borrow money from my father, who always said no."

"Did he work?"

"He was a painter. He was running around trying to get painting jobs. Even in my neighborhood. He claimed he was very good, but we didn't know for sure."

Jennifer paused for a moment.

"You know, even though we thought he was a little off the wall, we all thought he was a good dad given how Sharon turned out."

"What does that mean?" said Kumiega quizzically. "She was a stripper, a prostitute, dancing at clubs in Tulsa and in Florida and having children out of wedlock."

Jennifer snapped backward.

"Stripper? What are you talking about? Sharon wasn't a stripper or prostitute. The Sharon I knew, the one I was best friends with, was an honor student. She was in the ROTC. She received a scholarship to Georgia Tech University."

The two prosecutors and the FBI agent had received little information concerning Sharon Marshall's high school background. They knew she attended school and graduated, but never heard any details about honors or scholarships. They were surprised and, for a moment, unbelieving.

"Jennifer, we believe that Floyd had been sexually abusing Sharon for a very long time, probably from the day when he got her," said Yancey. "When she was older, in her late teens and early twenties, she was working as an exotic dancer and, from what we understand, a prostitute. She had numerous cosmetic surgeries, including breast enlargement, as well as several pregnancies. In addition, he was beating her, and she lived in absolute fear of him. She apparently died while planning to get away from him. Given what little we know about child abuse and the horrible conditions under which your friend was living, it's hard to understand, or accept, that she could possibly have been what you say she was in school, this all-American girl."

"But she was!" said Jennifer, her voice rising in anger. "Everything you're telling me doesn't sound anything like the Sharon I knew or my family knew. Stripping? Prostitution? That doesn't make any sense."

"Can you tell us if that's anything you're personally familiar with?" said Yancey.

"What? A prostitute? Dancing?" said Jennifer, visibly insulted and upset with the question. "I'm a married mother. A college graduate. My husband is in the Navy. Are you kidding? I was never into anything like that. I was just a kid who liked to chase boys. The Sharon I knew was the same, a normal, functioning teenager. Only she was better. She was smart and she was pretty. She read Shakespeare. She was a *Who's Who* in high school! She was going to college!

She had a scholarship! When I knew her she was an everyday teenager. What you're telling me I can't even comprehend. I knew her dad was weird but I had no idea to what extent."

Jennifer's eyes watered and Kumiega handed her a tissue box, exchanging glances with Yancey and Fitzpatrick, all shaking their heads in disbelief. Shakespeare, a college scholarship, a *Who's Who*? This was all news to them.

Kumiega asked Jennifer about Sharon's plans for college and the scholarship, keeping his voice at a soothing, comfortable level.

Jennifer could only stare at the floor.

"Georgia Tech. That was her dream, to go to Georgia Tech. It was all she ever talked about, from the moment we met at a student camp. She wanted to be an aerospace engineer. She wanted to work for NASA. She took the SATs twice, just so she was sure to score high enough to get in, and she did. The day she got that acceptance letter was the happiest I ever heard her sound. She was screaming, 'Jenny, I made it!' over and over again. She had her whole future ahead of her. It's funny, though. Now that we're talking about this. One second she was screaming that she made it, the next she was worrying about what her father would say. She didn't think that bastard would let her go. I didn't understand it at the time, but now we know why."

Jennifer's passionate defense of her friend warmed Kumiega, Yancey, and Fitzpatrick, their preconceived notions of Sharon melting away. Jennifer remained there for the balance of the day, answering dozens of questions about Sharon and Floyd and prodded to remember anything, no matter how small.

She recalled the story about the strange phone call from Sharon from South Carolina.

"It was weird. She was crying and begging me to come, but at the same time her voice was so monotone. It was like she was saying to me, 'Please don't come.' Then Warren, or Floyd or whatever you call him, gets on the phone and demands that I visit. Then he hangs up. I never understood that call," said Jennifer.

Fitzpatrick knew the answer.

"Jennifer, I believe if you had gone to South Carolina, you'd have been killed. It sounds like he forced Sharon to make that call, and in her way she was telling you not to come. I think she saved your life," said Fitzpatrick. "It was the same thing with Greg Higgs. If he'd taken Michael, Floyd would have gone back to him after he got out of jail in 1993 and no doubt would have killed Higgs to get the boy back."

It was all surreal to Jennifer, who by late afternoon was exhausted and emotionally spent. She didn't want to talk anymore, and slowly rose from her chair, offering a parting thought.

"I think about Sharon, and what I remember most is that she wanted so badly to be at our house. And right now that's the only comfort I have; in that I gave her an escape."

Jennifer returned to her hotel and flopped on the bed without undressing and fell into a deep sleep.

Kumiega, Yancey, and Fitzpatrick remained behind, discussing the day-long interview with Jennifer. She painted a profoundly different picture of Sharon Marshall, a mosaic that only compounded the human tragedy and heartbreak.

All believed that Jennifer would make a superb witness for the prosecution. She was passionate in her defense of her friend, and forcefully and clearly spoke of Sharon's accomplishments, her dreams, and her future, all of which were taken away by a predator.

Sharon never had a chance, and Jennifer's vivid memories of their time together won them over. By the end of the night as they walked out into the cold, all agreed that Sharon Marshall was, quite simply, remarkable.

CHAPTER 19

Franklin Delano Floyd wore a wrinkled blue suit as he entered the vast courtroom of U.S. District Judge Wayne E. Alley on Wednesday, March 29, 1995, the clanking shackles around his ankles sounding a warning bell that his trial was about to begin.

Ed Kumiega and Mark Yancey sat at the prosecution table on the right side of the courtroom, closest to the jury box. They were joined by Joe Fitzpatrick, since federal prosecutions allowed for the case agent in charge to sit with the attorneys.

The jury box was empty and would remain so because Floyd asked for and received a nonjury trial after his motion for a change of venue was denied. He unsuccessfully argued that the publicity surrounding the kidnapping tainted the jury pool. Judge Alley disagreed, though he did give Floyd one request: approving his motion to act as his own attorney.

Floyd claimed he did not feel comfortable with a public

defender, yet couldn't hire an attorney since he'd spent all of the insurance money he'd received following Sharon's death.

No one could argue his case better, he said, than himself. Floyd explained that he studied law in prison and even helped several friends, writing legal briefs in their defense. Judge Alley indulged Floyd's fancy, but decided that Floyd required legal help anyway, and Susan Otto from the federal public defenders office was appointed to serve as co-counsel.

Kumiega and Yancey were privately ecstatic when they heard the news about the "hybrid" defense team, even more so when they learned that Alley himself would decide Floyd's fate.

Juries were fickle. Judges like Alley were not. He was a former U.S. Army general, dean of the Oklahoma University Law School, and the chief appellate judge who denied the appeal of Lieutenant William Calley, the Army officer convicted of massacring hundreds in the Vietnam village of My Lai. An appointee of President Ronald Reagan, Alley was considered one of the best trial judges in the state. The prosecutors believed he would see this case for what it was, with the evidence presented before him, and render swift justice.

Floyd believed Judge Alley would be his savior.

He was seated at the defense table on the left side of the room with Otto. Behind the attorneys and the accused, the public pews were filled mostly with reporters. Members of the Choctaw Police Department attended along with Dorothy Leonard, who arrived dressed in black from head to toe.

The first witness called to testify was Special Agent Joe Fitzpatrick, who spent the day relaying the events of September 12, 1994—the day Michael was kidnapped—and the subsequent FBI investigation and Floyd's arrest on November 10.

By Friday, several other witnesses had testified, and court

was nearing the end of the day when Fitzpatrick felt his pager vibrating. He jotted down the number, then walked out to the hallway and called Special Agent Tom Jordan of the Oklahoma State Bureau of Investigation. Jordan said he had something Fitzpatrick should see, and it couldn't wait.

Luther Masterson was in his Mission, Kansas, garage early that Friday afternoon preparing to install a wiring harness for a trailer on the white 1994 Ford pickup he'd purchased from the State Farm Insurance company. The car had been stolen, and the insurance company sold it to reclaim some of the money it lost on the payout.

Masterson owned an auto body shop and pulled himself underneath the rear end. He looked up and saw what looked like a package wrapped in masking tape sticking out from above the gas tank. Masterson reached up and grabbed the package, which had been taped to the tank, and slid out from under the truck.

In his hand was a manila envelope, worn and ripped into several pieces and wrapped in tape. Masterson's first inclination was that it contained drugs. He turned it over to the other end, saw a slight opening, and looked inside. There were photographs. He decided to open the package and inside he found photos, dozens of them. His eyes opened wide with horror when he flipped through the pictures, and he immediately called the Mission police.

Officer Gary Hines arrived, confiscated the photos, and took down the vehicle identification number of the Ford truck.

When he returned to the police station, Hines ran a check on the car and verified that Masterson purchased the vehicle from State Farm. The car had been stolen out of Oklahoma City in September and later recovered in Dallas. It belonged to a James D. Davis of Midwest City, Oklahoma.

Hines called the Oklahoma Bureau of Investigation, who contacted Joe Fitzpatrick.

On Monday morning, day four of testimony had already begun, but Fitzpatrick remained at the FBI office, studying the photos.

There were ninety-seven pictures in all, most of them cropped pictures of young girls, from toddlers to teens. Many of the photos featured nude girls engaged in explicit sexual activity. Others were dressed in exotic clothing, posing provocatively.

Fitzpatrick studied each photo and was overcome with a deep sense of disgust and rage. There appeared to be four different sets of pictures. One set featured a boat, perhaps a twenty-two or twenty-four footer. The second set was of two girls, anywhere from ten to twelve years old, fully dressed but posing in clothing far too provocative for children to wear. The third group featured photos of what appeared to be one girl as she grew from toddler to teen. She was blond and had been photographed posing or performing in sexually explicit positions, often spreading her legs and exposing her vagina.

Fitzpatrick knew the girl was Sharon.

Fitzpatrick tried to remain stoic, but his heart sank, and he couldn't stop from imagining the absolute horror Sharon experienced during her years with Franklin Delano Floyd.

The fourth set of photos was equally, if not more, disturbing. They were of a young woman, perhaps in her late teens or early twenties. She was nude, her hands bound behind her back. She was blindfolded and obviously beaten. Her lips were swollen and bloody, with cuts and blood around her nose, which was also swollen. It was difficult to tell if she was conscious. She had long, dark curly hair, full breasts, possibly with implants, and a tanned, shapely body.

The woman had been positioned lying on her back and stomach, her legs spread apart, her vagina and anus exposed. There appeared to be small burn marks around the anal area. Many of the photos were close-ups of her breast and pubic areas.

Fitzpatrick returned to the courthouse and informed Ed Kumiega and Mark Yancey about the new, disturbing discovery.

Following the day's testimony the three men met at the U.S. Attorney's office to view the pictures, and Kumiega and Yancey were stunned. It was clear that the older girl had been tortured, forced into degrading positions, and was apparently near death.

"It looks like a snuff photo," said a disgusted Kumiega.

The photos of Sharon were devastating. They all had an idea that she had been abused living with Floyd, but the photos brought to life the real and unmitigated horror.

"This kid didn't have a chance," said Yancey. "He took her, abused her, then killed her, and killed her son. Absolutely horrible."

Kumiega pulled out a photo of Sharon wearing a leopard-skin outfit and high heels. She couldn't have been more than fourteen years old.

"He's dressing her up as a hooker," said Kumiega. "He did that to her. He put her in those strip clubs when she got older. That wasn't her choice. Jesus. That wasn't her choice."

It took a few minutes to recover from the initial shock revealed in the photos before the prosecutors and Fitzpatrick began discussing the legal ramifications of the find. Floyd clearly left the photos, his personal "trophy" case, underneath the truck after arriving in Dallas. That much was certain. All agreed that it was too late to file child-abuse charges, at least for this trial. It was also probably too late to introduce the photos during the trial.

It was clear that the young woman in the fourth set of photos, whoever she was, was probably dead, and Fitzpatrick returned to his office and sent out a nationwide alert hoping to find out her identity.

When the trial resumed the next morning the prosecution continued with its parade of witnesses: Gary Homan, Dr. William Schmid, and the other psychiatrists who treated Floyd in prison; Emilio Ayala, the Dallas police officer who found the stolen car; Gregory Panther, the Louisville man who worked with Floyd on the paint crew; James Davis; the school principal; and Merle Bean, who tearfully recounted Michael's profound turnaround under her care, all testified.

Greg Higgs was flown in from his home in Oregon and recounted his relationship with the girl he knew as Sharon. Prior to his testimony he met Jennifer Fisher Tanner in the victims' witness room provided by the U.S. Attorney's office. Inside the room were a support staff, couch, television, and food. Jennifer had flown in again from San Diego the night before. She was whisked downtown and asked to review several of the photos found in the Ford truck.

The prosecutors knew it would be painful and covered Sharon's genital area. Jennifer broke down when she saw the first photo. It was Sharon, dressed in the same sexy clothing Jennifer had seen in her dresser drawers so many years earlier. The second photo was of Sharon wearing the tiger-stripe suit Jennifer wore that night Floyd took them to the dance club.

The prosecutors showed Jennifer two more photos, both of Sharon when she was a child. Again, they covered her genital area. Jennifer was in agony.

The next day she met Greg Higgs. It was their first

meeting, and Jennifer could see why Sharon was attracted to him. He was handsome and clean-cut. They talked and expressed the same hurt, shock, and general disbelief. Greg was also deeply wounded over the loss of Michael.

"I never knew that I had a son. And now that I do know, he's gone," said Higgs. "If they ever find Michael I'm fighting for custody, and Jennifer, I want you to be his godmother, OK?"

Jennifer began to cry. She hugged Greg, thanked him for the thought, and then heard her name called.

It was time to go across the street and testify.

A court officer led Jennifer to the door leading into the courtroom. She was determined to bring the essence of Sharon into the court and wanted the judge and attorneys and all in attendance to see the real Sharon, to hear her voice, to hear the truth. Jennifer wanted to honor her friend, but she was nervous and needed help. So she closed her eyes and prayed for divine assistance.

The door opened and she confidently walked down the center aisle, her head held up high. She could see Floyd's back up ahead to the left. He was sitting at the defense table. He turned around, recognized her immediately, and appeared agitated. She walked past Floyd, not bothering to look at him, then walked to the witness stand, said the oath, and sat down. Now she was face-to-face with Floyd, and could see him clearly. It had been nine years, and he looked pretty much the same, just older, grayer, and balder.

Floyd returned the icy stare.

Kumiega and Yancey had taken turns interviewing witnesses, and it was Yancey who would lead Jennifer through her relationship with Sharon and Floyd, their phone calls, their letters, Sharon's dreams and aspirations. Each time Jennifer mentioned Sharon by name, she turned her stare toward Floyd.

Following a brief recess, Susan Otto cross-examined Jennifer, questioned her friendship with Sharon, and suggested that Jennifer held a negative opinion of Floyd based on information given her by the FBI.

"That's absolutely incorrect," said Jennifer. "I always had a very negative connotation about him. My parents absolutely could not stand him."

"Well, now, wait a minute. Your parents hired him to work for them," said Otto.

"No! We were terrified of him. He had a very violent temper," said Jennifer.

Otto stopped, turned to the judge, and said she had no further questions.

The judge excused Jennifer, who walked out of the witness stand and by Floyd. He looked enraged, his face red, his fists clenched.

She strode out of the courtroom feeling great satisfaction, confident that she had told the world about her friend Sharon, and knowing that her testimony was yet another nail in the government's case.

The hammer was Joe Fitzpatrick.

Following his testimony the first day of the trial, Fitzpatrick was called to the witness stand two more times as Kumiega and Yancey presented their case in chronological order.

It was Fitzpatrick's third and final time on the witness stand when he would be cross-examined by Floyd.

The only other time the two men had met face-to-face was in Louisville, and now Floyd believed he had the upper hand, given that he would be the one asking the questions. It was the moment Floyd had waited for, and he wanted to prove that Fitzpatrick was prejudiced and, despite his standing within the FBI, would resort to any means to help convict him.

But Floyd's examination was off-the-wall, his arguments more or less nonsensical, drawing even more damning evidence from Fitzpatrick concerning Floyd's years in Oklahoma City using the name Trenton Davis and allegations that he abused Sharon, then known as Suzanne.

"If you found evidence of abuse, tell the court what it is, and where you got it," said Floyd.

"The baby-sitter that took care of Suzanne Davis was highly suspicious that the child had been abused, that's why you left Oklahoma City," said Fitzpatrick.

Floyd tried to regroup, changing the subject to his travels throughout the country with Sharon, but only fumbled more on his words, giving Fitzpatrick the opportunity to toy with him.

For every question Floyd asked, Fitzpatrick returned either pointed answers or incredulous reactions, not understanding Floyd's incoherent line of questioning. Floyd looked and sounded foolish, and with each response from Fitzpatrick, he was becoming increasingly frustrated.

"Your Honor, the witness is not answering the question!" he'd bark.

Floyd prefaced impossible questions about his life with "Are you aware . . ." and incurred the wrath of Judge Alley, who repeatedly warned him not to assert a fact in the guise of a question.

At one point, Floyd painted himself as an "upstanding citizen" who was given a small child to care for, and asked Fitzpatrick what he thought of that.

"Mr. Floyd, an upstanding citizen in the community and you are not the same thing," said Fitzpatrick.

The rambling cross-examination continued through the morning, only to be mercifully stopped by Judge Alley, who'd had enough. He called for a lunch break, and instructed Floyd to allow Susan Otto to continue the cross-examination when court reconvened after lunch.

When they returned, Fitzpatrick was questioned by Otto

and Floyd sat slumped in his seat, emotionally and physically drained from the verbal beating he'd suffered at the hands of Fitzpatrick.

The trial was all but over, the time for Floyd's guilt to be declared separated only by the testimony of defense witnesses, one of whom unexpectedly provided the prosecution and investigators with clues to Floyd's whereabouts the week after he kidnapped Michael.

Susan Otto called Shashi Narottam, the owner of the Fulton Inn Motel in Atlanta, Georgia. Each day some thirty to forty people checked into the motel, which was next door to the Greyhound bus depot, and Narottam didn't think twice about renting a room, so long as the customer had cash in hand. Identification wasn't even a consideration if the person looked reasonably respectable and was ready to pay $27.62 per night, which included tax, for a clean room and bed. Checkout was the next day at 11 A.M.

Narottam testified that Floyd arrived in Atlanta on Tuesday, September 13, and rented a room under the name "Bill Blankenship." Floyd, a.k.a. Blankenship, said little other than he was staying in Atlanta for a while. He gave his address as 2640 46 Street, Phoenix, Arizona, and was handed the keys to room number 44, for which he paid eight days in advance. Floyd stayed at the Fulton Inn until September 21, when he checked himself into Grady Memorial Hospital. Narottam testified that during that week he never saw Floyd with a boy, supporting the defense claim that Michael was not in Atlanta with Floyd.

Kumiega, Yancey, and Fitzpatrick didn't believe that Narottam's testimony proved anything other than that Floyd was smart enough to rent the room by himself, without being seen with Michael. Dorothy Leonard's chilling story about the bathtub drowning now made even more sense, and the timeline was complete.

They all believed that Floyd arrived in Atlanta, with Michael, and rented the room at the Fulton Inn. A week later Michael was dead, and Floyd carjacked the Dodge Shadow, disposed of Michael's body, then checked himself into the hospital for nine days before boarding a bus for Louisville on September 30.

Narottam's testimony was, quite simply, a gift for the prosecution.

Testimony ended on Friday, April 7. Final arguments began on Monday morning, April 10, and Ed Kumiega was thankful he was speaking directly to Judge Alley and not a jury, which allowed him to shorten the time needed to deliver his closing.

Kumiega delivered a compassionate plea, addressing the legal issue of parental rights, maintaining that Floyd was never a parent to Michael Hughes and never satisfied the section 1201 requirement.

He then talked about Floyd's prior actions and the effect they had on others.

"The evidence also shows at this trial that the defendant has wreaked havoc on three generations of Michael Anthony Hughes's kin. Michael is missing, Michael's mother had to live since nineteen-seventy-five under many aliases, and we do not know the pain and suffering of Sharon Marshall's mother in this case. The statement that the defendant gave to the FBI is that she was an unwanted baby and he took the baby. That's all we know. That's all that the government, after many hours of—hundreds of hours, man-hours—can establish, is that Michael Anthony Hughes is the son of Sharon Marshall."

Susan Otto's closing argument centered on the legal definition of a parent, claiming that Floyd raised Michael during the first two years of his life, he fulfilled the definition of a parent in section 1201. She also argued that Michael "consumed" Floyd's waking hours, and that Floyd's love for

Michael led Floyd to subject himself to the Oklahoma Juvenile Court system, with little success.

"I respectfully submit that no one but a parent could have persisted," said Otto. "Mr. Floyd has lived a very remarkable life, remarkable in the sense that he has suffered great things and many things at the hands of adults when he was a child, at the hands of his peers when he was in prison. And as a result of this Mr. Floyd is very reluctant to trust institutions, to trust systems."

Otto concluded by saying that Floyd wished to speak, and he rose slowly, his legs shackled. Floyd had decided against taking the stand, and instead used his closing argument to state his case, reviewing the abuse he suffered as a child, then arguing that he was the sole parent of Michael Hughes, claiming that "blood is not the only ingredient to the love and cherishment of a child.

"I took my son because it was my right to live and care for him, unimpeded by an intervention by DHS unsupported by the law. It was not a stranger who held this beautiful child in his arms at birth and felt the warmth and glow of his love for me, and were bonded in that moment for life. It was not a stranger who nursed and cleaned and fed him while his mother worked at night. It was not a stranger who contracted his diseases and sicknesses while he cared for this fevered child and worried if he would die or not. It was not a stranger who walked with him in the park, pulling his wagon, and taking him to the fair and Easter egg hunts, taking him to the mall where he liked to shop until he dropped. Other children he played with, and he had deep feelings with them, a wonderful little boy. He loves Jesus and he sings it so sweet on the visit tape that I recorded."

Floyd's emotional speech was nauseating to the prosecution, but he had built momentum, and the words flowed like a Sunday sermon.

"It was not a stranger who paid child support and set up a trust fund for him, and spent four years fighting the court for his return. Oh, God, don't let these people stand between me and the love of my son and don't let them destroy the bond between us, and let my son come home. This is not a case of a stranger taking a child, it's the act of a loving father who can't stand to see the heartbreak of his child any longer."

Judge Alley called for an afternoon recess until 4 P.M., and when court resumed, justice was handed down as surely and swiftly as Ed Kumiega and Mark Yancey expected.

Franklin Delano Floyd was guilty of all charges.

Floyd stood still, showing little emotion, expecting the worst. Judge Alley read through his verdict, dismissing any argument that Floyd was Michael's parent. Alley believed that since Floyd was not a biological, adoptive, or step-parent, and that his marriage to Sharon was a "sham," Floyd simply had no right to claim himself a parent.

Alley, in essence, defined the word *parent* in the federal statute, to be used in federal prosecutions and courts throughout the country.

His fate sealed, Floyd was led to the back of the court-house and changed from his blue suit into a prison jump-suit. He was an inmate again, and come his sentencing in August, he probably would be for the rest of his life.

He was taken to a side door to a waiting prison transport, but the route was blocked by dozens of reporters and television cameras. The calmness Floyd exhibited earlier in the courtroom before Judge Alley evaporated before the media, and he became irate. He spit at one reporter, then raised his hands and stuck his middle fingers into the television cameras screaming "Fuck Oklahoma!"

CHAPTER 20

It was little more than a week after the Floyd trial ended when Joe Fitzpatrick arrived at his sixteenth-floor office early the morning of Wednesday, April 19. He was prepared to continue with his search to identify Sharon Marshall, the last resting place of Michael Hughes, and the identity of the brutally tortured woman in Floyd's photo album. Ed Kumiega and Mark Yancey had taken some well-deserved time off. Kumiega went fishing; Yancey played plenty of golf.

Fitzpatrick was pleased with the verdict in the Floyd trial and the work of the two prosecutors, but felt little satisfaction with the outcome. Questions remained, with so few answers. His personal record of closing every case during his twenty-five year career with the FBI was now in jeopardy. As he began to entertain thoughts of retirement, Fitzpatrick knew he could not leave the bureau without closure.

He spent the week following the trial focusing on the tortured woman. Nothing in the photos suggested a location. The woman was on what appeared to be a sofa. She was blindfolded, terrified, perhaps just moments away from death. She had long fingernails, and her T-shirt had been pushed up to her neck, exposing her breasts and stomach. Whatever type of pants or undergarment she had been wearing had been removed.

Fitzpatrick had already checked with the National Crime Information Center database, but there wasn't enough information to help wade through the tens of thousands of women reported missing each year. Fitzpatrick sent a teletype to bureaus throughout the country, seeking information on any women reported missing who might fit the general description of the victim.

As the new week began, and Fitzpatrick waited for responses on the unidentified woman, he directed his attention to Sharon.

He called social services and was sent a list of the missing-child clearinghouses from each state. Fitzpatrick intended to write to each and every one of them and include the copy of the photo of Sharon when she was a toddler, but decided he needed at least one day off to clear his head, and put in for a leave of absence on April 19 to go fishing.

When he woke that morning it was windy and he knew the fish wouldn't be biting, so he cancelled his leave and went to work. He decided he'd go to the courthouse and pick up the exhibits used in the Floyd trial, but telephone calls kept him at his office. At 9:02 A.M. he was on the phone again when he felt a slight vibration. Then came the loud noise. Startled FBI personnel looked out the window and could see the dark smoke and debris rising into the air from the downtown area some seven miles away.

Everyone in the office, including Fitzpatrick, stood up, unsure of what was happening. Some thought a plane had crashed, others that a gas line had exploded. Within minutes everyone knew that a massive explosion had destroyed the Alfred P. Murrah Federal Building, right across the street from the courthouse. The nine-story building had been blown in half, and it was clear there were fatalities, perhaps a great loss of life.

Throughout the FBI field office, agents and their supervisors managed to remain calm and focused, but other personnel, including secretaries, were beside themselves. Some there had family members who worked at the Murrah building, and the violent images of destruction and blood and chaos relayed over the television within minutes after the explosion were devastating.

Every one of the one hundred and twenty agents assigned to Oklahoma City was pulled off whatever cases they were working on and immediately assigned to work the bombing, including Joe Fitzpatrick. Before leaving the office for the makeshift command center near the destroyed Murrah building, Fitzpatrick took his Floyd file and photos and put them inside his desk.

Floyd, Sharon, Michael, and the unidentified woman would be forgotten as Fitzpatrick began his work on the Oklahoma bomber investigation.

Four months would pass before Fitzpatrick would be forced to take his attention off the bombing investigation to attend Franklin Floyd's sentencing in August.

A total of 168 people were killed in the bombing of the Murrah Federal Building; nineteen of the dead were children. Another five hundred people were injured. Timothy McVeigh, twenty-seven, had been arrested for driving without a license just ninety minutes after the explosion by an Oklahoma Highway Patrol officer. Two days later McVeigh was charged with the bombing, and the FBI's Oklahoma City field office coordinated the bureau's national investigation. The field office saw its ranks swell as agents were brought in from other bureaus throughout the country.

The probe replaced all activity at the field office, and other cases were pushed to the backburner as the government painstakingly collected its evidence with the ultimate goal of convicting Timothy McVeigh with 168 counts of murder.

Franklin Floyd remained at the Oklahoma County Jail and had plenty of time to prepare a statement to be read prior to learning his fate. When he was brought before Judge Alley on August 10, Floyd threw himself at the mercy of the court and requested the opportunity to read his entire statement.

"I'm a threat to no one. I'm an old man. I'm dying brokenhearted. And I'm going to die in prison, that's a fact. There's not but very little more you can do to me, so I'd like to have a little consideration."

Judge Alley sat back and let Floyd continue. It was a lengthy, rambling statement in which Floyd professed his love for Michael, the injustice in his life, and acceptance of the upcoming sentence. And as he did during his final argument during the trial, Floyd, who was now fifty-two years old, blamed his lot on the injustice of life and past abuse.

"I wrote the FBI from the dungeons of prison, in tears from being raped and beaten maliciously, and called names of untold horror, because of a conviction that I was innocent of, and used that as a tool to rape and abuse me. These people sitting out here don't know the truth. They can't handle the truth," said Floyd, pointing toward the prosecutors.

"When this case was brought up, the DHS personnel did everything in their power to crucify me, and took my son without a hearing, as required by law. And the judge said these words, 'No child molester will get this kid.' You're talking about a malicious society! I was seventeen years

Franklin Floyd, a.k.a. "Trenton Davis," posing with Sharon, a.k.a "Suzanne Davis" in Oklahoma City, circa 1976. *(Photo courtesy of the NCMEC)*

BELOW: Sharon Marshall, circa 1984. *(Photo courtesy of Jennifer Fisher McElhannon)*

Sharon's high school
graduation photo, May 1986.
*(Photo courtesy of Forest Park
High School)*

BELOW: Jennifer Fisher and
Sharon at the Fisher home
in Stone Mountain, Georgia,
July 1986. *(Photo courtesy of
Jennifer Fisher McElhannon)*

Sharon and her son Michael, circa 1989. *(Photo courtesy of the FBI, Oklahoma City)*

BELOW: Undated photo of Sharon posing for Floyd. The picture was one of dozens found by a Kansas mechanic and traced to Floyd. *(Photo courtesy of the FBI, Oklahoma City)*

Franklin Floyd following his arrest for assault in Oklahoma City, July 1994. *(Photo courtesy of the FBI, Oklahoma City)*

BELOW: Michael Hughes's missing poster. *(Courtesy of the NCMEC)*

Non-Family Abduction

MICHAEL HUGHES

DOB: Mar 21, 1988
Missing: Sep 12, 1994
Age Now: 15
Sex: Male
Race: White
Hair: Brown
Eyes: Brown
Height: 3'10" (117 cm)
Weight: 45 lbs (20 kg)
Missing From:
CHOCTAW
OK
United States

Age Progressed

Michael's photo is shown aged to 13 years. He was abducted at gunpoint from his school by a man who has since been taken into police custody. The child's whereabouts are still unknown. Michael has a scar on his forehead and has two new crooked bottom teeth. He was last seen wearing a blue T-shirt with red sleeves, a red and blue shorts, and black high-top sneakers.

ANYONE HAVING INFORMATION SHOULD
CONTACT
National Center for Missing & Exploited Children
1-800-843-5678 (1-800-THE-LOST)

Choctaw Police Department (Oklahoma) - Missing Persons Unit 1-405-290-7770 Or Your Local FBI

Assistant U.S. Attorney Mark Yancey
following Floyd's trial, April 1995.
(Photo courtesy of Mark Yancey)

Assistant U.S. Attorney Ed Kumiega (right) celebrates Floyd's conviction for kidnapping with David Walling, criminal chief for the U.S. Attorney's office, Western District of Oklahoma, April 1995.
(Photo courtesy of Ed Kumiega)

FBI Special Agent Joe Fitzpatrick. His pursuit for Sharon's identity revealed flaws in the nation's ability to track missing children. *(Photo courtesy of Joe Fitzpatrick)*

BELOW: Cheryl Ann Commesso, 1988. Her remains were found in 1995, six years after she disappeared. *(Photo courtesy of the St. Petersburg Police Department)*

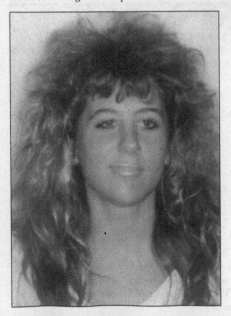

St. Petersburg, Florida, police detectives Mark Deasaro (left) and Robert Schock. *(Photo courtesy of Mark Deasaro)*

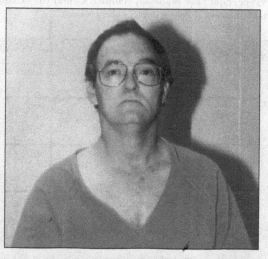

Franklin Floyd following his arrest for the murder of Cheryl Commesso, 1998. *(Photo courtesy of the St. Petersburg Police Department)*

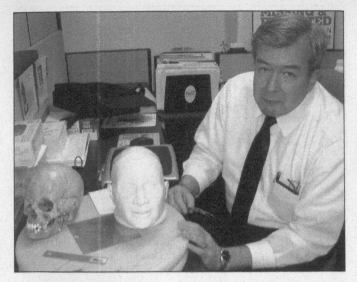

Gerry Nance, cold case manager, National Center for Missing & Exploited Children. *(Photo courtesy of Gerry Nance)*

Sharon's last resting place, Park Grove Cemetery, Tulsa, Oklahoma. "Tonya" was the name she was using when she died. *(Photo by Matt Birkbeck)*

without an arrest! I haven't had a conviction for any crime in thirty years! And all my time has been spent in prison or on the run. You don't know me. I got my hand scalded for playing with myself, had to eat cigarette butts for smoking, washed my mouth out with soap. When I was a kid at the orphans' home I cried out for help, but there were no laws back then, nothing about child abuse. They could beat you until your feet swoll up this thick with pus in them and no one would do nothing. When I got old enough to read a road map I took off, and I didn't care about starving."

Floyd turned toward Joe Fitzpatrick.

"Mr. Fitzpatrick wants to know why I don't go to him with what I know. I could clear up all his mysteries. The reason I don't is because he don't understand it, he wouldn't. He doesn't have any compassion. Just simple as that."

Floyd flipped over another page, and Judge Alley could see there were several more to follow. His patience was growing thin as Floyd continued.

"Judge, I had been a terrible person and man all of my life. A man can't go through my scars and come out all right. Oh, great one, you've not walked in my shoes, yet you stand in my judgment, and that's the law and your duty. You couldn't give me less time if you wanted, the guideline, you can show me no mercy, I ask you for none."

Before he could read another word Judge Alley stepped in, telling Floyd he had given him considerable time to speak, and now it was Ms. Otto's turn.

Floyd hobbled over to the defense table, satisfied that he had made his argument and hoping the judge had heard his plea.

Otto rose, and cited the difficulty of a case that presented challenging legal issues, particularly the definition of a "parent."

She then turned toward Floyd.

"Mr. Floyd is probably one of the most pain-filled people I have ever met, a person institutionalized to the extent that presents a very altered perception of the world when they're out among us and trying to explain themselves and their actions.

"Mr. Floyd is a prime example of what happens early in our childhood when our system, for whatever reason, whether it's the traditional nuclear family unit or our governmental substitutes for those units, somehow failed to address important issues. It is inevitable, it seems, that a person who lives in such a deprived circumstance finds it virtually impossible to live in the world with any degree of success. In many ways Mr. Floyd is still a six-year-old who wants to get you to listen to him about everything and all things, because life for Mr. Floyd is one long waking nightmare."

Otto asked the judge to sentence Floyd to the minimum set under the sentencing guidelines, which was 20 years.

Ed Kumiega quickly stood up and asked Judge Alley to throw the sentencing book at Floyd—a life sentence.

"Michael Hughes has been gone three hundred and thirty-three days," said Kumiega, reminding all that if Michael were still in Choctaw living with the Bean family he'd be entering second grade.

"He can't meet wonderful friends anymore. He doesn't have playmates. He can't experience learning something new, all because of some attitude, some fixation by the defendant toward this child. That's the real pain here. Mr. Floyd deserves everything he gets today. And the consistent core with his allocution and presentation today is that Mr. Floyd is a fraud."

Judge Alley agreed with Kumiega and sentenced Floyd to a total of fifty-two years and three months in prison, without the possibility of parole. It wasn't a life sentence, but Floyd would certainly die in prison.

Before Floyd was led out of the courtroom, assured of living his remaining years in a prison cell, Judge Alley offered one closing thought.

"I've viewed Mr. Floyd through the many proceedings in the case, concluding with today's proceedings, and I find that he has one conspicuous attribute, and that is the attribute of rationalizing his conduct, that he looks at the world in an extremely idiosyncratic way, an idiosyncratic way driven by his own needs, without regard to the rights of others or the dangers that his conduct might pose to others."

Floyd was gone, to rot in jail, and Ed Kumiega, Mark Yancey, and especially Joe Fitzpatrick couldn't have felt any more satisfaction.

They shared a hope that one day they would find the true identity of Sharon Marshall, along with the identity of the tortured woman and the remains of Michael Hughes. But those were investigations that would be continued another time. They all had other business at hand, and they returned to their offices to continue their respective work on the bombing investigation, work that filled their days and nights as Floyd did prior to April 19, 1995.

CHAPTER 21

St. Petersburg, Florida
July 1996

St. Petersburg Police Detective Robert Schock didn't know what to make of the phone call he received on July 16, 1996, from the FBI's Tampa field office. They had photographs of an unidentified woman that could pertain to Schock's case involving the Jane Doe of I-275, and wanted to meet.

Schock was surprised and taken off guard. His investigation had stalled a year earlier, and nothing since had surfaced to help identify the victim.

His probe began after the remains of a woman were found a year earlier, on March 29, 1995, off the side of I-275 by a laborer, Terry Lee Ricard, who was working with a crew clearing the east side of the highway just south of the Roosevelt Boulevard exit.

Ricard had to urinate and decided to walk through a three-foot hole in a chain link fence and relieve himself in the brush.

The fence, which was about five feet high and served as a

barrier to an old landfill, was some forty feet away from the interstate but ran parallel with the highway for about a half a mile before turning inland near Roosevelt Boulevard.

Ricard zipped up his pants, then retraced his steps through the hole and along the fence line, evading water that had typically collected through the year. The crew tried to clear the area in February, only to find it was still submerged and filled with the usual flotsam and cyprus knots, small stumps that grew from cypress trees but looked like otherworldly anthills that grew out of the water. Palmetto trees sprouted from the mini-lagoon and provided cover from the sun.

The crew decided to work another area and come back in a few weeks, expecting the area to have dried out, which it usually did for about a month during the spring months before filling up again.

As expected, much of the area had dried enough to complete the cleanup, though some water remained, and Ricard tiptoed along the fence until he reached a swath of ground where the water receded, leaving the ground wet and muddy. Ricard took two steps on the sloppy surface when he saw what looked like a faded white volleyball lying in the muck. It was half buried, and Ricard approached it slowly, pulled his leg back, then let go, kicking at the object and turning it over, revealing two holes that looked like eye sockets.

Ricard knew immediately this was no ball, and called out to his coworkers clearing out brush on the other side of the water.

"Hey guys, there's a skull over here."

He ran up and onto the side of the highway, flagging down a Florida State Highway Patrol trooper.

* * *

The search area was just inside the St. Petersburg city limit and Bob Schock was the first detective to arrive on the scene.

Schock was a native Floridian who had grown up in St. Petersburg. He attended St. Petersburg Community College, where he earned an associate degree in criminal justice, and remained in his hometown, joining the police department in 1977.

Schock was a self-proclaimed lifer, a "thirty-year man" who was respected for his careful approach and unassuming way. He was lower than low-key, so quiet some of his colleagues questioned whether he even knew the definition of "ego." Married with two teenage daughters, he looked older than his thirty-nine years, having developed soft pouches around his midsection.

When he arrived at the scene he had already been designated lead investigator, and he quickly parceled interviews to other detectives, who arrived one after the other.

Within a half hour, the entire side of the highway was roped off for a quarter mile in either direction. The right lane was closed, forcing traffic into the middle and left lanes, with motorists rubbernecking as the flashing lights from the dozen or so police cars parked off the road signaled the seriousness of the discovery.

It didn't take long to decide that the skull had apparently been submerged under the water for a long period of time, probably years. Exactly how long no one knew. All realized that if not for a series of coincidences—a receding water line and a worker with a full bladder—the skull would still be lying there, hidden and out of sight for at least another ten months when the area filled with water again.

A backhoe was brought in to help dig for more evidence, and over the course of two days, investigators found other bones, bone fragments, hair, and teeth, along with clothing, which included a worn bikini top and a striped short-sleeve shirt. They also found jewelry.

The human remains were sent to the medical examiner's office and to Dr. William Maples, a forensic anthropologist who was called in from the University of Florida in Gainesville to give an estimate of the age of the "Jane Doe" and an approximation of how long she had been left there. It had already been determined that the skull belonged to a woman, and two small holes in the back of the skull indicated she had been shot to death.

The medical examiner ruled the death a homicide.

Some forty personnel, including detectives and officers from the St. Petersburg police along with deputies from the Pinellas County Sheriff's office were involved during the first week of the investigation.

On April 4, 1995, Dr. Maples submitted his report. The victim was a white female, between sixteen and twenty years old. She had been badly beaten, with apparent fractures of the face. Two gunshot entry holes were marked in the back of the skull, just above the neck. Fragments from one of the bullets, a .22 caliber, were found inside the skull. Only three ribs were missing from the recovered skeleton, along with eight vertebrae and various elements of the hands and feet. The remains were in good condition, preserved by the water and muck. Estimation of time of death was extremely difficult, said Maples, but his best guess was two to three years earlier, perhaps around 1992.

Schock began checking missing-persons reports from neighboring police agencies, searching for women who fit the age range. But he added two years to Maples's estimate, and checked records dating back to 1990, just to be sure.

To help with the possible identification, the St. Petersburg Police held a press conference on April 6, hoping to generate leads. They received thirty calls, and Schock followed up on each one. In addition, Schock received another fifty possible matches from the National Crime Information Center.

Schock never realized there were this many reported missing women in the Tampa–St. Petersburg region, and these were only the women who fit the age of his Jane Doe. With eighty leads to search through, Schock needed help, and enlisted the aid of Detective Mark Deasaro.

Deasaro took part during the first few days of the investigation, combing the roadside for additional evidence and eventually finding a small bone, which he turned over to Schock.

A native New Yorker from Staten Island, Deasaro opted to attend college in a warmer climate and received a degree in criminology at St. Leo College in Pascal County, just north of St. Petersburg. He liked Florida and decided to stay, accepting a position with the Plant City Police and giving up earlier dreams of joining the New York City Police Department. Deasaro, thirty-six, later joined the St. Petersburg police in 1983 and eventually worked his way to detective with robbery homicide.

Deasaro and Schock made for a strange pairing—the quiet, unassuming native Floridian and the brash extrovert from New York. Deasaro was personable, impulsive, and loud; his friendly demeanor, charm, and good looks would take over a room in an instant. Deasaro was the hare, and Schock the turtle. But they worked well together, and Schock continued following leads with the phone calls while Deasaro contacted several clothing manufacturers, attempting to find more information on the garments found near the remains.

Some of the worn, dirty clothing still had labels attached, and Deasaro called the American Apparel Manufacturing Corporation in Arlington, Virginia, to help with the identification.

He passed along the registration numbers on the tags and was told the companies in question went out of business some ten years earlier. Another piece of clothing, a pair of black stretch pants, had the name Laurente on the label. Deasaro learned that the pants were cheap knockoffs of Yves St. Laurent, and that none of the clothing would be available in stores today.

Schock and Deasaro followed every single lead, but couldn't come up with a name to attach to the remains. After eight weeks the case remained open, but was just one of dozens of unsolved mysteries involving unidentified women found dead in the Tampa Bay area.

The call from the FBI more than a year later startled Schock, and he readily agreed to meet the following day with the Tampa police and FBI at a parking lot outside the Pinellas County Sheriff's office.

Schock stood in the parking lot and wiped his sweaty brow as he slowly reviewed the photos handed to him. He was taken aback by the brutality and sickness so plainly evident.

Schock quickly noticed the clothing pushed up toward the victim's neck. It was a white bikini top and striped shirt, similar to the worn clothing found near the skull of his Jane Doe.

Schock thought this was too good to be true.

It was explained that the photos were found more than a year earlier taped to the gas tank of a Ford truck in Mission, Kansas. The truck had been stolen during a kidnapping in Oklahoma in September 1994. The kidnapper was a Franklin Delano Floyd, who was currently in prison in Oklahoma City awaiting transfer to a federal facility to serve a fifty-two-year sentence following his conviction. Floyd lived in the Tampa area from 1988 to 1989 under the alias Warren Marshall. Included with the photos was an FBI file on Floyd, offering additional details of his troubled, disturbing, and violent history.

Schock returned to his desk downtown at police headquarters and read through the file. Attached was a contact
number for a Joe Fitzpatrick from the FBI's Oklahoma City
field office, who was the agent in charge of the Floyd case. It
was Fitzpatrick who had sent the photos to the Tampa FBI
field offices. He'd spent the past year working the Oklahoma City bombing investigation and recently returned his
attention to Floyd and the photos.

Fitzpatrick saw that the victim was well tanned, and figured she lived in a hot, sunny climate. Fitzpatrick knew
that Floyd lived in the Tampa area in the late 1980s. It was
a long shot, but he sent the photos to the Tampa FBI field
office, and they were now in Schock's hands.

Schock called Fitzpatrick that afternoon; their conversation was pleasant but to the point. Schock said judging by
the clothing worn in the photos, he strongly believed that
the woman and his Jane Doe were one and the same.

Fitzpatrick was stunned. It was his idea to send the photos to Tampa, but the sheer thought of connecting Floyd to
an open homicide investigation halfway across the country
was mind-boggling, even for a case that already stretched
the imagination.

Schock requested any and all information on Floyd, and
Fitzpatrick obliged, offering to help any way he could. Fitzpatrick always believed there was more to Franklin Floyd,
deeper, darker secrets that remained hidden. A new investigation, particularly a murder probe, could open new doors
to the mysteries surrounding Floyd and possibly those of
Sharon and Michael.

Over the next week Fitzpatrick sent Schock copies of files
on the FBI's investigation of Franklin Floyd, including the
names and contact numbers of all those involved in the kidnapping investigation, as well as acquaintances of Floyd in
other states, particularly Georgia.

Schock and Deasaro initially reached out to law enforcement in Oklahoma. The Choctaw police department filled in additional details on the kidnapping, and the Oklahoma City and Tulsa police departments eagerly offered background info on their investigations surrounding Sharon's murder in 1990.

On July 24, Schock and Deasaro drove across the bay to Tampa Police headquarters. A year earlier, during their original investigation, they reviewed missing-persons records dating back to 1990, based on Dr. Maples's belief that the remains were only a few years old.

Since Floyd lived in the area in 1988 and 1989, they expanded their search another two years to include missing-persons reports from that period. Tampa proved fruitless, so they drove to the Hillsborough County Sheriff's office to review two of their open cases. One had already been reviewed and eliminated. The other involved Cheryl Ann Commesso, a nineteen-year-old woman who had been reported missing in June 1989, but was last seen two months earlier, in April. Her car, a red Corvette, was reported abandoned by security at the St. Petersburg–Clearwater airport in May.

Commesso's description—including her height and weight—fit the Jane Doe. She also had breast implants, as did the woman in the photos. Schock compared the torture photos to a picture of Commesso's driver's license, and they appeared similar.

Schock requested, and received, all dental x-rays in the Commesso file along with a copy of the original missing-persons report. He and Deasaro then drove back across the bay to the Pinellas County Medical Examiner's office to compare the x-rays to those of the teeth found with the remains. The testing proved inconclusive.

Schock called Commesso's father, John, who lived in the Tampa area, and requested his daughter's dental records.

John said they were in New York, with Cheryl's mother, Lois.

Schock called Lois in New York, and she sent the records down the next day. With the dental records in hand, Schock and Deasaro returned to the medical examiner's office. That afternoon Dr. Ken Martin, a forensic odontologist, made a positive identification on the Jane Doe of I-275.

It was Cheryl Ann Commesso.

Schock notified her family with the sad news. He learned during the brief conversations that Cheryl had led a troubled life. She was the oldest of three children born to John and Lois, who were originally from New York and moved to Florida in 1985. Cheryl, who was born in June 1970, dropped out of high school when she was sixteen years old and ended up working as an exotic dancer in Orlando. She agreed to return home and live with her father after her parents separated during Christmas 1988, but a month later was gone, living in Tampa, dancing again and driving a 1985 red Corvette. She had placed eight thousand dollars down and her father cosigned the loan for the remainder. She spent another three thousand dollars on upgrades, including a rear spoiler. She also spent several thousand dollars for breast implants.

John said he received a call from the bank in May 1989 informing him that the Corvette had been abandoned at the St. Petersburg–Clearwater Airport. John figured his daughter had flown somewhere and left the car in the long-term parking lot, intending to return. But after several phone calls to family members he learned that no one had heard from Cheryl for a month or so, and by June a missing-persons report was filed.

Following his conversation with the Commessos, Schock called Oklahoma City and informed Joe Fitzpatrick they had an ID on the victim. Neither man was religious, but both had passing thoughts that a higher authority played a role in connecting photos found in Kansas to a murder in Florida.

With the torture photos and a positive identification in hand, the first order of business was connecting Cheryl Commesso to Franklin Floyd.

Prior to her disappearance Cheryl danced at the Mons Venus, a popular strip club on North Dale Mabry Boulevard near downtown Tampa. Schock and Deasaro visited the club with photos of Franklin Floyd, Sharon Marshall, and Cheryl Commesso. Employees at Mons Venus who worked at the club in the late 1980s recognized all three. Sharon and Cheryl were dancers, they said, while Floyd was some crazy coot known then as Warren Marshall.

On August 1, Joe Fitzpatrick and Mark Yancey flew to St. Petersburg to meet with Schock, Deasaro, and a representative from the Florida State Attorney's office. The Michael Hughes case was still open, and any information coming out of the Florida murder investigation could possibly lead to his remains, or even the true identity of Sharon Marshall.

Fitzpatrick provided an FBI timeline that revealed Floyd's whereabouts while in the Tampa area. He had lived in three different residences, all under the name Warren Marshall. Two homes were in trailer parks in Tampa, and the third and last address was at the Golden Lantern Mobile Home Park in Pinellas Park, just outside of St. Petersburg, from January 1989 to June 1989.

An arrest warrant had been issued for Floyd, a.k.a. Warren Marshall, on May 9, 1989, involving the reported theft of a boat and intent to defraud an insurance company. Floyd had allegedly drilled holes into the bottom of a twenty-two-foot motorboat he owned and sunk it in Tampa Bay, ostensibly to collect the insurance money. A month later, Floyd's trailer in Pinellas Park had been set on fire, but Floyd and his traveling companions—Sharon and her son, Michael—were gone.

Fitzpatrick and Yancey took the afternoon to describe the past events in Oklahoma, and shared the remaining photos of Sharon Marshall found in the truck in Kansas with the Florida investigators. Like their Oklahoma colleagues before, Schock, Deasaro, and the others sitting in the room were astounded. They already had a difficult time digesting the Floyd story, the kidnapping of Michael Hughes, and the tragic circumstances surrounding the life and death of Sharon Marshall.

The photos crystallized the repulsion felt by all.

Fitzpatrick's folder on Sharon was fairly complete and included much of the previously missing information, particularly her school years at Forest Park, Georgia.

Schock, Deasaro, and others in the room were astonished upon hearing of Sharon's accomplishments—from her selection as a *Who's Who Among American High School Students* in 1985, her elevation to Lieutenant Colonel in the ROTC, her senior class rank of twenty-six out of three hundred and fifty and finally her full scholarship to Georgia Tech University.

"You sure this is the same girl we're talking about?" said an incredulous Deasaro. "This can't be the same girl."

Fitzpatrick assured Deasaro and everyone else in the room hearing the story for the first time that this was, indeed, the same girl. She was also the same girl kidnapped by Floyd when she was a child, subjected to years of physical, sexual, and emotional abuse, and presumably killed by Floyd when she tried to leave him as an adult.

Her true identity was still unknown.

Fitzpatrick pulled out a copy of a 1988 hospital report from Louisville, Kentucky. Floyd, Sharon, and Michael suddenly bolted from Florida in November 1988 and lived for a short while at the Forsythia Apartments on Barley Avenue in Louisville. Sharon danced briefly at The Godfather club.

Around 8 P.M. on Christmas Eve, 1988, Sharon was found in her car, alone and unconscious. She had overdosed and was transported by ambulance to Humana University Hospital, where doctors revived her. Distraught and suicidal, Sharon wouldn't confide to doctors or psychiatrists the nature of her problem. During subsequent testing, doctors discovered that she was pregnant, probably in her first or second month. Sharon declined to tell them who the father was.

Floyd, a.k.a. Warren Marshall, was listed as a relative and notified by the hospital. He quickly checked Sharon out of the hospital, packed their bags, and they returned to Tampa, renting a trailer at the Golden Lantern trailer park in Pinellas County.

"You're kidding me, right? You've got to be kidding me?" said Deasaro, unable to fully comprehend all that he was hearing.

Fitzpatrick once again assured Deasaro and others seated that the story was, sadly, accurate.

"It's clear that whenever Sharon established a relationship with someone in a particular location or city, Floyd would move. Each time she became pregnant, in Georgia, Arizona, and Florida, they would leave. No friends, no ties, no attachments. This was one of the ways he controlled her all those years, by keeping her isolated," said Fitzpatrick.

Schock remained quiet through much of the meeting, as was his way. He was repulsed by Floyd, but deeply moved by Sharon's story. Aside from the ghastly photos of Cheryl Commesso found in the Ford truck, Schock focused on one particular picture in Fitzpatrick's file. It was Sharon's high school graduation photo. She wore a conservative, black off-the-shoulder dress, with small white pearls around her neck.

She had a slight smile, and to Schock's eyes was simply beautiful.

She appeared to be a young woman with a future filled with unlimited potential.

Schock decided that the Sharon in this photo could not be confused with the poor soul who was subjected to years of degradation and horror in the other photos laid out before him. No, Schock determined that this was the image of Sharon Marshall to be seared into his memory: an image of beauty, grace, and wholesomeness. She may not have had a real name, but this was the real woman, and the photo served to inspire Schock and Deasaro.

Over the course of the next month Schock and Deasaro would travel to Oklahoma to interview the witnesses who testified in Floyd's federal trial and others who came in contact with Sharon and Floyd in Tulsa.

Upon their return to St. Petersburg in mid-September, the two detectives began navigating the uncharted waters of Franklin Floyd and Sharon Marshall, a journey that would lead them to focus their attention on their last six months in Florida, from January to June 1989.

CHAPTER 22

The red Corvette sprinted past the handful of children playing basketball, ignoring the signs to "go slow—children at play." The driver, a young shapely woman with dark, wild hair and long, glossy fingernails, picked up her speed as she exited the Golden Lantern trailer park, her car screeching and smoke billowing from the rear tires as she turned right onto Park Boulevard.

Michelle Cupples had seen the car before, though she didn't think the driver lived in any of the singlewide trailers that made up the tawdry development in Pinellas Park. No, Michelle decided, she was definitely a visitor. No one in this neighborhood could afford a car like that.

It was mid-January, 1989, the weather on this day too cool even for the west coast of Florida. As they resumed their game, Cupples noticed a man and woman walking slowly up the street.

They were the new neighbors from down the block.

The man appeared to be older, while the woman was

probably in her twenties. She held a boy in her arms. He couldn't have been more than a year old or so.

When they reached the front of Michelle's home she jumped up and walked toward them, placing her attention on the boy.

"Hi, what's your name?" she said.

"That's Pookie," said the man.

"Well hello, Pookie. I'm Michelle. How old are you?"

The boy stared.

"He's just tired," said the man, who identified himself as Warren Marshall. The boy's real name was Michael. The woman standing next to him was his mother, and her name was Sharon.

"I'm his grandfather," said Warren. "You live here?"

"Right there," said Michelle, pointing to her trailer.

"You seem good with kids. How old are you?"

"Fifteen."

"Really," said Warren. "You know, my daughter here works nights and there are times we can use a babysitter. Would you be interested?"

"Sure," said Michelle.

"Well, I'll tell you what. Next time I need someone I'll just come and knock on your door. That sound OK?"

"Fine with me," said Michelle, who thought it was odd that Sharon didn't even say hello.

A week later Warren came knocking and Michelle was hired to sit for Michael.

The Marshall home was just around the corner from where Michelle lived and she recognized the trailer as the one with the boat in the driveway.

Three cars were parked in front of the house: the red Corvette convertible that had whizzed by Michelle and her friends the week before, and two others, a green Chevy and a red Ford pickup truck.

Inside, the trailer was typical. In the living room was a couch, which was really a hideaway bed. Next to the couch was a television, VCR, video camera, and dozens of black videotapes, perhaps a couple of hundred. The kitchen was in the middle and held a small table, three chairs, and a high chair.

Of the two bedrooms, one belonged to Michael, the other was Sharon's, which left Michelle guessing that Warren, the grandpa, slept on the sofa bed.

Michelle waited by the front door for several minutes before Warren emerged from Michael's room. Sharon stepped out from her room. With her was a friend, who was introduced as Stevie.

Stevie was thin and voluptuous. She had dark hair, wore plenty of makeup, and talked with what sounded like a New York accent. Sharon was quiet, much as she was when they first met. She said hello, but not much more.

Warren laid out the rules, and there were lots of them. Of most importance: Never enter Sharon's room.

"You can't go into Sharon's bedroom, understand? Ever. And you see this closet here?" he said, pointing to a small door near the entrance to Michael's room. "Don't ever go in there either. That's Michael's stuff in there. You git me?"

Michelle nodded and Warren said good-bye without leaving any instructions on what or how to feed Michael, or where to find his clothes and diapers.

Michelle looked out the front window and watched as Sharon entered Stevie's car and the pair drove off, with Warren right behind in his green Chevy.

Mons Venus was one of the more popular nightspots in Tampa, a strip club that served as a favorite hangout for a variety of individuals, famous and infamous. The single-floor building with the purple awning stood out among the Bennigan's and other fast-food restaurants that dominated the congested thoroughfare of North Dale Mabry. Women in outrageously colorful and exotic costumes could be seen entering the building at all hours of the day to entertain the male masses who found refuge behind the lavender doors.

Inside "Mons," as it was known, the dancers performed on an elevated circular stage with a hardwood floor and metal pole in the center. The club was clean and the clientele respectable, as far as strip clubs go. Some of the men were even wealthy.

Actors, athletes, and especially rock bands and their entourages stopped by whenever they were in town. A sense of extra excitement filled the club whenever musicians were around. The summer before, in May, members of Metallica had passed through the club. In June it was Van Halen, along with their roadies, who were seen handing out fistfuls of cash. Many of the girls were invited back to their hotel to finish off the night, and were paid for their services.

The women who danced at Mons Venus were required to adhere to several rules, and signed contracts stipulating that if they were found doing drugs or engaging in prostitution they could be fired. But drugs and prostitution were rife, and none of the girls signed the contracts using their real names anyway. Pimps were present. One was known to handle the business for more than half the girls. He even found them work outside the club, mostly at bachelor parties. Mons dancers were also prohibited from dating customers or leaving with them from the building. They got around that by meeting customers at area hotels and motels.

The performers at Mons Venus were well known within the world of nude dancing, and would travel throughout the southeast, from Miami to Atlanta, to appear at other clubs, private events, and bachelor parties.

Between the dancing and prostitution, some girls were

making as much as three thousand dollars per week.

The money was so good that one pimp, an older fellow named Harry, would drive down on weekends from his Georgia mansion. He had two girls who earned huge sums of cash through dancing and prostitution. They'd return to Georgia on Monday, only to come back the following weekend. Harry even acquired a third girl and gave her to his son.

Perhaps the most important rule to adhere to at Mons Venus was really the only rule the club enforced: No boyfriends or husbands were allowed inside.

Far too many times, a jealous lover would take out his anger on a customer who took interest in a dancer and a fight would ensue. The bouncers would roll into action, tossing out the boyfriend and the dancer, who'd be forced to look elsewhere for employment.

When Stevie and Sharon pulled up into the Mons parking lot, Warren was right behind them, taking a space near the front entrance. The girls rushed inside. Warren remained in his car. He had been banned from entering the club not long after Sharon began working there in 1988. His banishment was the result of management's belief that he had to be "strange" to come inside and sit at the bar watching as his daughter performed, which was too much even for a club like Mons.

Warren was asked to leave. Thrown out was more like it.

He protested, but couldn't do much about the six-foot, three-hundred-pound bouncers who escorted him to the door.

"And stay the fuck out you fucking weirdo," they said, the added dialogue intended to ensure Warren got the message.

He did. Warren remained in the parking lot most nights, by himself, waiting for Sharon to finish her shift.

No one asked Warren or Sharon who was watching her son.

Inside Mons, Sharon performed on the circular stage, and entertained customers between sets. She didn't socialize much with the other dancers, exchanging nothing more than passing pleasantries. She left the Mons for a few weeks in December, but was back, dancing again, in January 1989.

That's when she met Cary Strukel.

Strukel, twenty, was a bartender at the Brown Derby restaurant in Tampa and would stop in Mons several times a week before going to work. His sole interest was Sharon. He was drawn to her the first time he saw her. It wasn't the blond hair or blue eyes, or her easy, yet seductive, dancing. Strukel decided he liked Sharon after he bought her a Coke. She was personable and friendly, and deep inside, Strukel saw a softness to Sharon, something he didn't see in any of the other girls. A week after they met they began to date, and it wasn't long after that that Strukel would drive to the Golden Lantern trailer park to visit with his new girlfriend and meet her father, Warren, and son, Michael.

The first thing that struck Strukel was that Warren didn't work. He said he took a job in June 1988 with a painting crew after he spotted them working on a house. He talked the owner of Precision Painting into giving him a job. A couple of days later Warren fell off a ladder and claimed to have hurt his back. He was airlifted to a Tampa hospital and quickly filed for disability and workmen's compensation. He said he received nine hundred dollars per month, but at the moment he appeared to be living off the money Sharon made at the Mons.

As Strukel became more acquainted with his new girlfriend, it was clear there were two different Sharons—the quiet woman who danced at Mons, and the panicked woman he saw at home.

Sharon was always nervous around her father, and seemed to fear him. Strukel could easily see that she was under his control, no better than a dog. If Warren said sit, she'd fall to the ground butt first.

And Warren often made strange and disturbing comments. Strukel did a double take when he heard Warren suggest to Sharon that she get breast implants. He said he loved Stevie's, and thought implants would help Sharon's career. When Strukel casually asked what career that was, Warren said Sharon was aiming to appear in adult movies, and she needed every edge she could get—including the implants.

"These are going to be beautiful when she gets them done," said Warren, pulling at Sharon's nipple.

Strukel said nothing. He liked Sharon. She was sweet and pleasant and smart, far too intelligent to be dancing at a place like Mons Venus. Strukel figured people do what they have to do to get by, so he didn't question her profession. Sharon was always polite, and Strukel liked being around her. And deep down Strukel liked the idea that his girlfriend was a nude dancer. To Strukel, Sharon was a celebrity. She'd take off with Stevie to Miami or Fort Lauderdale to appear at other clubs or do parties, then come back the next day with large sums of cash, which Sharon always gave to her father.

Warren was another matter. The more Strukel saw of Warren Marshall, the more he believed he was a "nutcase and whack job."

He'd tell friends how Warren swallowed a handful of pills every day and kept a loaded shotgun near the front door. Every now and then Warren would suffer from "spells" in which he would talk to himself in a high-pitched voice. He also seemed to have a problem whenever Michael cried. Warren would scream out orders for Sharon to "shut that brat up." During one crying episode Warren put his hands to the sides of his head, bobbed his head from side to side, and shrieked, *"Stop the baby!"*

Sharon rushed over to Michael, picked him up, took him to her room, and locked the door.

Warren was also infatuated with sex, particularly sexual deviance. He spoke excitedly about a video he made on the beach with Sharon and Stevie. They wore string bikinis and rubbed oil over each other.

"Want to see it?" said Warren, his eyes opened wide.

Strukel said sure, but Sharon was embarrassed and ran to her room.

"Maybe another time," said Strukel, who decided that despite Warren's disturbing behavior, his feelings for Sharon were deep, and he would continue the relationship.

Sharon responded to Strukel's affection, and was heard one afternoon arguing with Warren.

Strukel fell asleep at the Marshalls' trailer but was awakened by voices coming from the living room. It was Sharon, and Strukel was the topic of conversation.

"Dad, but I love him, but I love him, but I love him," said Sharon.

"I don't care. He don't have no money and he's no good for you," said Warren.

Sharon joined Strukel in the bedroom moments later, and nestled into Strukel's arms. She appeared sad. When Strukel asked her what was wrong, she shook her head.

"Nothing," she said with a deep sigh.

Strukel knew that Sharon's problem was her father, and it was woefully clear she was under his thumb and either couldn't or wouldn't resist his wishes. There was a deep sadness to Sharon Marshall. Strukel would try to ask questions about Sharon's mother or her past, but Sharon always changed the subject. She'd kiss him, then they'd quietly make love, hoping that Warren wouldn't barge into her room, as he was prone to do.

Despite her present profession and her strange father, Strukel believed that Sharon was special, and he looked forward to every moment he spent with her.

* * *

Michelle Cupples became a regular at the Marshall trailer, baby-sitting four to six times a week. When she wasn't baby-sitting she'd visit the Marshall home after school just to hang out. She thought Warren was "cool." He didn't act like an adult, not someone trying to tell her what to do all the time. He'd say weird things every now and then, like pointing to Sharon's breasts and asking what she thought of Sharon getting a "boob job," or being overly concerned about what Sharon was wearing to work. It was Warren who picked out her skimpy and sexy clothing. Michelle would ask but neither Warren nor Sharon would tell her what Sharon did for a living.

All Michelle knew was that Sharon left the trailer at 7 P.M. every night and didn't come home until early in the morning.

Warren's peculiar comments aside, Michelle thought he was a good grandpa. Heck, he was more like the father. It was Warren who took care of Michael, who changed his diaper, who fed him his bottle, and who paid for the baby-sitting.

Sharon stayed to herself and barely ever said a word. It was almost like she wasn't there, maybe in body but not in mind. Michelle thought that was kind of weird, that Sharon never asked any questions or showed any interest in learning about the person taking care of her kid. Sometimes Michelle got the feeling that Sharon was afraid to talk.

Still, Michelle felt comfortable at the Marshall home, even after one night when she made a startling discovery.

Sharon was away at work, having received a ride from Stevie, and Warren remained home. Michelle and her teenage friend Jason decided to visit with Warren and Michael to watch a Mike Tyson fight on television.

Michelle was sitting on the sofa when she turned around and thought she saw a friend walk by on the street so she leaned over the back of the couch, straining to get a good look out the window. Warren began to yell, warning Michelle not to look down behind the couch.

"Why?" said Michelle.

"I've got some secret stuff back there and you don't want to get hurt," said Warren.

"Secret?" said Michelle, her teenage curiosity piqued. "What is it?"

"Yeah, what is it?" said Jason.

Warren walked to the side of the couch, reached down and pulled out a blue gun.

"What's that?" said Michelle.

"An electric stun gun. Don't ever touch this. You can get hurt," said Warren.

He placed the gun back behind the couch, and they diverted their attention to the fight on television. As soon as it was over, Warren announced that he had an idea—would Michelle and Jason want to see some good-looking women?

Jason jumped at the chance and said yes, and Warren eagerly pulled out a black VHS tape from among the hundreds he had lined up against the wall and put it into the video player.

On the television screen were two women, a blonde and a brunette, frolicking on the beach. They wore skimpy, string bikinis, and after a minute or two of dancing they sat down on a blanket and began to rub oil onto each other. Michelle immediately recognized Sharon as the blond girl. It took a few seconds longer to identify the brunette, but Michelle could see it was that Stevie girl, Sharon's friend with the red Corvette.

Warren stood with a big grin on his face as the video moved along, the girls rubbing the oil over each other's body, on their legs, arms, torsos and breasts. It was provocative, far too provocative for Michelle, who quickly got up and said she was leaving.

Jason said he would stay just a little longer.

CHAPTER 23

Cary Strukel's first reaction to his girlfriend's new breasts was, "What happened to you?"

They looked terrible, like two round rocks on a piece of paper. He didn't say anything to Sharon, who complained of constant pain around her chest and her hips, where she'd also had liposuction.

"This really, really hurts," said Sharon, almost near tears.

Sharon wasn't thrilled with the idea of breast enlargement, but gave in to Warren, who had been pushing the surgery for months.

"Bigger tits means more money," said Warren, who also talked about Sharon testing for and appearing in adult movies.

"You could be a star, you could be famous," said Warren.

They found a cheap surgeon outside of Tampa and paid fifteen hundred dollars for a procedure that typically cost five thousand dollars or more.

The result looked like a fifteen-hundred-dollar surgery, and it took nearly a week before the intense pain subsided.

Aside from the pain, Sharon didn't complain. None of this—the dancing at Mons, the boob job, the talk about movies—seemed to be anything she wanted to do. Strukel could see clearly that Sharon was just going through the motions, solely to please her father, who would react angrily whenever Sharon said no to him.

He wanted her to get bigger breasts, she said fine.

Liposuction? OK to that too.

Warren was pleased with Sharon's new look. He'd tell anyone and everyone that he thought she looked great.

"Don't her tits look nice, and doesn't Sharon's ass look great in those shorts," were passing comments made to Michelle Cupples and her friend Jason.

When Michelle asked Sharon how she liked her new look, Sharon remained quiet. Michelle thought Sharon was stuck-up, a quiet woman who never really talked to anyone.

Cary Strukel thought his girlfriend was a zombie, but there was little he could do. He'd strike up conversations, even asking about her father, but she'd quickly divert the discussion. Their time together was spent watching television or meeting for breakfast, and on rare occasions driving her home in the early morning hours when Warren didn't feel the need to wait in the parking lot.

Each time Strukel drove up to the Marshall trailer under the darkness of early morning, he'd see Warren peering out the window, watching.

When Sharon Marshall first walked into the Mons to apply for a job in January 1988, she was told to lose some weight.

"You need to shape up a little, honey," said Kenna Blood-worth, the night manager.

Sharon said the extra weight was due to a recent miscarriage, but in reality she was six months pregnant. Management couldn't help but notice she was carrying a baby when it became painfully obvious to all that her midsection was getting bigger, not smaller. Management was even more surprised when several customers voiced their approval of a pregnant performer, so Sharon was kept on and danced right through to April 21, when she gave birth to a boy at Tampa General. Sharon named him Michael Gregory Marshall. He was six pounds, twelve ounces, and nineteen inches long.

Sharon returned to the Mons soon after, and as she did before, she kept to herself. Compared to some of the extroverts and can't-miss-in-a-crowd personalities at the Mons, Sharon was a virtual nonentity. She rarely spoke, never got into trouble, didn't cause any problems, and was always on stage when she was supposed to be.

Her quiet way was often mistaken for having an "attitude" in a dressing room filled with constant chatter. Though she said little, Sharon managed to make a few friends at Mons through 1988. She particularly became close with a bisexual dancer named "Heather Lane."

Heather gained notoriety for having a female pimp who looked like a guy. Heather didn't mind. She liked women, socially and sexually, though she wasn't necessarily homosexual. She was attracted to Sharon, and felt sorry for her, which was something she had in common with the few girls who weren't put off by Sharon's silence. All believed Sharon's problems stemmed from her father, who rarely ever let her out of his sight. Everyone knew he was sitting out there in the parking lot virtually every night. If Sharon was hungry when Mons closed and she wanted to accompany some of the other girls for breakfast, Warren would insist on coming along.

He'd even escort Sharon to her private parties. They'd drive to some dingy motel, pull up to the front, and Warren would reach into the glove compartment, pull out condoms, and give them to Sharon. He'd watch as she walked inside, and emerged a half hour later. She'd come back into the car, give him the money, and they'd drive off.

Other times Warren would chauffeur Sharon and Heather to bachelor parties.

Heather organized the parties, which usually contracted for two girls to perform. Sharon heard about the work, said she needed to make extra money, and asked to come along. They'd perform together, as a team, and simulate lesbian acts.

Driving to and from the events, Heather shared her complaints with the business, particularly the prostitution, and Warren was sympathetic and understanding, offering inspirational speeches in the car.

"Well, I know it must be hard," he'd say, "but you make an awful lot of money, much more than you'd be making if you had a day job, so I'd suggest you stay with it for a little while longer."

Sharon, as was her way, said little. She'd stare out the car window while Warren continued the conversation, expressing interest in the porno business, and his plans for Sharon.

"She got the boob job and she's good to go into these movies," said Warren. "Now she can make some real money. Maybe you can introduce us to some people."

"I don't know much about movies, but I'll keep a lookout for anyone that might have an 'in' for you," said Heather, who turned to Sharon. "How do you feel about movies? Something you want to do?"

Sharon didn't reply. She remained slumped against the back seat, keeping her focus outside the car.

"Of course she wants movies!" said Warren, raising his voice in anger. "How can she not do movies with these!"

Warren reached into the back seat and pinched Sharon's breast.

"Damn right she'll do movies," said Warren.

The exchange, and Warren's grab at Sharon's chest, took Heather by surprise. She later spent a night at the Marshall home, where she heard more of Warren's strange, sexual remarks toward Sharon, and Heather couldn't resist reporting what she'd heard to the girls at Mons.

"I think he's sleeping with Sharon," said Heather. "Even the baby looks retarded."

The rumors that Warren was the father of Sharon's baby ran rampant throughout the club, and by the fall of 1988 the sordid stories eventually reached Sharon's ears.

Sharon confronted Heather in the dressing room, and tearfully denied an incestuous relationship with Warren, saying the baby's father lived out west, in Arizona.

"You know your dad is strange," said Heather.

"I know, I know. But it's nothing like you're thinking," said Sharon.

Heather remained unconvinced, and Sharon became even more reclusive, arriving to work and then leaving without saying much to anyone.

Two months later, in December 1988, the Marshalls disappeared. Everyone at the Mons thought they fled due to the rumors.

But Sharon returned in January, saying they took a brief vacation, and the Marshalls rented the trailer at the Golden Lantern trailer park.

She soon met Cary Strukel and became friendly with Stevie.

In March, Strukel and others noticed that Sharon wasn't looking right. She appeared to be gaining weight, especially around the hips and midsection. Sharon said she suffered from stomach problems and was bloated, giving off the appearance she was gaining weight.

Strukel didn't question Sharon, and would occasionally

meet her for breakfast after she got off of work. If Strukel was good for anything in Warren's eyes it was that he served as a chauffeur on those rare nights when Warren didn't feel up to driving Sharon to and from work.

Warren had a new toy, a twenty-two-foot boat that he kept on a trailer in the driveway. He'd take it to Tampa Bay, or one of the neighboring lakes late in the afternoon while Sharon worked. Everyone knew he was living off Sharon's money, and there wasn't a night she didn't work, leading to whispers at the Mons that Warren wasn't just Sharon's father but her pimp.

CHAPTER 24

Cheryl Ann Commesso wanted to be a star.

A free spirit who performed under the name "Stevie," she arrived at the Mons in January 1989 believing, like some of the other performers, that her dancing and appearances at local beauty contests could earn her a ticket to Hollywood.

After arriving at the Mons she dated the son of Harry the pimp from Georgia, and lived for a while with Heather Lane and another girl.

By March, Cheryl's penchant for walking around the house nude annoyed her roommates to the point that they kicked her out. She needed a place to stay and moved in temporarily with Sharon and Warren.

Cheryl took a liking to Warren, who boasted to having contacts in the entertainment industry. Cheryl agreed to appear in a video, taped on the beach at dusk. Warren, camera in hand, directed Cheryl and Sharon to frolic in the sand, then lie on a blanket and massage each other, then later engage in sexual acts.

Warren claimed he was going to send the video to producers he knew in Los Angeles to serve as an audition tape, and the girls would be called to Hollywood to appear in adult films. Cheryl was excited with the possibility.

Warren also talked Cheryl into posing nude, claiming he was a still photographer and had contacts with *Playboy* magazine.

Warren complimented Cheryl on her tight body and large breasts, telling her how beautiful she was and intimating they should have sex. Cheryl wasn't attracted to Warren but gave in anyway.

Warren thought he had a girlfriend.

Word about the video eventually found its way to the Mons, along with Warren's unbelievable claim that he and Cheryl were an item.

When Heather Lane heard the stories, she confronted Cheryl, asking what the hell she was doing with a freak like Warren Marshall.

"He said he was going to get me into *Playboy*," said Cheryl.

"Warren Marshall? Are you insane?" said Heather. "Stay away from him, you hear me."

Cheryl ignored Heather's advice and continued to visit the Marshall home, pulling up each afternoon in her red Corvette. She even took a trip alone with Warren on his boat on Lake Okeechobee. When Warren sought sex, Cheryl resisted, infuriating Warren, who punched Cheryl in the mouth, then tried to choke her. She was on the floor of the boat shaking off the effects of the blow to the head when she saw Warren coming toward her with a fishing net in his hands. She picked herself up and, fearing for her life, jumped off the boat into the water. Warren flung the net overboard but missed his target, and Cheryl swam the quarter mile to shore, hitchhiking home.

Cheryl decided to get even with Warren through Sharon, calling Florida social services to inform them that Sharon had been collecting welfare but earned more than fifteen hundred dollars a week as a nude dancer. Social services subsequently called Sharon to inform her that the welfare checks would be stopped pending an investigation.

Warren was furious.

It was Heather who answered his angry call to the Mons. He wanted to know where to find Cheryl. Heather said she couldn't help him and hung up the phone.

Later that night Warren was at his usual spot in the parking lot when Cheryl arrived for work. He grabbed Cheryl and tried to pull her into his car. The screaming drew the attention of Heather, who ran outside to intervene.

"You don't understand. That bitch turned Sharon in to welfare," said Warren, who wouldn't let go of Cheryl.

Heather went inside and told the bouncers that a crazy man was trying to kidnap Cheryl. They ran outside and Warren let her go, but not before more angry words were exchanged.

Warren sped off into the night.

A week later, Cheryl Ann Commesso disappeared.

By mid-April it was clear that Sharon Marshall was pregnant again, and the sordid rumors about Warren were resurrected.

Even in a place like the Mons folks had their ideas about respectable behavior, and incest was crossing the line. Many of the dancers had personal experiences with child abuse, and the thought of Sharon with her father was revolting and unacceptable.

Heather decided to confront Sharon and waited until the two were alone in the dressing room as Sharon changed into her short skirt and bobby socks.

"Sharon, everybody can see you're pregnant, and we all think your father is the dad," said Heather. "That's something a lot of people here can't take."

Sharon started to cry before Heather could finish the sentence. She slumped into her chair, tears streaming down her cheeks. She raised her arms, trying to explain with her hands since she could only stutter, unable to speak in any intelligible form.

"Sharon, honey, I know this is tough. Your father is fucked up. We all know it. We all see it. C'mon, you can talk to me. A lot of girls have been there before," said Heather.

"You don't understand," said Sharon between the tears. "He's not my real father."

"Then who is he?" said Heather.

"He's my stepfather. He's been molesting me for years, ever since I was a child."

Sharon crumpled onto a chair, her head buried between her legs, the crying now more like an anguished squeal. She had finally admitted something she had kept hidden all her life.

"Sharon, listen, father or no father, you're going to have to leave this guy. Go to the police. Go to somebody. Get your kid and get away from him," said Heather.

"I can't do that!" shrieked Sharon. "You don't understand, He's done things. I saw it. I know what he can do and if he ever heard me talking like this he'd kill me and Michael. He has friends everywhere. I can't leave him. I just can't. I know he would find me. And I know he'd hurt Michael."

Sharon shot up from her chair as terrible thoughts crossed her mind.

"Heather, you can't say anything about this. Please promise me you won't say anything."

Sharon was scared for her life and the life of her son, and Heather could see the terror in her eyes.

"OK, Sharon. It's your secret."

In late May 1989, Vicki Bahan heard that Sharon Marshall was looking for a home for a Maine coon cat.

Bahan was the night bar manager at the Mons and a one-time dancer named "Cherry Pie" who now lived on a farm outside Tampa. For reasons known to no one but herself, Bahan preferred the company of animals to humans, and didn't associate with any of the girls at the Mons.

All she cared about were her horses.

Sharon heard Bahan lived on a farm and approached her one night, saying she was leaving town and asking if Bahan wouldn't mind taking in her cats.

"If I don't find a home for them I'll have to drop them off at the pound, and you know what happens to them there," said Sharon.

She had two cats, and one was the Maine coon cat. Bahan had never seen one before and figured, why not?

"It's my father's favorite cat," said Sharon.

"Well, I'll do it for you. Not for your father, but for you, OK?" said Bahan. "And one other thing. They'll have to stay in the barn."

"Well, they're house cats. We keep them inside," said Sharon.

"Sorry. I don't let any animals inside my house. I'll let them go in the barn. If they hang around, they hang around," said Bahan.

A week later Warren, Sharon and her year-old son, Michael, pulled up to Bahan's farm in a late-model Ford pickup truck, the flatbed filled with boxes. Sharon stepped out with the cats in her arms, and thanked Bahan again for taking in the animals.

"I didn't ask you, where you heading?" said Bahan.

Sharon stammered, saying she wasn't sure, but that her father needed a better climate, a place with less humidity for his ailing back.

"Maybe somewhere out west."

"So you're done dancing?"

"I'm done dancing at the Mons," said Sharon, putting her hand to her belly. "Besides, I've got other things to worry about now."

Sharon offered a weak smile and said good-bye, and Bahan watched as the Marshalls drove down the dirt road and out of sight.

Cary Strukel saw the dozen roses that had been left at the Brown Derby when he walked into work that day, and asked who they were for.

"They're yours," said a hostess. "A pretty lady stopped by earlier in the day and dropped them off, and I'd say you made a good impression."

There was no card attached, but there were two gold charms. One said "Special Lover." Judging by the description of the woman from the hostess, Strukel knew it had to be Sharon who left the flowers.

He called Sharon at home but there was no answer. He called the Mons but was told she'd quit. The next morning Strukel drove to the Marshalls' trailer and rang the bell, but no one was home. He looked inside a window and could see the trailer was empty. Everything had been cleared out.

Sharon didn't mention anything about leaving. No phone call, no warning. Just a dozen roses and gold charms.

She couldn't leave like that, thought Strukel, who figured she'd eventually call. So he waited.

Two weeks later Strukel received a call at home. Only it was Warren. He asked if anyone had been by to question Strukel about Warren's boat. It had sunk the month before, and Warren had grown increasingly nervous, even more so after he was quizzed by insurance investigators. They fished the boat out of Tampa Bay after Warren filed a claim and found someone had drilled holes through the boat's bottom.

"No, why would anyone ask me about your boat? Where are you guys?" said Strukel.

"Oh, just on vacation," said Warren.

"I went by your trailer and everything was gone."

"Well, we put all the stuff in closets so nobody would want to break in."

"The furniture too? In the closets?"

"Well, yeah, that too."

"Is Sharon with you? Can I talk to her?"

"No, she's not feeling well. She's out on the beach. I'll tell her you asked about her and I'll call you later."

Warren didn't call, and Strukel would never speak to Sharon again.

Like Cary Strukel, Michelle Cupples thought something was wrong when she stopped by the Marshalls' trailer only to find it empty. The Marshalls had left without even saying good-bye.

A week later she received a call at her home from Warren asking her to take the mail out of his mailbox and burn it. Michelle said no and handed the phone to her mother, who also said no.

Several weeks later, on June 16, the Marshall trailer at the Golden Lantern trailer park burned to the ground.

Pinellas Park fire investigators determined that the blaze had started on the kitchen stove. A combustible liquid was placed over the left front burner, which was turned on, and the mixture soon ignited. The trailer was destroyed, along with everything inside.

The fire was determined to be arson.

CHAPTER 25

Bob Schock closed the thick folder stamped "Cheryl Ann Commesso" and sat still at the long conference table, looking at the men and women who were seated around him, all of whom were unable to say a single word.

It was March 1997, two years after the skeletal remains were found on the side of the highway, and eight months after Schock first saw the shocking photos. Schock and Mark Deasaro were in Oklahoma City, completing their report on the investigation into the murder of Cheryl Ann Commesso for Joe Fitzpatrick, Mark Yancey, Ed Kumiega, and others involved in the Michael Hughes kidnapping.

Schock's report was sickening, sad, and sobering.

The two Florida detectives spent considerable time on the Commesso case, interviewing numerous acquaintances of Floyd and Sharon, and drawing a comprehensive listing of their activities in Florida from 1988 through June 1989.

The chilling details deflated all in attendance, particularly Fitzpatrick, Yancey, and Kumiega, who thought they had heard the worst about Sharon Marshall.

They now knew they had been wrong.

Veteran lawmen sitting at the table shook their heads or let out deep sighs as Schock continued his report.

"After leaving Florida sometime in June they drove to New Orleans where, according to the FBI timeline, on June 15, Floyd and Sharon were married as Clarence Hughes and Tonya Hughes," said Schock. "The only reason I can see for the marriage is that Sharon knew that Floyd killed Cheryl Commesso, and by marrying Sharon, Floyd believed that as his wife, Sharon would be barred from testifying against him in the event he was ever arrested. We're entertaining a theory that after Floyd killed Cheryl, it was Sharon who helped Floyd get rid of the car at the airport. Someone had to drive it there."

Someone said that if Floyd was in New Orleans on June 15, who burned down his trailer on June 16?

"Good question," said Schock. "We don't know."

Following the FBI timeline, Schock said that while in Louisiana, Sharon or Floyd apparently stole the Social Security number of a man who lived in nearby Gulfport, Mississippi. The man remembered being at a mall in June and filling out numerous credit card applications. Somehow, Sharon or Floyd got hold of his number.

They remained in New Orleans, where on August 11, 1989, Sharon gave birth to a girl, who was immediately adopted by a young couple. The identity of the birth father was unknown.

After leaving New Orleans in September they traveled to Tulsa, where Sharon danced at the Passions club the last months of her life. It was clear to all she reached the depths of despair in Florida, where Floyd cast her into a seamy world of prostitution and hopelessness.

After arriving in Tulsa, it was clearly evident that Sharon had somehow found the courage to see a life beyond Floyd.

She was reading again, as she had in high school, devouring books and magazines between her sets at Passions. With the help of her new boyfriend, Kevin Brown, Sharon planned her escape from Floyd. She warned Kevin that it would be dangerous, and she was right. Floyd had contacts in Tulsa, including sheriff's deputies who knew the women and clientele at Passions, and he somehow learned of Sharon's plans, which cost Sharon her life.

Her death, it was conceded, was inevitable. Floyd was, at his core, a murderous pedophile, and as Sharon grew older his interest in her diminished to where her only purpose in life was to support Floyd. Under daily threats of physical and verbal abuse, Sharon worked every day for Floyd as a nude dancer and prostitute. Floyd's full attention, his focus, was now on Michael. The little boy had become Sharon's replacement, and it didn't matter to Floyd if she lived or died.

He was obsessed with Michael, and as long as Sharon served a purpose, she lived.

Schock said Cheryl Commesso apparently lost her life because of a single phone call. Floyd became enraged when Cheryl turned Sharon in to social services, and his anger was evident in the violence plainly displayed in the horrifying photos. Schock reminded all that Cheryl wasn't killed right away. Floyd toyed with her, tortured her, took delight in her misery as he degraded her, burned her, beat her to near death, and then finally ended her life with two shots from a .22 to the back of the head.

Schock said the photographs and evidence collected to date were to be sent to the FBI's special photo unit in Washington, D.C., for review. In addition, Oklahoma County Assistant District Attorney Lisa Hammond sought a court order to photograph Floyd's hands. In two of the Commesso pictures a thumb was clearly visible inside the victim's right thigh. Investigators believed it was Floyd's thumb, probably holding her leg back as he took his photos holding the camera with his right hand.

Whatever the outcome of the thumb investigation, it wouldn't take an expert to tell Bob Schock that Cheryl Commesso's death was an execution.

The next day, he and Deasaro had an appointment to meet the executioner.

Franklin Floyd was led into the interview room at the Oklahoma City County Jail at 9 A.M. on March 25, 1997. Waiting for him were Bob Schock and Mark Deasaro, who on first sight didn't think much of Floyd.

He wasn't a physically intimidating presence, that was for sure. He was of medium size, wore glasses, and his hair had plenty of gray. He had no remarkable physical features, and was so plain he looked to be someone who could be easily dismissed or ignored.

Floyd became angry and agitated upon his introduction to the detectives, saying he knew why they were there.

"My sister sent you. She's crazy. Did you know that? She's always calling cops about me," he said.

Floyd rambled on for fifty-five minutes, and Schock and Deasaro let him go without interruption. They were warned by Fitzpatrick and others to just let him talk and get it out of his system, or else he'd just shut up and remain silent.

Schock and Deasaro traveled to Oklahoma City hoping, at best, for a confession from Floyd. They knew the evidence to date was overwhelming: They had a motive, they had a means, and they had the pictures.

But when Schock broached the subject of the murder of

Cheryl Commesso around 10 A.M., Floyd became angry, reiterating he had heard about the murder from his sister Dorothy but claiming to know nothing about Cheryl Commesso.

"That homicide took place in 1994. I was in Oklahoma. Couldn't've been me," said Floyd.

"No, the victim was found in nineteen-ninety-five, but we believe the homicide occurred in nineteen-eighty-nine," said Schock.

Floyd threw off a look of surprise.

"Well, that changes everything," he said, throwing his hands up in the air. "I was in Florida in nineteen-eighty-nine."

Schock produced a photo of Cheryl and gave it to Floyd, who said he didn't recognize her.

"She could have been a friend of Sharon's."

"Sharon? That's the girl that was living with you in Florida. She was your daughter, right? You want us to call her Sharon?"

"Yes, Sharon. She wasn't my daughter. I just raised her. She was a good girl until she got older, and then she became bad. She was involved in dancing, drugs, and other stuff. She danced at a club in Tampa, off of Dale Mabry."

"You mean the Mons Venus?"

"I don't remember the name. But Sharon knew a lot of shady people at that club, and some of them would come up from Miami. Sharon did parties there, and in Fort Lauderdale. I told you, she wasn't a good girl. And she wasn't my daughter. I raised her, but she wasn't my blood."

Schock continued his interrogation, drawing even more anger from Floyd, who didn't want to hear anything about Cheryl Commesso.

"Did you meet any of Sharon's friends from the club?" said Schock.

"Hell yeah, knew lots of the girls. Sharon would bring them home. Sharon knew lots of people. And a lot of them were weird. She'd have parties in the house. Sex parties. I told you, she became a bad girl."

Floyd changed the subject away from Sharon to how he fell off a ten-foot-high ladder while working a painting job, and drew nine hundred dollars a month in disability payments. The injury caused severe back pain and forced Floyd to wear a brace.

"If you were hurt that bad, how could you go on a boat? You had a boat, didn't you?" said Schock.

"Yeah, I did. Don't you know that boats are good therapy, that riding on the water is like a good massage? Doctors told me to get on the boat."

"I like boats," said Deasaro, drawing a satisfying grin from Floyd, who had developed a clear dislike for Schock. Floyd reacted favorably to Deasaro and eased a bit, talking about his arrival in Florida in 1988, thanks in part to word of mouth from ex-cons he knew, who said Tampa was a good place to live.

"I've got friends. Not going to tell you who they are, but they're around and they know where a guy like me can live and prosper. We did all right in Tampa," said Floyd.

"You mean Sharon did all right. You weren't working, right?" said Schock.

"I told you, I hurt my back. Fell of a ladder and got nine hundred a month. And she had her own money and did whatever she wanted to do. There was little I could do about it," said Floyd. "I just hung around the house and fished."

Schock asked if he remembered a red Corvette. Floyd said he remembered the car but not the color. Schock pulled out a picture of the car, and Floyd said yes, the car was at the trailer.

"She was probably friends with Sharon. She'd go out on weekends, on junkets to Miami with those people. You know, parties. They'd do terrible things. We had to leave

Florida because Sharon stole from them. Half-a-million dollars," said Floyd, leaning over the table and reducing his voice to a whisper. "We had to change our names, so we went to Alabama, to a cemetery in the town of Andalusia. I took Clarence Hughes. She took Tonya Tadlock. We went to New Orleans and got married. I had to do it. To give Michael a name. Couldn't raise him without one, you know. Then we went to Oklahoma and buried the money. But they found us and we had to give it back."

Floyd told his bizarre story with great zeal and conviction. Schock thought he was mad.

Deasaro, who was somewhat amused, asked about Sharon.

"Where did Sharon come from, can you tell us that?" said Deasaro.

"I'll never tell ya' anything other than it was near Chicago. Near the warehouse where they made the snuff films," said Floyd.

"Didn't you tell the FBI that she was from Indianapolis? That her mother was a prostitute?" said Schock.

"Don't remember what I told the fucking FBI. I know what I'm telling you now," said Floyd.

Schock nodded, looked to Deasaro, then asked the question he wanted to ask two hours ago.

"Mr. Floyd, did you kill Cheryl Commesso, the woman in these photos?" said Schock.

"No, I didn't," said Floyd, appearing incredulous. "I may have known her, but I sure didn't kill her."

The following morning Schock and Deasaro drove to the federal prison in Lexington, Oklahoma, to meet with an inmate, Allen Dwight Dowdy. He was just a kid, only eighteen years old, but had befriended Floyd months earlier when they were cellmates at the Oklahoma City County Jail.

Dowdy said they spent much of their time talking, though the conversations were heavily one-sided, with Floyd doing the talking, even recalling several startling events in his life.

Schock pressed Dowdy to share his conversations with Floyd, and Dowdy thought for a second or two.

"He first told me something about burying a body and putting lye on top of it to help it decompose. He didn't say where it was or who it was. I just figured he killed somebody and didn't want to give me any more details."

"Did he ever talk about his wife, Tonya?" said Deasaro.

"Yeah. He said he hit her in the head and left her on the left side of the road. Another time he said he ran her down in his car while she was walking on the side of a highway. He talked a lot. Said lots of things. Not sure if anything is the truth, you know?"

"Did he say why he killed her?" said Schock.

"I think she was going to leave him. He heard she was going to take his son and run away. Franklin blamed the people she worked with. Said they were whores who pushed her to leave him, and he wouldn't have it. He didn't really like talking about her much. Didn't seem like he really cared about her. He only cared about the boy. That's really all he talked about. That kid, Michael. But he always spoke in the past tense, like he was dead. Franklin said one night that he was in jail in Kentucky after he was caught and told a con there that he threw the boy off a bridge and he screamed the whole way down until he hit the water."

"What did you think of that?" said Deasaro.

"Not much," replied Dowdy. "I mean, he told so many stories I figured he was just telling me a lot of shit. Pumping himself up. I didn't think he was a bad guy, maybe a little crazy, but he was OK as a cellmate. I've had worse."

"How about Florida?" said Schock. "Did he talk about

living there, about his involvement with a girl, a girl with a red Corvette?"

"Only thing he said about Florida was that he owned a boat and he'd get rid of his enemies by wrapping them in a net and throwing them in the water," said Dowdy. "He also said he didn't like strippers and people involved in pornography. Again, I just figured he was telling stories, you know, to pass the time. Ain't got much else to do. Really didn't think much of it."

Franklin Floyd was seated again in the interrogation room at the Oklahoma City County prison, and appeared even more disturbed than he had two days earlier. Under each arm were papers and envelopes, which he called his "stuff pertainin' to his situation."

He dropped the papers on the table, then started talking much like he had before, without allowing any interruption.

Schock and Deasaro, as they did during the first interview, allowed Floyd to carry the conversation. And much like the first interview, Floyd told a convolution of stories, even changing statements he'd made before. Floyd continued for an hour before Deasaro finally cut him off.

"Let me ask you a question," said Deasaro.

"No, I have more to show and tell you," said Floyd.

"No, I'm going to ask you a question. If the police could prove the photos of Cheryl Commesso were yours, what would be your explanation?" said Deasaro.

"They're not my pictures. They were intermingled with the FBI to make us think they were mine. I'd be able to fuck you in court just with the chain of custody alone," said Floyd. "I'm not stupid. I studied the law."

Floyd continued on for another fifteen minutes and Schock and Deasaro were about to cut him off again when he unexpectedly admitted that he knew Cheryl Commesso.

"She hung around with Sharon. Drove that red car. Now I remember. I didn't see her much, but I know she was around," said Floyd.

"So let me ask you again, Mr. Floyd, now that you're saying you did know her. Did you kill Cheryl Commesso?" said Schock.

"I told you before no and I'm sayin' it again, no," said Floyd.

Schock and Deasaro flew back to Florida, and over the summer months interviewed more witnesses, solidifying their case with further identification of the furniture in the Marshall trailer at the Golden Lantern trailer park, particularly the sofa in the living room. The color of the sofa matched the color and design of the sofa in the photos, which was identified as the sofa bed in the living room.

In November, Floyd pled guilty to state kidnapping charges filed in Oklahoma, claiming he was "sick and tired" of the Oklahoma City County Jail and its menu of beans and bologna. By pleading guilty, it was agreed that Floyd would be transferred to the federal prison in Atlanta, the same prison where he served a year from 1971 to 1972 just prior to his parole to a halfway house in November 1972.

Unbeknownst to Floyd, a grand jury was impaneled in the circuit court for the Sixth Judicial Circuit of Florida in Pinellas County, Florida, to consider evidence presented by Bruce Bartlett, the chief assistant state attorney for the Sixth Judicial Circuit.

Bartlett alleged that Floyd bound, beat, and eventually killed Cheryl Commesso in his rented trailer home at the

Golden Lantern trailer park. The photos found in the stolen truck revealed that Cheryl was either dead or near death before Floyd allegedly shot her twice in the head, disposed of her body off the side of I-275, then left her red Corvette at the St. Petersburg–Clearwater Airport.

On November 12, the grand jury returned an indictment for first-degree murder, a capital felony in Florida. A week later Floyd received a third and final visit from Schock and Deasaro, who believed there was a slim chance that Floyd would finally admit to the crime.

Floyd was angered by their presence, and greeted them with a four-hour-long harangue, insisting that several others were responsible for Cheryl's murder.

"Sharon had so many friends, could've been anyone that did it," said Floyd. "I have an idea who did it, but I ain't no snitch."

At that point it was clear to Schock and Deasaro that Floyd would not admit to the murder, and it was Schock who delivered the news to Floyd that a grand jury had returned an indictment against him for murder.

Floyd flew into a rage and cursed the two detectives, who got up to leave the room.

"You don't have shit on me!" he yelled. "I'm going to make fools of you! I didn't kill that woman!"

The detectives stood side by side, a sheriff's deputy behind them waiting to take Floyd back to his cell.

"Mr. Floyd," said Schock. "Be informed that you are under arrest for the murder of Cheryl Ann Commesso."

CHAPTER 26

During his twenty-seven years as a special agent for the Federal Bureau of Investigation, Joe Fitzpatrick took special pride and satisfaction in his ability to close every case assigned to him. It was a personal barometer of his achievements within the bureau, a feat that also served to drive him emotionally and professionally, and no doubt led to his continued success.

By 1997, Fitzpatrick entertained thoughts that perhaps he'd spent enough time with the bureau, and envisioned spending lazy days fishing or playing with his grandchildren. He had also remarried, following a divorce several years earlier from his first wife, and he wanted to spend less time at work.

As retirement became increasingly enticing, Fitzpatrick had some unfinished business, his personal record now in jeopardy.

Two mysteries remained from his successful pursuit of

Franklin Floyd: finding the last resting place of Michael Hughes and the true identity of Sharon Marshall.

There was little Fitzpatrick could do with the Hughes investigation. Michael's remains were believed to be twelve hundred miles away in the Atlanta area, and the search was now in the hands of the Atlanta FBI field office. All Fitzpatrick could do was press hard on the Atlanta agents, pushing and prodding them to follow every possible clue and grill every witness, particularly Floyd's friends David Dial and Rebecca Barr.

Fitzpatrick assumed Dial knew more than he was saying, and even believed that Floyd confided to Dial the exact whereabouts of Michael's remains. But Dial remained mum, claiming he knew little about Michael, but a lot about Floyd.

"Franklin was a nicer person back in prison," said Dial in one interview. "Now he's all twisted."

Rebecca Barr had previously agreed to help the FBI and had taped Floyd's phone calls from prison. But by the time of Floyd's federal trial she publicly expressed her love for Floyd and planned to marry him in prison, a union that prison authorities thought unwise and suspect.

As he did with David Dial, Fitzpatrick and others believed Barr knew more than she was letting on about Michael and Sharon, but Barr refused to say anything that would incriminate Floyd.

His secrets were her secrets.

With the Michael Hughes trail cold, Fitzpatrick decided to take it upon himself to search for Sharon's true identity.

Sharon's story affected Fitzpatrick like no other investigation before. He never knew Sharon, and she died four years before he ever heard of her. But it was clearly eating him alive that she remained unidentified, and it bothered

him more that a convicted felon and pedophile could actually kidnap a girl and raise her as his daughter without so
much as a blip on any radar screen.

Fitzpatrick asked himself over and over, *Why didn't she
ever say anything?*

Hoping to find an answer, he turned to the interviews at
Forest Park High School. Agents from the Atlanta field office visited the school, where teachers and administration
personnel who remembered Sharon were still dealing with
raw feelings that mixed between guilt, rage, and confusion.
All were stunned when they first heard the news in November 1994, and all were unable to understand or comprehend
how Sharon and her "father" could fool so many people for
such a long period of time.

The more they talked about Sharon, the more they remembered the subtle, and not so subtle, signs that something was amiss. Teacher Terry Magaro remembered
Sharon's quiet way during their first interview, and could
still see "Warren" sitting before her, espousing his "daughter's" talents and accomplishments, even answering questions directed toward Sharon.

Carol Worley clearly remembered Sharon's insistence
that she return home by 4:30 every afternoon to cook and
clean for her father. Everyone knew why she was leaving,
but no one thought to interfere with what all believed was a
somewhat strict dynamic between father and daughter. Further blurring the lines of reasoning was Sharon's performance: She was a gifted student with a high IQ and all felt
Warren's firm parenting was something to admire, not crit-
icize. As Worley, Magaro, and others looked back in disbelief, no one could comprehend how a young woman could
perform at such a high level while subject to the kind of tor-
ment and abuse that Sharon suffered.

And she hid it so well. It was clear that Sharon had developed a skill at covering up her past, never approaching any teacher or student to share her pain. Instead she maintained the ruse, easily shifting back and forth between stories, telling most students that her mother died in a car accident, then supporting her father's later statement that she died of cancer.

Everyone had questions, but felt it wasn't their business to pry. School was an environment where parental alcoholism, drug abuse, and sexual abuse were problems that never went away, and teachers were experienced at dealing with the resulting dysfunctions exhibited in students of all ages. In the event a student suffered apparent physical or emotional harm, social services, or even the police, were called.

What made Sharon's story all the more devastating and incomprehensible to the staff at Forest Park was that she appeared to be highly functional, and her intelligence and inner strength apparently worked against her in that it allowed her to separate her two lives—the one she had with her father, and the one she had at school. A weaker, less intelligent person would have, in all probability, fallen apart at some point, and given away his or her personal secrets.

Earle Lewis, Sharon's ROTC instructor, thought it stretched the limits of comprehension to figure where the genes came from to develop that type of character.

Lewis had never known anyone like Sharon Marshall.

Joe Fitzpatrick had worked dozens of kidnappings during his lengthy career, but never one that involved a child stolen two decades earlier.

There were so many questions, the most important of which was, How would he go about finding her true identity?

Fitzpatrick began his search in earnest by obtaining a list

of missing-child organizations throughout the country. Clearinghouses served as registries for all missing-children cases reported within each state, and Fitzpatrick found at least one clearinghouse in all fifty states. He personally wrote fifty letters, describing Sharon and the approximate year she was believed to have been taken, anywhere from the summer of 1973 to the fall of 1975, when she first appeared with Floyd in Oklahoma City.

Fitzpatrick spent half his working days on the phone with the clearinghouses, focusing his attention on places where Floyd was known to have traveled in the mid-1970s, including Georgia and Illinois. Floyd's mother, Della, died in Chicago in 1968 and Floyd was said to have visited her grave in 1974. Della lived a hard life. She was an alcoholic who turned to prostitution, who later married and moved to Illinois. Floyd last saw her in 1960 in Indianapolis prior to entering the Army.

But information coming from the various clearinghouses shed little light on Sharon's plight, and responses soon became predictable since few states maintained records older than five years.

Some went back ten years, but none longer.

Several leads did surface through conversation and networking: California authorities suggested two possible identifications, but they quickly washed out. Another possibility emerged out of Florida concerning a woman and her daughter, who had both disappeared. Fitzpatrick thought he might have a hit since the photo of the missing girl looked like Sharon, but the father and brothers of the girl were certain they were not identical.

With each new lead, particularly the Florida connection, Fitzpatrick would share the promising news with Mark Yancey and Ed Kumiega. All were excited with the possibilities, discussing the leads long into the night at the U.S. Attorney's office. Fitzpatrick would stop by at the end of the day, share the information, and Yancey and Kumiega could see and sense Fitzpatrick's excitement.

They could also plainly see his complete dejection when it became clear there was no match.

As months went by, the search had become a frustrating and, to a large degree, impossible exercise. Even Fitzpatrick, with nearly three decades of experience, was surprised at the lack of information available in searching for a missing child from the not-too-distant past. There was simply no place to go to find detailed information on missing children prior to 1990.

If one girl could go unnoticed after being kidnapped and held for so many years, Fitzpatrick wondered, how many others shared the same predicament?

To understand the gravity of problem, Fitzpatrick decided to research the issue.

The lesson was eye-opening.

CHAPTER 27

Define a missing child in America prior to the mid-1980s and the typical answer would be anyone under the age of eighteen who willingly left their home.

A runaway.

And runaways were considered the problem of parents, teachers, and social workers, not the police. That attitude prevailed for decades as law enforcement agencies throughout the country virtually ignored missing children. There are more than eighteen thousand police departments throughout the United States and all routinely failed to take reports, imposed waiting periods before considering taking a missing-person report, and after 1975 either ignored or simply refused to input missing children cases into the FBI's National Crime Information Center database.

And in cases where police did take reports, there was little communication between the thousands of police departments. Given the low priority placed on missing children, a child could be abducted from one jurisdiction, and no other police agency, not even a neighboring department, would know about it.

The criminal justice system, which ultimately dictates police response, showed even less concern for missing children. There were few criminal statutes prior to 1982 that addressed family-abduction issues, giving police no real authority to deal with runaways even if they wanted to. Runaways were considered *status offenders*, not criminals.

In essence, Congress, the courts, and law enforcement paid little attention to the plight of missing children in America.

No one even bothered to gauge the problem until 1975, when the National Statistical Survey on Runaway Youth, a federally funded study, estimated that approximately 500,000 children ran away from home each year. The report was criticized for being incomplete, since it relied on a sampling of inferior statistics maintained by clearinghouses in each state, which received their information from local police departments, which failed miserably in monitoring and acting on missing-children reports.

Testimony before Congress in 1982 suggested that the actual number of children who disappeared each year hovered near two million, with estimates of as many as five thousand children murdered every year through kidnapping and abduction. Thousands more were never seen again.

The numbers were not verified but were shocking enough. Even more unsettling was that the U.S. government provided zero dollars for the search and recovery of missing children.

There was no agency, no department, no investigators—no one—aligned with or supported by the federal government charged with the task of coordinating and investigating missing-children reports throughout the country. Aside from placing pictures on milk cartons, the plight of missing children in America was a nonissue.

Individual cases did emerge over the years, leading to public outrage and federal legislation, but they were few and very far between. The first was in 1932, when the infant son of Charles Lindbergh was kidnapped and killed in New Jersey. The nation reacted angrily, given Lindbergh's status as a national hero, and Congress responded with the Lindbergh Law, legislation that authorized the U.S. Department of Justice, in the form of the FBI, to intervene in kidnapping cases that crossed state lines.

Congress later passed the Uniform Child Custody Jurisdiction Act in 1968, which stopped parents involved in custody disputes from "judge shopping," or traveling to different states to seek favorable custody decisions.

In 1975 the FBI instituted a missing-persons file in its National Crime Information Center, an automated information sharing system that allowed law enforcement throughout the country to input and review cases in one centralized file. But few law enforcement agencies took the time to input cases, much less investigate missing-persons reports. Most reports involving missing children were treated as runaways or children taken in domestic disputes, and were ignored.

The nation remained in the dark to the plight of missing children until 1982, when Congress adopted the Missing Children Act, legislation enacted following three unsettling events that occurred over a two-year span.

The first was the abduction of a seven-year-old boy, Etan Patz, from his downtown New York City neighborhood in May 1979.

Patz persuaded his parents to allow him to walk alone to the bus stop two blocks away. His mother watched him stroll down the first block, then went inside. He never made it across the second block.

New York newspapers published Patz's heart-tugging photo daily, and the publicity surrounding an abduction off a city street in broad daylight caused a national furor. It had happened countless times before throughout the country, but none of those cases received the scrutiny or notoriety as the Patz abduction.

The second event involved the murder of twenty-nine young men and boys in the Atlanta area. Their bodies were found from 1979 to 1981 throughout the greater-Atlanta region. The nation followed along as body after body washed up in local lakes and rivers.

The third and final event occurred in July 1981, when six-year-old Adam Walsh was abducted from a Florida shopping mall. His head was found two weeks later in a ditch, his body was never recovered.

His parents, John and Reve, desperately sought answers, but were surprised and disturbed to learn there were few coming from law enforcement. The Walshes' profound grief, personal frustration, and anger attracted thousands of parents of other missing or lost children whose stories were tragically similar to the Walshes' but never heard.

Children of all ages were taken at all hours of the day, from homes, parks, supermarkets, schools, hospitals, amusement parks—anywhere.

It was clear to all concerned that that these violent acts toward America's children were not isolated events, and the furor reached Washington, D.C., Congressional hearings in 1982 revealed the untold violence and tragedy surrounding the disappearances of thousands of children and their parents' desperate need for resources to investigate each and every case.

Legislators were bombarded with stories of children routinely beaten, bludgeoned, burned, and sexually abused by predators who easily retreated into the shadows, with little fear of capture and prosecution.

The Missing Children Act of 1982, signed into law by

President Ronald Reagan, was a milestone. It announced to all that after decades of ignorance, the federal government now perceived the investigation and recovery of missing children a priority.

The new legislation called on police departments throughout the country to investigate every missing-person report involving a child and to enter all pertinent information into NCIC. It also required the FBI to intervene where appropriate and confirm NCIC entries for parents of the missing.

Another milestone occurred just two years later, when Congress enacted the Missing Children's Assistance Act, which recognized that federal assistance was urgently needed to "coordinate and assist the national problem of missing and abducted children."

Later that year, Congress directed the establishment of the National Center for Missing & Exploited Children. Formed as a direct result of the lobbying efforts led by John and Reve Walsh, the National Center was formed as a nonprofit agency funded by the federal government and private donations. Its mandate was to help families find missing children. The National Center was charged with creating and maintaining a national clearinghouse of information on missing children, running a toll-free hotline, and providing technical assistance to law enforcement ill-suited for the task.

The National Center opened in April 1984 in Washington, D.C., with a small staff of retired police detectives, a general but unfocused purpose, and an initial budget of $3.3 million.

It was the first quasi-federal agency with a sole responsibility for missing children.

Soon after its historic creation, it became clear that the National Center's greatest attribute would be its lobbying power. The National Center was not a lobbying center, but Congress found it difficult to say no to the rising tide of anger expressed by parents of the missing, the numbers of which no one really knew.

With previous testimony alluding to the number of the missing at a staggering two million annually, Congress sought more tangible statistics, and through the Missing Children's Assistance Act called for a new study, the National Incidence Studies of Missing, Abducted, Runaway, and Thrownaway Children in America (NISMART), to accurately estimate the number of missing children in the United States.

The study took six years to complete, the results of which were published in 1990.

NISMART focused on a target year of 1988, and found that the plight of missing children was really five different and distinct problems: family abduction; nonfamily abduction; runaways; thrownaways; and lost, injured, or otherwise missing children.

Combined, NISMART revealed that over a million children were reported missing in 1988. Of that number 450,000 were considered runaways while 438,000 were considered "lost/injured/otherwise missing."

Joe Fitzpatrick's interest in his search for Sharon's identity was in nonfamily abductions, which included the "unauthorized" taking of a child by someone other than a family member who detained the child more than an hour or lured the child for the purposes of committing another crime, such as kidnapping or sexual assault.

The NISMART study determined there were 114,600 attempted nonfamily abductions, which encompassed all efforts to gain custody of a child, including luring children into cars, in malls, near schools, from parks—just about anywhere. Many attempts were unsuccessful. Either the child refused the advance or a parent or another adult interceded, driving the potential abductor away.

Still, Fitzpatrick saw that anywhere from 3,600 to 4,600 children were successfully taken against their will each year, with many of those children subsequently sexually or physically abused, or both. Of those taken, two hundred to three hundred were considered "stereotypical kidnappings," which meant the child was killed, ransomed, or the perpetrator intended to keep the child permanently.

Pedophiles such as Floyd who kidnapped rarely kept the child longer than seventy-two hours, when the child would either be set free or murdered. Fitzpatrick realized that Floyd's case was most unusual in that he not only kept Sharon alive but maintained custody, even under the pressure of his status as a federal fugitive.

There was no other case on record where a pedophile, convicted felon, and federal fugitive kidnapped a child and successfully raised her as his daughter—successful to the extent that he maintained custody of the child for fifteen to seventeen years. What made the case even more baffling was Sharon herself, a beautiful, tender, and highly intelligent girl who could easily have told someone, anyone, about her plight, but remained silent.

The efforts of parents and the National Center throughout the 1980s led to another major piece of legislation in 1990, when Congress passed the National Child Search Assistance Act, which greatly improved the Missing Children Act of 1982 by mandating that no federal, state, or local law-enforcement agency could establish or observe a waiting period before accepting a missing-child case. And police were required by law to input information into NCIC within two hours of receiving reports of missing children under eighteen years of age.

Law enforcement agencies throughout the country were

now mandated to act, and the new guidelines resulted in direct improvements in the recovery of missing children, which reached 75 percent of all reported cases by 1995.

For Joe Fitzpatrick, the success of the missing children movement from 1982 to 1990 did little for his investigation into the disappearance of a girl from the early to mid-1970s.

Fitzpatrick realized the ease with which a predator like Franklin Floyd could conceivably kidnap a girl during that time, travel to another state, and go unnoticed. Floyd was clever enough to obtain documents, including Social Security numbers and birth certificates, from a vast network of resources and contacts, including ex-cons, that spanned the country.

Once Floyd enrolled Sharon in first grade in Oklahoma City, he began a legitimate paper trail where legal parentage was never a consideration. No one—teachers, guidance counselors, neighbors, or acquaintances—ever sought actual proof that Floyd was the legal parent. No one had reason to. As long as Floyd could provide transfer records from each of Sharon's previous schools, and without any signs or signals from Sharon herself, the ruse was complete.

To all who knew Floyd and Sharon, he was simply a single father struggling to raise a daughter.

Prospects for identifying Sharon Marshall were dim at best, and Fitzpatrick was running out of options. So he turned to the National Center.

The National Center opened a file on Michael Hughes on September 15, 1994, three days after Michael had been kidnapped, and through the Hughes case Fitzpatrick developed a relationship with the agency.

Since its creation in 1984, the National Center had grown from a small agency with a handful of employees and small working spaces with typewriters to an efficient organization that relied on increased funding, state-of-the-art computers, and the expertise of experienced investigators from various local, state, and federal police agencies.

By 1995 the National Center privately estimated, based on statistics from the FBI and studies such as NISMART, that some 800,000 children went missing each year. But thanks in part to the work of the National Center a solid 75 percent were recovered, which was far better than the estimated 50 percent recovery rate recorded by law enforcement when the agency opened its doors in 1984.

Ron Jones was the case manager in charge of the Michael Hughes investigation for the National Center. A veteran homicide detective with the Washington, D.C., police, Jones joined the National Center after retiring from the D.C. force in 1987.

His job upon receiving the Michael Hughes case was to publicize the kidnapping within law enforcement circles throughout the nation as well as the media. Jones sent out flyers with Michael's picture and made numerous phone calls, which produced leads from all over the country that subsequently were passed along to the FBI.

To Fitzpatrick's dismay, the National Center never opened a file on Sharon Marshall since its Congressional mandate stipulated that services were offered only to children under eighteen years old.

Sharon was, by all accounts, believed to have been well past her eighteenth birthday at the time of her death.

Still, Jones helped Fitzpatrick however he could, alternately serving as a buffer and an advisor. Jones easily sensed Fitzpatrick's frustration and despair. The two men spoke every other month, and it was clear that the veteran FBI agent placed great importance on finding Sharon's identity.

And like Fitzpatrick, Jones also wanted to answer all the questions that began with "Why?"

Why did Sharon remain with Floyd? Why didn't she tell someone her predicament?

Jones received a partial answer from a 1995 study commissioned by the Office of Juvenile Justice and Delinquency Prevention.

The report focused on the prostitution of children and, in part, on the relationship between an adult, or pimp, and child prostitute. A pimp is described as someone who becomes the primary person in a young woman's life, who lulls a girl into believing they have a mutually developing relationship, and then she becomes emotionally and psychologically dependent on the adult.

After creating this dependency, the adult dominates the girl and becomes an integral part of her life. He then "seasons" the girl for a life of physical and verbal abuse. "Seasoning" is described as "breaking her will and separating her so that she does not know where to turn for help. He may change her identity and move her around because constant mobility breaks any personal ties she may have developed and ensures new ties are only temporary."

The study revealed that the adult's relationship to the girl parallels the dynamics of a battering relationship, where the girl is first isolated from family and friends and the adult uses threats and intimidation to control her through emotional, sexual, and physical abuse. He creates an environment of total emotional deprivation and uses violence to establish and maintain power.

While the relationship between Floyd and Sharon closely mirrored that of a pimp and prostitute, what was unusual was Sharon did not appear to be vulnerable or have low self-esteem, as was typical of girls who generally fell under the spell of a pimp.

During her high school years Sharon was vivacious, appeared to have a positive, healthy outlook on life, and was upbeat. Only after Sharon left Forest Park High School was her will finally broken. The study did not account for how Sharon found the strength to attempt an escape from Floyd. That attribute, Jones believed, came from Sharon's own personal strength, a force that drew in Fitzpatrick, who spent the last year of his career focused on Sharon Marshall. It was a personal endeavor supported by his superiors, who virtually looked the other way, knowing how much it meant to the veteran agent.

Despite Fitzpatrick's determined and heartfelt efforts, his retirement day approached with little progress in the search for Sharon's identity.

Given the time period when she was believed to have been kidnapped, there were simply no records available to continue the search.

In mid-July Fitzpatrick visited with Mark Yancey and Ed Kumiega to say good-bye. Both men felt for Fitzpatrick, and both appreciated the zeal and effort he had placed into his search.

Fitzpatrick officially retired from the FBI on July 18, 1998, submitting his papers just two months in advance so as to not give the special agent in charge of the Oklahoma City field office time to talk Fitzpatrick out of leaving the bureau.

When he left the building that day, Fitzpatrick felt a profound sense of sadness. For the first time during his distinguished career, he was unable to close a case. He left that day still asking himself: Where was Michael Hughes, and who was Sharon Marshall?

CHAPTER 28

Franklin Floyd remained in the Atlanta federal prison through 1999, when he was brought to Florida and transferred to the Pinellas County jail.

The murder indictment slowly worked its way through the courts, and successfully stood against several legal challenges. In 2001, Floyd's court-appointed attorneys sought to have him declared mentally incompetent to stand trial.

Assistant Public Defender Jill Menadier told Pinellas-Pasco Circuit Judge Nancy Moate Ley that Floyd had a history of mental problems, including schizophrenia, and throughout his life had undergone psychiatric care.

Three court-appointed psychologists examined Floyd, and two agreed that Floyd was not competent to stand trial.

It would be up to Judge Ley to make the final decision.

The judge had raised her own concerns about Floyd's competence after she received several letters from Floyd, all rambling thoughts, theories on his life, and the identities of Cheryl Commesso's "real" killers. One letter was particularly memorable, with Floyd remarking that *"I will trudge the last miles to the death house crumpled before the legal system towards the electric chair which awaits me like the mother I once loved."*

Floyd did not want to be declared incompetent. He actually fought against it.

Bob Schock and Mark Deasaro didn't believe for one minute that Floyd was crazy. They visited the federal prison in Atlanta in April 2000, hoping to gain additional insight and information from several inmates whom Floyd had befriended.

Inmate Kenneth Birchfield told of one of Floyd's strange hobbies.

Floyd was described as a "freak" over child-porn magazines. He obtained titles such as *Barely Legal* and *Barely 18* from other inmates, then would cut out the pictures, then the private parts, which he'd place in a photo-type album.

During prison "shakedowns" some of the albums would be confiscated. Floyd gave others to inmates to hold for safekeeping.

Floyd wrote to Judge Ley, objecting to any effort to have him declared incompetent, going so far as to request his attorneys be removed and Floyd be allowed to defend himself.

"No psychiatrist in his right mind would find me incompetent," wrote Floyd.

On March 2, 2001, Judge Ley disagreed with Floyd's assessment and ruled that Floyd was mentally incompetent to stand trial. She ordered Floyd to undergo further mental evaluations.

Floyd called the ruling "insulting."

Prosecutor Bruce Bartlett worried that Floyd would escape from the mental hospital.

"This guy is no dope," said Bartlett.

Two months later, Schock visited with Robert Messina,

an inmate at the Pinellas County Jail who spent a month in lock-down solitary confinement in a pod next to Floyd.

The pods were single cells separated only by iron bars. Inmates could see and talk freely with other inmates, and Floyd apparently talked a lot, and often.

It was Messina who contacted the State Attorney's office via letters sent by regular mail, relaying that he had information pertaining to Floyd.

Messina had been jailed for resisting arrest with violence and was awaiting trial. He had previously been arrested before for resisting arrest.

Floyd bragged about beating the Commesso murder rap, claiming all the prosecution had was pictures. There was no witness nor did Floyd ever confess. Floyd often spoke about his past, and talked freely about how he kidnapped his son and put him to rest.

"He said, 'If I can't have him, no one would,'" recalled Messina.

Schock and Deasaro were interested in what Messina had to say next, about how Floyd claimed he dated some of the girls at the Mons Venus, and that he had no problem killing some girl with an Italian-sounding last name.

"Was her name Commesso?" said Schock.

"Sounds about right," said Messina.

Schock, Deasaro, and Bruce Bartlett all believed that Floyd had toyed with Judge Ley and the psychiatrists who examined him and in July, Judge Ley agreed, reversing her earlier ruling based on subsequent psychiatric evaluations. After watching Floyd over several months, psychiatrists determined that Floyd was competent to stand trial after all.

More than a year later, on September 9, 2002, Floyd would finally face the jury.

Unlike his previous federal trial in Oklahoma City,

where Floyd limited his outbursts before Judge Wayne Alley, he battled daily with Judge Ley, arguing and often hurling obscenities.

On several occasions he was physically removed from the courtroom.

Floyd was particularly incensed over Ley's ruling that jurors would know of Floyd's prior conviction for the Michael Hughes kidnapping.

"You'll know I'll be convicted, so don't worry about that," said Floyd sarcastically.

Floyd's trial lasted nine days. He wore glasses and a blue prison jumpsuit and each day scribbled furiously into a notebook, alerting his attorneys to his thoughts and questions as witnesses who once knew Floyd as Warren Marshall described his violent temper and uneven demeanor.

Jennifer Fisher Tanner testified, as did Merle Bean and others involved in the Michael Hughes kidnapping case.

Cary Strukel, Sharon's old boyfriend from Tampa, repeated his belief that Floyd was a "nutcase and whack job."

Even Joe Fitzpatrick was brought down to testify.

Fitzpatrick intended to spend his retirement fishing. Instead he was a highly sought private investigator working for several insurance companies. He was busier now than he had been with the FBI. He also spent a considerable amount of time helping Schock and Deasaro as they built their case against Floyd, providing a sounding board for the Florida detectives.

As the trial continued, Floyd's attorneys argued that there were no witnesses to the slaying of Cheryl Commesso, and no confession. The most damning evidence were the photos found in the truck in Kansas.

Floyd claimed the pictures were planted by the FBI, a claim that was rebuked by prosecutors Bruce Bartlett and Glenn Martin, who argued that Floyd took the photos prior to killing Cheryl, then kept the photos to "memorialize" the event, a typical trait of pedophiles and sexual sadists.

Hand experts also testified that it was, indeed, Floyd's thumb that appeared in several of the photos.

Floyd was prone to outbursts throughout the trial, maintaining his innocence as he screamed at the judge and witnesses as they walked by the defense table.

Floyd's temper, the overwhelming evidence, and the testimony from those most affected by his past deeds did him in.

On September 28, 2002, following nine days of testimony, the jury deliberated only four hours before finding Franklin Floyd guilty of murder.

After the verdict was read, Floyd stood at the defense table and screamed at the jury.

"Look me in the face!" he cried. "Look me in the face."

Floyd then turned to Bartlett and Martin.

"They framed me," he yelled. "It was the FBI that put those pictures there. I was framed."

The guilty verdict secure, the penalty phase of the trial would begin on October 1, but not before Floyd would explode again with rage, screaming at the judge and jury that he was framed. Floyd also objected to the disclosure of his his 1962 child abuse conviction, which he unsuccessfully fought to keep from the jury during the penalty phase.

Floyd's outburst forced Judge Ley to suspend court until the following day, when Floyd calmly took the stand and answered questions for more than an hour, talking about his troubled life as a youth, the alleged sexual abuse at the orphanage, and his brutal years in jail as an adult.

His newfound serenity did little to sway the jury, which returned after deliberating but one hour. Floyd stood, surrounded by seven bailiffs, and listened solemnly as the jury announced their unanimous decision to recommend Floyd be put to death by lethal injection.

Floyd said nothing as he was led out of the courthouse and back to his cell at the Pinellas County jail. He remained there until late February 2003, when he was transferred to death row at the maximum-security prison at Raiford.

On April 9, two weeks before his sixtieth birthday, Floyd was admitted to the prison hospital following what was described as a complete emotional breakdown. He was hospitalized for three weeks, then returned to death row, where he remained in total lockdown.

Two cars traveled slowly on the thin roads of the Park Grove Cemetery in Tulsa, Oklahoma, the female drivers searching in different directions for the long-forgotten marker.

It was spring 2003, a time for renewal. Once-brown grass, dormant through the winter, displayed a fresh green hue.

The small cemetery was empty of visitors except for the two cars, a red Mustang and blue Ford minivan. Each would stop in front of a marker or tombstone to read a name, then slowly move on again. After ten minutes, the Mustang pulled up in front of one marker, and Karen Parsley jumped out of her car, waving her arms back and forth and calling to Lavernia Watkins in the minivan.

"It's here! It's here!" yelled Karen.

Lavernia pulled her van behind the Mustang, and walked up to the gravesite just off the road. It was a simple gray marble marker, identified by only one name, Tonya.

The soft ground in front was bare. It had been some time since anyone had come to visit, much less placed flowers at the site. Karen hadn't visited since Tonya was buried in 1990. Same for Lavernia.

The two women still worked at Passions, both giving up dancing for different jobs. Both were mothers with children of their own, and Karen was the day manager while Lavernia worked as a hostess serving drinks. They kept their stage names, Connie for Karen, and Bambi for Lavernia.

Franklin Floyd's trial in Florida had been reported in the local papers. His subsequent death sentence, by lethal injection, was too good for him, as far as they were concerned. The electric chair would have been their preferred manner of death. A few minutes of high-voltage electricity passing through his shaking body, with smoke billowing out of his ears and nostrils, still wouldn't have been enough to pay for the pain he caused their friend and her son. But it would have been far more desirable than lying on a gurney, getting stuck with a needle, and falling asleep forever.

The two women stood in front of the marker, not quite sure what to do next other than stand there, their presence apparently enough to show their respect.

"We should have brought flowers," said Connie.

"Didn't think of it," said Bambi.

"Looks like no one cares about her," said Connie, looking down at the marker, a tear running slowly down her cheek.

"We're with you, baby," she whispered. "That bastard's gonna be gone soon."

Connie had hoped that someday the marker would be replaced with another bearing Tonya's real name, but that day had yet to come. All Connie knew was that the FBI had tried to identify her friend, but Tonya had been taken so long ago, it was deemed an impossible task.

She knew that Franklin Floyd knew the answer, but he continued to resist, offering different versions to different people, saying Tonya was given to him by her prostitute mother, or by her father, who couldn't care for her.

Floyd would never tell the truth, and it appeared the mystery would remain just that.

Bambi stood there, deep in her own thoughts, while Connie knelt down before the marker.

"I hope one day we find out who you really were," she said. "I hope one day I'll know your real name, and I'll meet your real family, and I can tell them that I once knew a girl who tried to save herself and her son. And I can tell them I was your friend."

EPILOGUE

Alexandria, Virginia
February 2003

Gerry Nance sat in his cubicle on the second floor of the National Center for Missing & Exploited Children, staring at his computer as he typed out an e-mail.

The letter was written to Shelley Denman, a Kansas City, Missouri, woman who had spent the last three years searching for three members of her husband's family who had disappeared in 1974.

Nance was interested in helping Denman, particularly since two of the missing were children—a four-year-old niece and ten-month-old nephew. Nance had written many similar letters since joining the National Center in December 1998, following twenty-five years of service with the U.S. Naval Criminal Investigative Service.

The change of careers had not been planned.

In 1996, Nance was the deputy assistant director for felony criminal investigations for NCIS, investigating major felony crimes, counterintelligence, and espionage. He was in the process of rewriting investigation protocols, focusing at the time on missing-persons reports. He had heard of the National Center, and its stellar work with missing children, and decided to pay a visit to see what information they could offer for his project.

His tour was life-changing.

By the end of his visit that day Nance was so taken with the work of the National Center he let it be known that if a position ever became available, he was interested.

Two years went by, and Nance was working as an advisor to the Department of Defense Inspector General's office when he received a phone call from Ben Ermini, director of the missing-children's division. The National Center had received additional funding in its new budget to create and operate a cold-case division, and they were looking for someone to run the new department.

Nance retired on a Thursday in December 1998, and reported to his new job the following Monday.

His official title was case manager for special cases, but Nance knew that he'd be working on the coldest of cases, investigations where a child had been missing for at least five years and there was no active participation by police or a family member in finding the child.

Some cases went back twenty, even thirty years.

Nance, fifty-six, was a tall, even-tempered, and deliberate man who knew from experience that laying a good foundation—through analysis, programming, fact-finding, and evaluation—was the key to a successful investigation.

He also knew going in that his new job would be tough, and in some respects impossible. The culture of noncooperation and noncommunication that plagued law enforcement in the U.S. for decades in missing-children investigations was slowly evaporating, as many police agencies welcomed the National Center and its resources. But a good number of the nation's 18,000 police agencies still maintained the old ways.

They refused to cooperate or take advantage of the resources offered by the National Center, holding tightly to their well-entrenched belief that no one enters their jurisdiction, no matter what the circumstances.

In researching his new caseload, which stood at slightly more than four hundred inactive cases, Nance was greeted with open arms by some police departments and found plenty of resistance from others. In his attempts at researching cases from the resisters, Nance was often forced to find other means to gather information on a particular case, even required to read through back issues of local newspapers to find the names of the investigating detectives or officers originally involved in a long-dormant case.

It was painstaking work but Nance persevered, knowing that the keys to solving a cold case, along with technological breakthroughs in forensic science, were determining what had changed in the investigation over the course of time, and what had changed in the relationships between those involved.

In a cold case, somebody knew something somewhere, and a witness could have been reluctant to offer information to police at the time of the disappearance for a variety of reasons. As years passed, Nance found if those same people were tracked down and interviewed, they'd usually offer honest, and helpful, answers.

By the end of 1999, Nance established protocols for cold-case investigations at the National Center, which included gathering all information previously collected by local police, new interviews with family and friends, and new information provided by independent investigators hired by the National Center to serve as case managers (a group known as Project ALERT, for America's Law Enforcement Retiree Team; they are usually retired law enforcement officers who are hired to work as case managers as well as field investigators at the request of police departments).

All the information gathered was brought under one umbrella and solvability was then separated into three groups: good solvability; something there but don't know what; and nothing is hopeless.

Nance hated the term *hopeless* and for cases that fit into the third group, information was warehoused with the belief that additional clues would someday turn up. Nance maintained a collage of photos on the wall next to his cubicle, photos of dead children, some horribly burned or maimed, set against other photos of smiling children. The children ranged in age from infant to teens and all had been missing for years. The photos served to remind Nance and his staff that the long-term missing had names and families and loved ones, and for every case that was solved, a family could finally find closure. *Hopeless*, said Nance, was not a word to be used in his department.

Perhaps a hunter or fisherman would one day walk over a pile of bones, or a witness with a guilty conscience would one day come forward. More likely an identification would come thanks to the use of advanced technology—specifically DNA testing—to help identify long-lost remains that suddenly surfaced.

Since its introduction in England in 1985, nearly one hundred years after another major breakthrough—fingerprinting—was conceived (also in the U.K.), DNA testing revolutionized forensic science and improved significantly with each passing year. The standard test, called nuclear DNA testing, compared the nucleus of a cell from one sample to a sample from a family member, preferably a parent. Nuclear testing was usually performed using "wet" samples, either blood or saliva, semen, or other bodily fluids.

DNA testing helped the National Center identify the remains of twenty-five missing children, and by 2003 the technology had become so advanced that trace amounts of blood, saliva, bone, or tissue, invisible to the naked eye, could be amplified and tested, with results delivered within days.

DNA, or "genetic fingerprints," helped police close rape cases, exonerate innocent inmates in prison, particularly those on death row, and secured guilty verdicts for prosecutors with little other evidence.

By the turn of the new century a new technology had revolutionized DNA testing.

Called mitochondrial testing, it was different than the standard nuclear testing in that it traced the maternal bloodline, the hardier proteins outside of the nucleus extracted and compared.

Known as the "dry" method, mitochondrial testing was used to compare DNA taken from bones or other human samples where the nucleus of a cell had degraded. Mitochondrial testing was labor intensive and far more expensive, up to ten thousand dollars per test, than a standard nuclear DNA test. By 2003 only a handful of labs in the U.S. had the capability of performing mitochondrial DNA testing. One was the FBI lab in Quantico, Virginia; the others were private companies, including the Bode Technology Group of Springfield, Virginia, the largest private forensic DNA lab in the country.

Known as Bodetech, the scientists there perfected mitochondrial DNA testing in the aftermath of the attacks on the World Trade Center.

Some thirty thousand bones and bone fragments recovered at Ground Zero, labeled DM for Disaster Manhattan, were sent to Bodetech for analysis. Many of the samples had arrived in generally poor condition, having been shattered during the collapse of the buildings or burned under the intense heat.

Initial testing identified a small percentage of the remains.

The scientists and technicians at Bodetech persevered, and the specific testing techniques utilized to extract mitochondrial DNA were significantly enhanced and improved as a result of the thousands of bone samples collected at Ground Zero. The high volume shaved several years off the time needed to perfect mitochondrial testing and Bodetech was producing results in 2002 not expected until 2005. By the end of 2002 Bodetech had completed processing of the Trade Center remains, having processed one thousand bone samples per month and eventually identifying more than six hundred additional victims.

By 2003 the Bode Technology Group, through its parent company, Choice Point, of Atlanta, Georgia, had entered into an agreement with the National Center to perform as many as a dozen mitochondrial DNA tests annually. The work was pro bono, and reserved for investigations by Gerry Nance and his cold-case division.

Nance and his staff had performed admirably since forming the new division, solving 226 out of 409 cold cases, a remarkable 55 percent average. Many children thought lost forever were found alive and reunited with their families. Others were found dead. In each case Nance and his growing staff provided closure for the family of the missing child.

Identification of the long-term missing added yet another feather in the cap of the National Center, which by 2003 was a $25 million federal/private nonprofit enterprise with a sparkling new headquarters in Alexandria, Virginia, and a website that drew 3.5 million hits per day.

Just across the river from Washington, D.C., the five-story building was outfitted with top-of-the-line, state-of-the-art equipment that offered cutting-edge technology in the recovery and location of missing children, including age-progression and facial-reconstruction services to help law enforcement throughout the country.

Since its formation in 1984, the National Center had developed the most complete database of missing children in the country; operated a twenty-four-hour toll-free hotline to report missing children in the United States, Canada, and Mexico; provided complete year-round classes, training programs, and technical assistance to individuals and law enforcement professionals focusing on prevention, investigation, prosecution, and treatment of cases involving missing and exploited children; and despite their own denials became a powerful lobbying force to effect state and federal legislation.

Even the FBI, when faced with a federal investigation involving a missing child, turned to the National Center. Within its five floors thousands of photos of missing children lined every hallway on every wall; large flat-screen television monitors displayed the sad pictures and even sadder stories of the missing. Law enforcement professionals from small and large departments throughout the nation traveled to Alexandria to attend daily training sessions, filling first-floor classrooms and learning new preventive techniques or advances and suggestions in missing-child investigations, their expenses fully absorbed by the National Center.

Forensic services were now available, including handwriting analysis, polygraph services, Automated Fingerprint Identification System database searches, and photo enhancement, including computerized age progression for long-term missing children. Reconstructionists even created facial images for investigators from morgue photographs of unidentified dead children.

The National Center also worked to support the AMBER Alert plan. Created in 1996, the AMBER Alert is an early-warning system designed for broadcasters to offer special "alerts" whenever a child is confirmed to have been abducted. It was named after Amber Hagerman, a nine-year-old girl who was kidnapped and murdered while riding her bike near Dallas, Texas. By 2003, a growing number of states, thirty-three, had enacted AMBER Alert legislation. And thanks to laws that require police to take action whenever receiving a report of a missing person under eighteen years of age, 95 percent of the estimated 800,000 children who go missing every year are recovered.

Despite the National Center's startling success, the number of missing and abused children remained high.

A second NISMART study, released in 2000, revealed that of the 800,000 children reported missing each year, 58,200 had been abducted by nonfamily members. And more than half of those children were sexually abused. Another 115 children were victims of long-term abductions, or stereotypical kidnappings, of which 40 percent were killed each year.

The efforts of the National Center and other groups notwithstanding, violence toward America's children continued unabated.

Nance and the National Center were on the front lines of a never-ending battle, and with each identification of a long dormant missing child, they earned a victory.

Shelley Denman of Kansas City, Missouri, was a mortgage loan underwriter who in 2000 embarked on a search for several missing members of her husband Robert's family.

Robert Denman, sixty, grew up in rural Wisconsin with ten brothers and sisters. A middle sibling, Freda, was living in Independence, Missouri, in 1974 with her husband, Michael Johnson, and two children, Sherri Lynn, four, and Michael, ten months, when they all suddenly disappeared.

Shelley, forty-eight, who had been with Robert since 1991 and married him in 2000, heard the whispers of the missing sister, a story too tragic and too painful to repeat in general conversation. Growing up in Wisconsin, the Denmans were farmers, simple people who had put their faith and trust in the police to find Freda and her children. All that the Denmans knew was that Freda and her family were last seen in November 1974. The Independence police closed the case in June 1975 after learning that Freda's husband, Michael, was really a petty thief and ex-con named Henry Harbison.

Freda met Harbison, a.k.a. Michael Johnson, at a bus stop in Chicago in 1969. Harbison worked in Chicago as a window washer, while Freda was simply passing through. A quick romance resulted in a pregnancy, and Freda gave birth to a daughter, Sherri Lynn, on September 21, 1970. The couple married three years later in December 1973, though Freda remained oblivious to her husband's real identity. She was also unaware, at the time they met, of his violent behavior and criminal record, which dated back to the 1950s.

In 1954 Harbison was convicted of stealing a car and attempting to escape arrest and served time from 1954 to 1959 at Leavenworth and the infamous federal prison at Alcatraz. He was arrested again in Kansas City in 1960 for stealing cars and served nine years. He was released in May 1969.

Following Sherri Lynn's birth, Harbison and Freda moved to Alabama, where he was arrested again in 1971, this time for counterfeiting and forgery. He served twenty-two months in a state prison in Alabama and upon his release married Freda and moved his family into a rented house in Independence, Missouri.

Harbison was a violent man and abusive to his young wife,

who left him for a short time, only to return when he threatened to kill her entire family. In August 1974, Freda told a friend at a local Kmart that her husband was beating her. She said she was scared for her life and if anything should happen to her, the friend should take care of her children.

Three months later, Freda, her husband, and the children were gone. Their landlord didn't report them missing until March 1975. The Independence police investigated and learned that Harbison was wanted by the FBI. Believing that Harbison fled the area with his family, the police closed the case.

The family was never seen or heard from again.

Intrigued, Shelley contacted her sister, Shannon Kaye Stevens, who lived in Dallas, Texas, and worked for a private eye. In 2000, Shelley and Shannon decided to try to solve the mystery of the missing sister and her children.

The novice detectives requested and received a portion of the Independence police file, which offered a number of clues. The latest TV guide found in the house after the family disappeared was dated November 1974. More ominous information included a report of dried blood found on, around, and under a chair in the living room. The blood was identified as type O, the same type as Freda's. The blood had been smeared, as if someone had tried to clean the chair. In the bedroom was a bloodstained pair of women's slacks. There was women's clothing in the closet, while most of the men's and children's clothing were gone.

Also found was an envelope with a return address of a John Price of Iowa City, Iowa. It was a P.O. box that had been opened in August 1972 and closed in 1974.

The address belonged to the Church of the New Song. The police report indicated that Harbison entertained friends at the Independence home, mostly ex-cons who were passing through the area.

Neither Shelley nor Shannon had ever heard of the Church of the New Song, so they called Iowa City, hired a researcher, and waited.

Penal Digest International was a newspaper published in Iowa City, Iowa, and conceived during some very heady, and culturally revolutionary, times. It was 1970 and the Vietnam War, the Black Panthers, and the recent assassinations of Martin Luther King, Jr., and Robert Kennedy all helped to create a radical melting pot that pervaded the national consciousness, particularly in the nation's prisons.

The *PDI* published stories of concern to inmates across the country, including prisoner rights, their accomplishments, and major court cases. The *PDI* also published newsworthy stories, even following the bloody events at the state penitentiary in Attica, New York, in 1971 where inmates took over the prison, an act that ultimately resulted in the deaths of prison guards and inmates.

PDI was, at its core, an underground newspaper that was made available to virtually any inmate in America. Sold by subscription, if an inmate wanted to read *PDI* but had no money, a copy was provided.

The newspaper had its own reporters, sales representatives, and representatives within each prison. Those who took an interest in *PDI* were commonly jailhouse-lawyer types who turned to the prison library as a means to escape the utter boredom of prison life.

The staff, which started with two people, grew to twenty-five, nearly all the staffers ex-convicts. Joe Grant, an ex-con who served time in prison for forgery, was the publisher and founder of *PDI*.

Some fifteen hundred miles away at the federal prison in Atlanta, another movement began in concert with the *PDI*.

Harry Theriault was a violent career criminal serving a lengthy sentence in 1970 at USP Atlanta for bank robbery. He often split his time between solitary confinement and the prison library, where he took an interest in religion and the United States Constitution. During one lengthy stint in solitary an idea took hold, and that was the creation of a "religion" for inmates supported by inmates. Theriault named it the Church of the New Song, or CONS. With the help of several other inmates, including Jerry Dorrough, who was serving ten years for bank robbery, Theriault filed a petition on June 18, 1970, in the federal district court for the Northern District of Georgia seeking recognition of the Church of the New Song.

Theriault sought the same rights afforded other inmates who were Protestant or Catholic, and also introduced "communion" to his new church. Only instead of wafers and wine, Theriault suggested steak and Harvey's Bristol Cream.

Theriault's petition included 165 signatures from inmates at USP Atlanta.

Soon after filing the petition for recognition of his new church, prison officials decided to nip the church in the bud and Theriault was transferred to the USP in Marion, Illinois. Only the plan backfired. Theriault spread the word of his church at Marion while Jerry Dorrough and others carried it on in Atlanta. News of the church spread throughout prisons across the country and instantly gained new members. Theriault was returned to USP Atlanta in 1971, where he acted as lead counsel and the principal witness at hearings to determine recognition for his church.

On February 25, 1972, Theriault and his followers earned a stunning victory when a district judge ruled that the Church of the New Song was a legitimate religion and inmates were to be afforded the right to gather.

The decision shocked prison officials, who transferred

Theriault on March 3, 1972, to USP at La Tuna, Texas. Three days later the first "church" service was held at USP Atlanta and attended by six hundred inmates who gathered in the prison auditorium.

Penal Digest International reported on the service and spread the gospel of the new church through its pages. Joe Grant became a crucial member of the Church of the New Song and continued to report on the Church and events surrounding the new "religion" through the *PDI*.

Inmates in Atlanta and throughout the country earned a temporary victory, but the Federal Bureau of Prisons fought the new church, and legal battles ensued for two years before the church met its ultimate, and predictable, demise. Still, the damage had been done. From 1970 through 1974 inmates were connected by the comraderie offered by the Church of the New Song and *PDI*, and upon their release many ex-cons would find themselves drifting throughout the country, many finding refuge at *PDI* headquarters in Iowa City, where Joe Grant provided a place to sleep and food to eat as they passed through.

Living in Iowa City and working for *PDI* was John Price, another ex-con from Mobile, Alabama, who served time for possession of an unregistered shotgun at USP Atlanta in 1971 and 1972. Price was one of the original organizers of the Church of the New Song, which by now had opened an office in Iowa City. The Church also had flophouses throughout the country, one of which was in south Chicago.

Letters written by Henry Harbison and later recovered by Shelley and Shannon revealed Harbison's interests and participation in the Church of the New Song. Harbison knew Jerry Dorrough from a previous stint at USP Atlanta in 1968. Harbison was also friendly with John Price. But it wasn't clear how they met and, despite the best efforts of the sisters, the connections ended there.

By January 2003, Shelley and Shannon hit a dead end in their search for Freda and her two children. All they knew was that Henry Harbison, his wife, Freda, and their two children had disappeared, and that Henry was an active member of the Church of the New Song.

The Independence, Missouri, police offered the sisters little assistance aside from providing the file on the case. The sisters' research into the Church of the New Song provided some interesting clues, but little else. With nowhere else to go they turned to the Doe Network.

During the course of their search the sisters had turned to the Internet for help and found several websites devoted to missing persons. The best of the bunch was the Doe Network.

Created in 1999 by Jennifer Marra, a Michigan woman who took an interest in missing-persons cases, Marra began to post photos and file information on her new website. She soon attracted queries from others interested in the plight of missing persons in America, particularly members of a cold case chat group who met regularly on the Yahoo! website.

The Doe Network posted a photo of the missing person, along with pertinent details, which were confirmed by law enforcement surrounding the disappearance, and a contact number for anyone with information.

By 2001 Marra bowed out and the site was taken over by several members of the cold-case chat group from Yahoo!. By 2002 the Doe Network had attracted the attention of law enforcement and had, though unintentionally, become a vital resource in the search for missing persons. The Doe Network had 277 members and received more than one thousand hits per month. It listed 2,220 missing persons and operated out of the homes of the network of volunteers that spanned around the globe.

Shelley and Shannon found the Doe Network while surfing the web, and decided to contact one of the volunteers, Angela Ellis, to share their story.

Ellis immediately listed Freda, Sherri Lynn, and Michael on the Doe Network, posting photos of all, along with Henry Harbison.

They then searched through the Doe Network files, and Shelley and Shannon and Angela made a startling discovery: A listing for a Sharon Marshall and her son Michael, along with photos of both. The little girl sitting on Franklin Floyd's lap in a distant photo from the mid-1970s resembled the equally distant photos of Sherri Lynn. They weren't exact matches, but familiar enough for Shelley to contact Ellis and tell her of the suspected match. Ellis had already seen it herself, and she contacted Gerry Nance, asking if he'd talk to Shelley Denman. Nance said fine. Ellis forwarded Nance's e-mail address, and Shelly responded, explaining her story. Before speaking with Shelley in March 2003, Nance called the Independence police for background and was told there was no point in pursuing this, that Henry Harbison and his family had left of their own free will.

Nance relayed that information to Shelley, and added that in order for the National Center to become involved in the investigation he needed the police to input Sherri Lynn into the NCIC database, but the Independence police refused.

"Did their response blow us out of the water?" asked Shelley.

"Pretty much," replied Nance, who said that the Independence police chief, Bill Trotter, provided information on the case that was pretty convincing that Sharon Marshall could not be Sherri Lynn.

But Nance wasn't convinced, and he decided to take matters into his own hands.

During the summer of 2002, I received an e-mail from an acquaintance who was combing through the Doe Network website when she happened upon the photo of a cheerless little girl sitting on the lap of an equally cheerless man in a suit.

Described below the disturbing photo was a horrendous story: a convicted felon, fugitive, and pedophile named Franklin Floyd who apparently kidnapped the girl sitting in his lap, raised her as his daughter, later married her, and presumably killed her and her young son. The girl, who had many names during her short life, had never been identified, despite the dogged efforts of several police agencies and the FBI.

Making the story even more heartbreaking was the photo: There was no doubt, given the pained expression of the girl, something was terribly wrong.

Intrigued, I researched the story for several months, my interest not necessarily in Franklin Floyd but in the girl, who was known as Suzanne as a child, Sharon as a teenager, and Tonya at the time of her death.

For now, we'll call her Sharon.

By October 2002, I had spoken to several people familiar with the case, including retired FBI Special Agent Joe Fitzpatrick. His feelings about Sharon, Floyd, and Michael were still very raw, even seven years after Michael's kidnapping.

It was clear after but a few minutes on the phone that the case touched Fitzpatrick in a way no other investigation had during his lengthy career. He was cautious, talking to a reporter, but there was no doubt that he was pained, particularly with the inability to discover Sharon's true identity.

Terry Magaro shared that pain. The former teacher at Forest Park High School still lived in the Atlanta area and spoke admiringly of Sharon, describing her beauty and brilliance in the classroom. Yet Magaro was haunted by the events that transpired so many years ago, and she was still unable to explain why Sharon kept her terrible secrets to herself, never trusting anyone to help.

In November, following Floyd's conviction for the murder of Cheryl Commesso, I contacted his attorney in St. Petersburg, Florida, and requested an interview with his client.

Several days later Floyd called from the Pinellas County prison. I told him I was considering writing a book, though I didn't give him too many details during our twenty-minute conversation. He agreed to talk to me at a later date, though he told me in no uncertain terms that he would never reveal Sharon's true identity or the fate of her son Michael. He also denied killing Cheryl Commesso. Floyd was unfocused and rambled throughout the conversation, in one breath saying he wasn't such a bad guy ("I'm no Ted Bundy," he said) then in the next breath he'd say "no body, no crime," indicating there was more to Franklin Floyd.

My next call was to the National Center for Missing & Exploited Children, which had become the preeminent authority on missing children in America.

After several phone calls I was directed to Gerry Nance.

Nance was somewhat familiar with the Floyd case since the National Center had an open file on young Michael Hughes, but he was unfamiliar with the details. Nance was a quick study, and after several weeks was up to speed on Floyd and Sharon Marshall and, like Joe Fitzpatrick, Terry Magaro, and others, was both perplexed by and admired Sharon.

Through Nance I learned more about the National Center and received an overview of missing children in America.

By February 2003, I had begun my research in earnest and traveled to St. Petersburg to visit Franklin Floyd.

Floyd had remained at the Pinellas County prison longer

than expected as he awaited his transfer to death row at the state prison in Raiford. When I arrived on February 18 the deputies from the sheriff's office took me inside to a room reserved for inmates to meet their attorneys. There were no windows in the rectangular room and but one door. Inside, a long table filled the room. Floyd stood behind the table, surrounded by several deputies, his hands cuffed behind his back. He didn't look like much, and upon first glance I was struck by his nonthreatening appearance. He was near sixty years old and appeared weak, his skin pale white. Floyd brought paperwork with him, perhaps six inches thick, and asked for and received permission to have his handcuffed hands in front of him so he could flip through the pages.

When I arrived at the prison I hoped for enough time with Floyd, maybe twenty minutes, to describe him and write down some quick responses to several questions. Instead I spent four hours with Floyd, alone, with a guard outside the door.

Like he did during his interviews with police over the years, Floyd spoke without interruption and became irritated whenever I tried to get him to pause so I could ask a question. I let him talk, which he did for ninety minutes, and he explained his life, from his days at the Baptist home through prison and on the run with Sharon.

As he did during our phone conversation in November, Floyd reiterated that he would not discuss Sharon's true identity, the whereabouts of Michael, or the Cheryl Commesso murder.

But during the interview he touched on all.

He was complimentary of Sharon and recalled how she called for her "daddy" as she was transported to the hospital after she was struck.

"That broke my heart. In her unconscious state she called out to me to help," said Floyd.

And like a proud "parent" he relished her accomplishments in high school as he pointed to copies of her report cards.

"I'm telling you straight out, she was a perfect child. Just like an angel from heaven. She didn't complain, she didn't whine, she didn't cry, she didn't beg. I don't mean she didn't get her feelings hurt when I was going to leave her at that orphan's home. I'm saying she was dependable, she cleaned, she loved everybody, she loved God, she had faith in Santa Claus, she defended me, she protected me, she tried to find me work then got on them for not paying me. She was so special that when she saw me she made up her mind that I would be her daddy. I told her I can't do it, I don't know nothing about girls. But I said I will take you because I don't want him to strangle you. I knew he was going to do that. I heard that."

Floyd wouldn't tell me who "him" was, nor would he explain anything of his other statements, which didn't make much sense.

Included among his paperwork was a photo album with pictures of himself and Sharon at a St. Louis Cardinals baseball game sometime in the early 1980s.

"I was a Cardinals fan," said Floyd as he flipped through the album, pointing to photos of Sharon holding Michael when he was an infant. The mother and son appeared to be close, with Sharon holding her son face-to-face, smiling at him while Michael returned the smile with equal affection.

Floyd's demeanor changed as he gazed at Michael's picture. He talked about how much he loved the boy, then dismissed Sharon, saying "I raised her and all, but I was never really attached to her. I was attached to Michael."

Floyd claimed to have given the boy to a shadowy underground group who took him out of the country, first to

Europe then later to South America. Communication with the group, said Floyd, was accomplished through advertisements in *USA Today*.

Floyd pulled out letters he had written in his jail cell to Michael, rambling declarations of love for the boy and promises to one day reunite.

He returned to his stack of papers, and he changed the subject from Sharon and Michael to Cheryl Commesso.

Having represented himself during his trial, Floyd was given access to all the prosecution files and exhibits given to the defense via discovery. Amongst the paperwork were the startling and horrible photos of Cheryl Commesso as she was being tortured.

Floyd proclaimed his innocence, and spoke about Commesso without any regard to the suffering endured by the young woman. Instead he argued that the FBI illegally "cropped" the photos, and they should have been ruled inadmissible in court.

"I was framed, I tell ya," said Floyd.

He pushed his paperwork across the table. Included were official letters from the Baptist home and from the various prisons where he had been incarcerated, along with family information, court documents, and records of Sharon's schoolwork, including report cards and test scores.

It was, quite literally, a treasure trove of information, and I left with copies of all his paperwork, some of which was of great value and included in these pages.

A week later Floyd was transferred to death row at Raisford.

The following day I sat down with Robert Schock and Mark Deasaro.

Schock had retired from the St. Petersburg police and was now working for the State Attorney's office. He was a soft-spoken, gentle man who was kind enough to take me to all the important sites, including the area where Cheryl Commesso's remains were recovered.

I was also provided with interviews, court transcripts, and other valuable information, without which I could not have told the story of their investigation. I visited St. Petersburg a second time in March 2003, and it was there I learned that a new lead had developed in the search for Sharon's identity.

I was told that a family from Missouri searching for several missing relatives made a connection that possibly involved Franklin Floyd. It had to do with the husband of the missing relative, who may have served time in prison with Floyd. The family had recently contacted Gerry Nance at the National Center. I called Nance and asked him if he could put me in touch with the family. Nance said he'd get back to me.

From St. Petersburg I flew to Atlanta, Georgia, where I interviewed several of Sharon's teachers from Forest Park High School. Their feelings and memories, some seventeen years after Sharon graduated, were unmistakable and vivid, and served to reinforce that Sharon was indeed special.

It was in Atlanta where I met Jennifer Fisher.

Jennifer had married for a second time, her name now Jennifer McElhannon. She had four children and was living and working in her hometown, serving as the head of IT purchasing for a large media company. I initially spent six hours with Jennifer, and she recalled every last detail of her friendship with the girl she knew as Sharon Marshall. Jennifer gave life to Sharon, her memories clear and vivid. Jennifer also provided me with a folder full of paperwork, several photos and two letters from Sharon.

Two weeks later, in early April, I visited with Gerry Nance at the National Center for Missing & Exploited Children. I had spoken with Nance regularly since our first phone contact in November, and I came to appreciate his knowledge and his help. I knew nothing about missing kids in

America, yet Nance obliged me, answering every question that came his way.

He also put me in touch with Shelley Denman and her sister, Shannon Kaye Stevens.

The two women had searched since 2000 for Shelley's missing sister-in-law, Freda Denman Johnson, and her two children, Sherri Lynn and Michael, who disappeared in 1974.

The sisters had provided photos of the family to the Doe Network, and upon first glance there was a physical resemblance between Sherri Lynn and Sharon. They had the same style hair, with bangs on the forehead, though Sherri Lynn was a brunette and Sharon a blond. The timeline seemed to fit, with the family last seen in November 1974 and Floyd first appearing with Sharon, then known as Suzanne Davis, in 1975 in Oklahoma City.

Prior to arriving at the National Center I had several conversations with Shelley and Shannon, and became very interested in their developing theory that perhaps Franklin Floyd met Freda's husband, Henry Harbison, in prison. All the sisters knew was that Henry was an apparent member of the Church of the New Song, and that he knew another church member, another ex-con named John Price.

The sisters had retrieved Harbison's prison record from Alcatraz, which was a matter of public record given that he served time there in the 1950s. All records of Alcatraz inmates, along with any other incarcerations, were now part of the national archives. Those records indicated that Harbison and Floyd did not meet in prison, having served their sentences at different facilities. It was a setback, but there was other information that strengthened the belief that Sharon Marshall could really be Sherri Lynn Johnson.

Jennifer Fisher McElhannon allowed me to take her folder of papers and letters and photos of Sharon, two of which were taken during the summer of 1986 during Sharon's emotional return to Atlanta.

Sharon bore a striking resemblance to Freda Denman, whose photo had been posted on the Doe Network.

In early April I visited the National Center for Missing & Exploited Children. I spent two days there and came away with a profound sense of admiration for the people who worked there and their commitment to missing children.

Nance took the two photos of Sharon given to me by Jennifer Fisher McElhannon and had them analyzed by his forensics imaging department. While not definitive, their conclusion was they could not discount that Sharon was Sherri Lynn given the clear likeness between Freda and Sharon.

In addition, the imaging specialists compared photos of a four-year-old Sherri Lynn prior to her disappearance and of a five- or six-year-old Sharon soon after she came into custody of Franklin Floyd. Again, there were no discernable features that would discount the possibility that they were one and the same.

Given the resources at the National Center, including their relationship with Bodetech labs to provide DNA testing, I told Nance that Sharon's old friend Jennifer Fisher gave me two envelopes sent to her by Sharon in the 1980s, the original stamps still affixed to the envelopes. Would it be possible to secure Sharon's DNA from the stamps?

Nance believed it was possible, but to move forward with any testing he first had to have Sherri Lynn Johnson listed with the National Center. Since the Independence, Missouri, police closed the case in 1975, Sherri Lynn had never been entered into NCIC. The sisters, Shelley and Shannon, asked the Independence police to place Sherri Lynn in NCIC and contact the National Center for assistance, which would give the National Center jurisdiction to open a file. The Independence police refused.

Convinced that he was on to something, Nance broke protocol and opened a file on Sherri Lynn anyway.

I had also begun reviewing the paperwork given to me by Floyd during our interview in February and found a letter from the Oklahoma firm that harvested and donated Sharon's organs the day she died in 1990.

The firm still had Sharon's file on record, along with her blood type, which was A negative. According to the sisters, Henry Harbison had A positive blood, while Freda had O blood, making it possible to have a child with A negative blood. Since we couldn't discount Sherri Lynn by her blood type, the mystery deepened.

In May I traveled to Oklahoma City and Tulsa, and spent nearly two weeks interviewing a host of people, including Joe Fitzpatrick, Mark Yancey, Ed Kumiega, and several of Sharon's former coworkers at Passions.

I was cautiously optimistic that perhaps we were on the right road since the National Center was zeroing in on Henry Harbison and Freda Denman as Sharon's real parents, given the blood type, physical resemblance, and time of her disappearance.

I shared the information with Joe Fitzpatrick, whose idea for an interview was sitting in a fishing boat on a small lake surrounded by snakes and other interesting creatures. We later spoke at length at his home, and Fitzpatrick was helpful and earnest, though somewhat guarded when it came to revealing details of the inner workings of the FBI.

Fitzpatrick was still very much interested in the Floyd case, having testified at his murder trial eight months earlier in St. Petersburg, Florida, and took great interest in the new information involving Henry Harbison, someone whom he had never heard about. He asked to be informed should something develop.

Mark Yancey and Ed Kumiega were also interested in the new lead, the case having affected them as much as anyone. The two prosecutors were very helpful in relaying the events surrounding the Michael Hughes kidnapping trial and provided access to the paperwork and information required to accurately depict the events that transpired before, during, and after the trial.

Like Fitzpatrick and others, the mystery surrounding Sharon Marshall gnawed at them. I also interviewed Gary Homan, Floyd's old parole officer, and the Bean family, who were still haunted by the loss of Michael.

In Tulsa I met Karen Parsley, a.k.a. Connie, and Lavernia Watkins, a.k.a. Bambi. We sat in a restaurant for several hours as they shared their stories of Sharon. They knew her for less than a year, yet Sharon left an indelible imprint on each of the women. Like everyone else who ever met Sharon or heard her story, they wanted to know her real identity.

Both Connie and Bambi were still employed at Passions, though now well into their thirties they had given up dancing. We visited the dank club, the trailer park where Sharon and Floyd had lived, and Sharon's grave. They knew Sharon as Tonya, and the simple, marble marker bore that name.

The two Sharon letters were forwarded to the National Center in June, and all concerned, including Shelley, Shannon, and Gerry Nance, would wait through the summer for an answer.

In the interim, research on the Church of the New Song, along with the prison records of several church leaders, revealed all had been at the federal prison in Atlanta the same time as Franklin Floyd, among them Jerry Dorrough, John Price, and founder Harry Theriault.

Floyd arrived at USP Atlanta in November 1971 to serve out his time for the 1962 escape attempt at the federal prison in Chillicothe, Ohio. Floyd was there in March 1972, when the Church of the New Song held its first "service" at the Atlanta prison with six hundred inmates in attendance.

During the summer I contacted Joe Grant, former editor of the *Penal Digest International*, who said he did not know or remember Floyd. I also found Jerry Dorrough, who was living in Texas. Dorrough visited a public library to go on-line and pulled up the Doe Network website. He didn't recognize Franklin Floyd, but did remember Henry Harbison, with whom he served time together in the 1960s. He described Harbison as a "good guy," though somewhat intense.

Dorrough thought he remembered the name John Price but wasn't sure.

Price was said to be a deeply troubled and violent man who took an interest in the "church" while at USP Atlanta in 1971 and 1972. He was released from prison in 1972 and ended up at the "church" headquarters in Iowa City, where he lived and worked fixing grain silos.

While delving further into the Church of the New Song, on July 17 we received some very encouraging news from Gerry Nance: Lab technicians at Bodetech were successful in extracting DNA from one of the stamps on Sharon's envelopes.

With what was believed to be Sharon's DNA in hand, Nance moved quickly. He sent out a retrieval kit to one of Freda's sisters to complete a mitochondrial DNA test since the DNA that had been extracted from the stamp was too degraded to perform nuclear DNA testing.

To complete the test, Bodetech needed a sample from a maternal member of the Denman family, and received permission to obtain a "swab" from a sister. A kit was sent out, the sister took a Q-tip, put it into her mouth and rubbed it against the inside of her cheek, then placed it in a clear package and sent it back to the National Center.

Again, we waited.

In the interim the search continued to connect the dots between Floyd and Henry Harbison, and the dots had begun to connect quickly.

By September the story came into focus.

In November 1971 Franklin Floyd was transferred from the state prison in Reidsville, Georgia, to the federal prison at Atlanta. Floyd became a regular at the prison library, studying the law and meeting other jailhouse-lawyer types, nearly all of whom were involved in the new Church of the New Song.

John Price was already at USP Atlanta, having arrived in August 1971 on a gun charge.

Price and Floyd were at the prison when the Church was officially recognized in February 1972, and both attended the first official gathering of the new church in March 1972.

John Price was paroled later in 1972 and moved to Iowa City, where he took part in a number of church activities. Price was six-feet-one, about 190 pounds, and strong. He had a slight southern accent and was said to be quite the ladies' man. But Price was also considered dangerous and, like most other ex-cons who had served lengthy prison sentences in tough prisons, he was a survivor, capable of taking care of himself and striking first if he believed he was in danger.

Though it's not clear, somewhere along the line Price connected with another dangerous individual, Henry Harbison, a.k.a. Michael Johnson. Price wrote at least one letter to Harbison, an Iowa City P.O. box listed as the return address, the same P.O. box used by the Church of the New Song.

Harbison always had "guests" staying at his Independence home, men he introduced to neighbors as his "brothers."

The sisters, Shelley and Shannon, learned about Harbison and Price through the Independence police file, and also from Joe Grant, whom they tracked down in Phoenix, Arizona, and traded several e-mails with.

During one exchange, Grant relayed how he recently received a visit from Harry Theriault, the founder of the Church of the New Song.

Theriault spent most of the 1970s in solitary confinement, the effects of which led to what Grant believed was mental instability. Theriault believed he was a "prophet" and went by the name of Shiloh. During Theriault's visit to Arizona, Grant said he asked him about John Price, but Theriault was in no mental condition to remember much of anything.

The sisters also learned of a letter written by Theriault to Jerry Dorrough in the early 1970s, with Theriault referring to Price saying, "The Bishop has ordered Brother John Price, S.R.M. to stay out of the Habazinian. It's spiritual stuff on a physical plane." (According to Jerry Dorrough, S.R.M. meant Special Revelation Minister, a title concocted by Theriault and given to most members of the Church of the New Song.)

Grant then sent an e-mail to Shelley, saying he was "thinking about the missing kids" and that Freda was "probably murdered."

"Brother John [Price] was capable of such acts," wrote Grant.

There was no mention of Harbison, though the sisters were very aware of his violent reputation, his threats to the Denman family, and the physical abuse he inflicted on his young wife, Freda, who was twenty-seven when she disappeared. Given that Harbison was wanted by the FBI at the time the entire family disappeared, along with the blood found at the Independence home, which the sisters learned matched Freda's blood type, the sisters believed that Freda had been killed and the children taken away. By whom, they weren't sure.

In late September 2003, Gerry Nance called with some astonishing news: Initial results from the DNA testing revealed that Sharon's DNA, retrieved from the stamp affixed to the letter sent so long ago to Jennifer Fisher, appeared to be consistent with that of the Denman family.

A definitive answer would come soon, perhaps in weeks, said Nance.

The added time allowed for further investigation and conjecture concerning Harbison, Price, and Floyd. Given the evidence in hand, it appears that Henry Harbison and Franklin Floyd may have met somewhere near Chicago. Both were in and around the city at the same time, the Independence police having tracked Harbison to Rensselaer, Indiana, just southeast of Chicago, after he wrote several bad checks. Harbison was on the run from the FBI, and if Freda was killed back in Independence, carrying two children with him was a liability.

Floyd was known to be in Freedom Village, Illinois, also just south of Chicago. Both were members of the Church of the New Song, which had a flophouse in Chicago run by a *PDI* photographer where wayward ex-cons and church members would be given a warm meal and place to spend the night. Among the several stories told by Floyd about gaining custody of Sharon was one where her father gave him the child, saying he couldn't care for her.

Three weeks later, in mid-October, Nance called again. Only this time the news was not good: Further testing on the DNA sample proved fruitless. Technicians at Bodetech found cross-contamination coming from any number of sources, including the glue from the stamp and the handling of the letter over the years, which precluded them from further examination.

All we would get from the stamp would be a host of unanswered questions.

Still, Nance was encouraged and emboldened by the initial DNA results and decided to "pull out all the stops."

Nance began the process of obtaining permission to obtain DNA samples from Sharon's third child, a daughter adopted by a family in New Orleans. Nance also contacted Dr. Henry Lee, a noted forensic pathologist in Connecticut, to obtain a tissue sample taken from Sharon at the time of her autopsy in 1990. Sharon's organs helped more than a dozen people improve and lengthen their lives considerably, many of whom are still alive today. Lee's office obtained Sharon's tissue sample in 1995 in a bid to identify a missing person.

In February 2004, I visited Franklin Floyd again and, surprisingly, he acknowledged he knew Henry Harbison (from a 1974 photo) but insisted he "didn't want to talk about it." He also dismissed the suggestion that Sharon was Sherri Lynn Johnson. The mystery would unfold three months later when it was learned that, unbeknownst to all, the Oklahoma City police had two vials of Sharon's blood and hair samples in storage, taken when she died in 1990.

In May 2004, the samples were shipped to Bodetech for analysis and DNA testing confirmed that Sharon Marshall was not Sherri Lynn Johnson. The news was deflating to all who worked on this lead for over a year and served to reinforce the extreme difficulty in searching for the long-term missing. But all was not lost. Floyd's disclosure that he knew Henry Harbison raised questions about what role, if any, he had in the disappearance of Freda Johnson and her children. More importantly, Nance now had a profile of Sharon's DNA, a crucial development. The DNA profile will be input into a national database for comparison against other DNA profiles collected across the country. Nance firmly believes that someone searching for a long-lost little girl will come forward, their DNA compared, and the mystery of Sharon Marshall's true identity will finally be revealed.

AFTERWORD

In the weeks after the September 2004 publication of the hardcover edition of *A Beautiful Child*, I received hundreds of heartfelt letters and e-mails from readers who were traumatized, saddened, and angered by Sharon's story.

Among those were notes from former classmates at Forest Park High School, many familiar with the story but unaware of the tragic details. All shared good memories, including Sharon's tenderness, her photographic memory, and the ease with which she navigated through her schoolwork.

Also e-mailing from Atlanta was a woman whose daughter was a classmate and friend of Sharon's. The woman told me that Sharon and "Warren" were at her home in November 1985 celebrating Thanksgiving and, like the accounts from the Fisher family, this family embraced Sharon, though all considered "Warren" to be an oddball.

But again, like the Fishers, no one ever thought or considered that something so sinister and diabolical was afoot.

I also received an e-mail from a man who lives in Cincinnati, Ohio. He met Sharon during a visit to the Mons Venus in Tampa in March 1988, and then again upon a return visit that summer. They exchanged lengthy letters, and Sharon wrote of one day attending college and working in the aerospace field. She also wrote that she was nineteen years old and born in Detroit, Michigan.

The man was so taken with Sharon that, sixteen years later, he still had her four-page letter, which was written in blue ink on pink paper and in pristine condition.

He contacted me after he happened to walk by a bookstore and, quite innocently, noticed the cover of *A Beautiful Child*, which features Sharon's photo. He immediately recognized her, ran inside and bought a copy. In his e-mail he described Sharon as a "bright, lovely young woman who seemed quite out of place at the Mons Venus."

Word of the book and Sharon's story circulated throughout the country, and the world, and within several months there were more than 20,000 hits on my website, www. mattbirkbeck.com, with readers from as far away as the UK and Italy searching for more information, and trading their own thoughts and opinions in the forum section.

There were, they wrote, so many questions left unanswered, most of which centered on Sharon herself. Why, they asked, didn't Sharon tell someone about her predicament and seek help?

It's a question I thought I addressed in the book, but given the number of queries, was quite certain I did not.

To help find a more definitive and satisfying answer I turned to Dr. Robi Ludwig, a psychotherapist and regular commentator on various programs such as *Larry King Live*, *Nancy Grace*, and *Oprah*, who, after reading *A Beautiful Child*, provided a clear and concise analysis.

Sharon's relationship with Floyd was all about power, says Ludwig. Floyd had it. Sharon did not. She had been stripped at a very young and tender age of any power to make decisions, thus becoming totally dependent on Floyd. And given the nature of their relationship, in which Floyd was, in fact, the only parental figure Sharon had ever known, he was her only constant in what was a dysfunctional and dangerous life, which produced a somewhat strange and even bizarre mixture of loyalty and fear.

It was that combination, says Ludwig, that kept Sharon from telling anyone.

Perhaps most important for Sharon, says Ludwig, is that her life with Floyd was all about survival.

She was an abused child and abused wife all wrapped into one, yet through her inner strength she found a way to survive—and excel—under horrendous conditions. And as a testament to that inner strength and courage, Ludwig believes that, after all those years with Floyd, by attempting to leave Floyd, Sharon was, in large measure, finally doing something for herself.

And as further testament to her courage, says Ludwig, Sharon was not only acting for herself, but was also trying to save her son, Michael. She was acting like a mother.

Despite the odds, and facing almost certain death, Sharon's attempt to finally break free from Floyd's grasp and control was her final emancipation, says Ludwig.

Perhaps the one single question most asked, and pursued, is he one concerning Sharon's identity. Soon after publication, suggestions came forward via e-mail and letters, particularly from those involved in searching for missing persons via Internet sites such as The Doe Network (www. doenetwork.org) and Websleuths (www.websleuths.com).

The first and most promising lead was Jennifer Klein, a three-year-old kidnapped in 1974 from a campsite in Moab, Utah. Klein had a cowlick, as did Sharon, and Floyd was in the region at the time and believed to have broken into the

Boulder, Colorado, home of his sister Tommye. Given that Floyd was camping during the week before he kidnapped Michael, the lead developed strong interest.

Two other leads came directly from law enforcement. One retired detective from the Toronto, Canada, area was keen on Cheryl Hanson, a seven-year-old who disappeared near her home in Aurora, Ontario, in 1974. Another detective from San Jose, California, was investigating the case of Cynthia Sumpter, a child who also disappeared in 1974.

In all three cases, Sharon's DNA profile, taken from the blood delivered by the Oklahoma City police, was sent to test against the DNA profile of family members of each of the missing girls.

The California Department of Justice lab handled the testing of Jennifer Klein. In December 2004 word came that the test proved negative.

By mid-March 2005 testing had yet to be completed on Cheryl Hanson or Cynthia Sumpter.

But that same month there was a curious and disturbing development concerning Sharon's blood samples: Questions arose concerning the validity of the blood, specifically, whether it was really Sharon's blood. During their investigation following the kidnapping of Michael Hughes, the FBI in Oklahoma City searched for but was told no DNA evidence from Sharon existed. Authorities also questioned why, if it was indeed Sharon's blood, it had been held in custody for so many years after her death. With Floyd in jail, and no open investigation, samples are usually thrown away.

Was there a mix-up of some kind? No one knows for sure but officials are investigating and while as of this writing the answers still are not clear, the DNA testing continues under the premise that the blood is indeed Sharon's.

Matt Birkbeck
March 2005

Sources

So many people involved in this story never met Sharon Marshall yet were deeply touched by her story and were very agreeable to sharing their experiences. This book is based on interviews with those people, and on countless pages of personal documents. I also had access to thousands of pages of interviews and notes from police files in St. Petersburg, Florida, and Oklahoma City, Oklahoma, and court documents from Franklin Floyd's federal trial in Oklahoma City and his subsequent murder trial in Pinellas County, Florida.

Dialogue found in *A Beautiful Child* was culled either directly from those interviews and notes or from personal recollections of the participants.

ACKNOWLEDGMENTS

Writing this book was not easy, and given the subject matter and research required to tell the story in depth, it simply could not have been written without the help of the following people, to whom I am deeply indebted:

Robert Schock, investigator with the Florida State Attorneys Office; Mark Deasaro, St. Petersburg, Florida Police Department; Mark Ginan, Corporal, Pinellas County, Florida, Sheriff's Office; Bobbi Sue Bacha; Jennifer McElhannon; Terry Magaro; Karen Parsley; Lavernia Watkins; Ed Kumiega and Mark Yancey, Assistant United States Attorneys, Oklahoma City, Oklahoma; Joe Fitzpatrick, FBI retired; Merle and Ernest Bean; and Gerry Nance, Cold Case Manager of the National Center for Missing & Exploited Children, Alexandria, Virginia.

I would also like to thank Paul Moses, a journalist and associate professor of journalism at Brooklyn College, and Helen Yanulus, a journalist and adjunct professor of English at Northampton Community College, Tannersville, Pennsylvania, for their continued support and invaluable guidance; and my agent, Andrew Stuart, of the Stuart Agency, and Natalee Rosenstein at Berkley Books, who believed in this project and in me.

And finally, thanks to my mom, Patricia Birkbeck; and to my understanding wife, Donna, who held down the home front caring for our two sons, Matthew and Christopher, while her husband was off traveling throughout the country following a story.

RESOURCES

NATIONAL CONTACTS FOR MISSING PERSONS

National Center for Missing &
Exploited Children
Charles B. Wang International
Children's Building
699 Prince Street
Alexandria, VA 22314-3175
(703) 274-3900
(800) THE-LOST
Website: www.missingkids.org

The Nation's Missing Children
Organization/Center for
Missing Adults
2432 West Peoria Avenue, Suite
1286
Phoenix, AZ 85029
(602) 944-1768
(800) 690-FIND
Website: www.nmco.org

The Doe Network
Website: www.doenetwork.org

CLEARINGHOUSES FOR MISSING CHILDREN IN THE U.S. AND CANADA

ALABAMA

Alabama Bureau of
Investigation/Missing
Children
P.O. Box 1511
Montgomery, AL 36102-1511
(800) 228-7688
Website: www.dps.state.al.us/abi

ALASKA

Alaska State Troopers
Missing Persons Clearinghouse
5700 East Tudor Road
Anchorage, AK 99507
(907) 269-5497
(800) 478-9333 (in-state only)
FAX: (907) 338-7243

ARIZONA

Arizona Department of Public
Safety
Criminal Investigations
Research Unit
P.O. Box 6638
Phoenix, AZ 85005
(602) 223-2158
FAX: (602) 223-2911

ARKANSAS

Office of Attorney General
Missing Children Services
Program
323 Center Street, Suite 1100
Little Rock, AR 72201
(501) 682-1020

(800) 448-3014 (in-state only)
FAX: (501) 682-6704
Website: http://www.ag.state.ar.us

CALIFORNIA

California Department of
Justice
Missing/Unidentified Persons
Unit
P.O. Box 903387
Sacramento, CA 94203-3870
(916) 227-3290
(800) 222-3463 (nationwide)
FAX: (916) 227-3270
Website: http://ag.ca.gov/missing

COLORADO

Colorado Bureau of
Investigation
Missing Person/Children Unit
710 Kipling Street, Suite 200
Denver, CO 80215
(303) 239-4251
FAX: (303) 239-5788

CONNECTICUT

Connecticut State Police
Missing Persons
P.O. Box 2794
Middletown, CT 06457-9294
(860) 685-8190
(800) 367-5678 (in-state only)
FAX: (860) 685-8346

DELAWARE

Delaware State Police
State Bureau of Identification
1407 N. DuPont Hwy.
Dover, DE 19903
(302) 739-5883

DISTRICT OF COLUMBIA

D.C. Metropolitan Police Dept.
Missing Persons/Youth Division
1700 Rhode Island Avenue, N.E.
Washington, DC 20018
(202) 576-6768
FAX: (202) 576-6561

FLORIDA

Florida Department of Law
  Enforcement
Missing Children Information
  Clearinghouse
P.O. Box 1489
Tallahassee, FL 32302
(850) 410-8585
(888) 356-4774 (nationwide)
FAX: (850) 410-8599
Website:
  http://www.fdle.state.fl.us

GEORGIA

Georgia Bureau of Investigation
Intelligence Unit
P.O. Box 370808
Decatur, GA 30037
(404) 244-2554
(800) 282-6564 (nationwide)
FAX: (404) 244-2798

HAWAII

Missing Child Center—Hawaii
Department of the Attorney
  General
235 S. Beretania Street, Suite 206
Honolulu, HI 96813
(808) 586-1449
State Office Tower
FAX: (808) 586-1424
Hotline: (808) 753-9797
Website:
  http://launch.hgea.org/hsc

IDAHO

Idaho Bureau of Criminal
  Identification
Missing Persons Clearinghouse
P.O. Box 700
Meridian, ID 83680-0700
(208) 884-7154
(888) 777-3922 (nationwide)
FAX: (208) 884-7193
Website:
  http://www.state.isp.id.us

ILLINOIS

Illinois State Police
500 Iles Park Place, Suite 104
Springfield, IL 62703-2982
(217) 785-4341
(800) 843-5763 (nationwide)
FAX: (217) 785-6793
Website: http://www.isp.state.il.us

INDIANA

Indiana State Police
Indiana Missing Children
  Clearinghouse
100 North Senate Avenue
Third Floor
Indianapolis, IN 46204-2259
(317) 232-8310
(800) 831-8953 (nationwide)
FAX: (317) 233-3057
Website:
  http://www.state.in.us/isp

IOWA

Missing Person Information
  Clearinghouse
Division of Criminal
  Investigation
Wallace State Office Building
E. 9th and Grand
Des Moines, IA 50319
(515) 281-7958
(800) 346-5507 (nationwide)
FAX: (515) 281-4898
Website:
  http://www.state.ia.us/missing

KANSAS

Kansas Bureau of Investigation
Missing Persons Clearinghouse
1620 S.W. Tyler Street
Topeka, KS 66612-1837
(785) 296-8200
(800) 572-7463 (nationwide)
FAX: (785) 296-6781
Website:
  http://www.ink.org/public/kbi
Website: http://www.ksamber.org

KENTUCKY

Kentucky State Police
1240 Airport Road
Frankfort, KY 40601
(502) 227-8799
(800) 543-7723 (nationwide)
(800) KIDS SAF
FAX: (502) 564-4931
E-mail: kentuckych@ncmec.org
Website:
  http://www.state.ky.US/agencies/
  KSP/mchild.htm

LOUISIANA

Louisiana Department of Social
  Services
Clearinghouse for Missing &
  Exploited Children
Office of Community Services
P.O. Box 3318
Baton Rouge, LA 70812
(225) 342-8631
FAX: (225) 342-9087

MAINE

Maine State Police
Missing Children Clearinghouse
1 Darcie Street, Suite 208
Houlton, ME 04730
(207) 532-5404
FAX: (207) 532-5455

MARYLAND

Maryland Center for Missing
  Children
Maryland State Police–
  Computer Crimes Unit
7155 Columbia Gateway Drive,
  Suite C
Columbia, MD 21046
(410) 290-1620
(800) 637-5437 (nationwide)
FAX: (410) 290-1831

MASSACHUSETTS

Massachusetts State Police
Missing Persons Unit
470 Worchester Rd.
Framingham, MA 01702
(508) 820-2129
(800) 622-5999 (in-state only)
FAX: (508) 820-2128

MICHIGAN

Michigan State Police
Prevention Services Unit
714 South Harrison Road
East Lansing, MI 48823
(517) 333-4006
(517) 336-6100 (24 hour,
  emergency)
FAX: (517) 333-4115

MINNESOTA

Minnesota State Clearinghouse
MN Bureau of Criminal
  Apprehension
1430 Maryland Ave.
St. Paul, MN 55106
(651) 793-1107
FAX (651) 793-1101

MISSISSIPPI

Mississippi Highway Patrol
Criminal Information Center
3891 Highway 486 West
Pearl, MS 39208
(601) 933-2657
FAX: (601) 933-2677

MISSOURI

Missouri State Highway Patrol
Missing Persons Unit
P.O. Box 568
Jefferson City, MO 65102
(573) 526-6178
(800) 877-3452 (nationwide)
FAX: (573) 526-5577

MONTANA

Montana Department of Justice
Missing/Unidentified Persons
P.O. Box 201402
303 N. Roberts Street, Room 471
Helena, MT 59620-1402
(406) 444-2800
FAX: (406) 444-4453

NEBRASKA

Nebraska State Patrol
Criminal Records &
  Identification Division
P.O. Box 94907
Lincoln, NE 68509
(402) 471-4545
(402) 479-4918
FAX: (402) 479-4054

NEVADA

Nevada Office of the Attorney
  General
Missing Children Clearinghouse
555 E. Washington Ave., Suite
  3900
Las Vegas, NV 89101-6208
(702) 486-3539
(800) 992-0900 (in-state only)
FAX: (702) 486-3768

NEW HAMPSHIRE

New Hampshire State Police
Investigative Services Bureau
  Major Crime Unit
91 Airport Rd.
Concord, NH 03301
(603) 271-2663
(800) 852-3411 (in-state only)
FAX: (603) 271-2520
Website:
  missingpersons@safety.state.nj.us

NEW JERSEY

New Jersey State Police
Unidentified Persons Unit
P.O. Box 7068
W. Trenton, NJ 08628
(609) 882-2000
(800) 709-7090 (nationwide)
FAX: (609) 882-2719

NEW MEXICO

New Mexico Department of
  Public Safety
ATTN: Law Enforcement Rec-
  ords
P.O. Box 1628
Santa Fe, NM 87504-1628
(505) 827-9191
FAX: (505) 827-3388

NEW YORK

New York Division of Criminal
  Justice Services
Missing and Exploited Children
4 Tower Place
Albany, NY 12203
(518) 457-6326
(800) 346-3543 (nationwide)
FAX: (518) 457-6965
General e-mail:
  missingchildren@dcjs.state.ny.us
Website:
  http://criminaljustice.state.ny.us

NORTH CAROLINA

North Carolina Center for
  Missing Persons
4706 Mail Service Center
Raleigh, NC 27699-4706
(919) 733-3914
(800) 522-5437 (nationwide)
FAX (919) 715-1682

NORTH DAKOTA

North Dakota Clearinghouse
for Missing Children
North Dakota Bureau of
Criminal Investigation
P.O. Box 1054
Bismarck, ND 58502-1054
(701) 328-5500
FAX: (701) 328-5510

OHIO

Missing Children Clearinghouse
Attorney General's Office
Crime Victims Services Section
65 East State Street, 5th Floor
Columbus, OH 43215-4231
(614) 466-5610
(800) 325-5604 (nationwide)
FAX: (614) 728-9536
Website:
  http://www.ag.state.oh.us/
  juvenile/mcc/missing.htm

OKLAHOMA

Oklahoma State Bureau of
Investigation
Criminal Intelligence Office
6600 N. Harvey
Oklahoma City, OK 73116
(405) 879-2645
FAX: (405) 879-2967

OREGON

Oregon State Police
Missing Children Clearinghouse
400 Public Service Building
Salem, OR 97310
(503) 378-3720
(800) 282-7155 (in-state only)

FAX: (503) 363-5475
PAGER: (503) 361-1935
Website:
  http://www.osp.state.or.us

PENNSYLVANIA

Pennsylvania State Police
Bureau of Criminal
Investigation
1800 Elmerton Avenue
Harrisburg, PA 17110
(717) 783-0960
FAX: (717) 705-2306

RHODE ISLAND

Rhode Island State Police
Missing & Exploited Children
Unit
311 Danielson Pike
North Scituate, RI 02857
(401) 444-1125
FAX: (401) 444-1133

SOUTH CAROLINA

South Carolina Law
Enforcement Division
Missing Person Information
Center
P.O. Box 21398
Columbia, SC 29221-1398
(803) 737-9000
(800) 322-4453 (nationwide)
FAX: (803) 896-7595

SOUTH DAKOTA

South Dakota Attorney
  General's Office
Division of Criminal
  Investigation
East Highway 34
c/o 500 East Capitol Ave.
Pierre, SD 57501
(605) 773-3331
FAX: (605) 773-4629

TENNESSEE

Tennessee Bureau of
  Investigation
Criminal Intelligence Unit
901 R.S. Gass Blvd.
Nashville, TN 37206
(615) 744-4000
FAX: (615) 744-4655

TEXAS

Texas Department of Public
  Safety
Special Crimes Services
Missing Persons Clearinghouse
P.O. Box 4087
Austin, TX 78773-0422
(512) 424-5074
(800) 346-3243 (in-state only)
FAX: (512) 424-2885
Website:
  http://www.txdps.state.tx.us/
  mpch

UTAH

Utah Department of Public
  Safety
Bureau of Criminal
  Identification
3888 West 5400 South
P.O. Box 148280
Salt Lake City, UT 84114-8280
(888) 770-6477 (nationwide)
FAX: (801) 965-4749

VERMONT

Vermont State Police
103 South Main Street
Waterbury, VT 05671
(802) 241-5352
FAX: (802) 241-5349

VIRGINIA

Virginia State Police
  Department
Missing Children's
  Clearinghouse
P.O. Box 27472
Richmond, VA 23261
(804) 674-2026
(800) 822-4453
FAX: (804) 674-2105

WASHINGTON

Washington State Patrol
Missing Children Clearinghouse
P.O. Box 2347
Olympia, WA 98507-2347
(800) 543-5678 (nationwide)
FAX: (360) 664-2156

WEST VIRGINIA

West Virginia State Police
Missing Children Clearinghouse
725 Jefferson Road
South Charleston, WV 25309-1698
(304) 558-1467
(800) 352-0927 (nationwide)
FAX: (304) 558-1470

WISCONSIN

Wisconsin Department of
  Justice
Division of Criminal
  Investigation
P.O. Box 7857
Madison, WI 53701-2718
(608) 266-1671
(800) THE-HOPE (in-state only)
FAX: (608) 267-2777

WYOMING

Wyoming Office of the
  Attorney General
Division of Criminal
  Investigation
316 West 22nd
Cheyenne, WY 82002
(307) 777-7537
FAX: (307) 777-7252
Control Terminal: (307) 777-7545

CANADA

Royal Canadian Mounted Police
National Missing Children's
  Services
1200 Vanier Parkway
P.O. Box 8885
Ottawa, Ontario, CN K1G 3M8
(613) 993-1525

(877) 318-3576 (toll-free)
FAX: (613) 993-5430
Website:
  http://www.ourmissingchildren.ca

PUERTO RICO

Missing Children Program
Centro Estatal Para Niños
  Desparecidos y Victimas de
  Abuso
P.O. Box 9023899
Old San Juan, Puerto Rico 00902-3899
(800) 995-NINO (limited calling
  area)
(787) 729-2523
FAX: (787) 722-0809
Website: www.niepr.org

NETHERLANDS POLICE

National Criminal Intelligence
  Service
P.O. Box 3016
2700 KX Zoetermeer
The Netherlands
011-31-79-345-8880
FAX: 011-31-79-345-8881
Website: http://nl.missingkids.com

THE AMECO ROSTER

Nonprofit Organizations
Serving Missing and Exploited
Children

AMECO, the Association of
Missing and Exploited
Children's Organizations, is a
membership organization
founded in 1994. AMECO

supports the endeavors of the membership on behalf of missing and exploited children, their families, and the community at large. The activities of AMECO and its member agencies are strictly noncommercial and not-for-profit.

ARIZONA

The Nation's Missing Children Organization and Center for Missing Adults, Inc.
2432 W. Peoria Avenue, Suite 1283
Phoenix, AZ 85029
(602) 944-1768
Toll-Free Hotline: (800) 690-3463 (FIND)
FAX: (602) 944-7520
E-mail: nmco@aol.com
Website:
  http://www.theyaremissed.org
Website:
  http://www.missingadults.org

ARKANSAS

Morgan Nick Foundation, Inc.
P.O. Box 1033
Alma, AR 72921
(501) 632-6382
Toll-Free Hotline: (877) 543-4673 (HOPE)
FAX: (501) 632-0795
E-mail: morgannick@aol.com
Website:
  http://www.morgannick.com

CALIFORNIA

Amber Foundation for Missing Children, Inc.
P.O. Box 565
Pinole, CA 94564
Phone: (510) 222-9050
Toll-Free Hotline: (800) 541-0777
FAX: (925) 680-4861
E-mail:
  amberjeansmom@yahoo.com
Website:
  http://www.missingchild.org/

Child Quest International, Inc.
1625 The Alameda, Suite 500
San Jose, CA 95126
Phone: (408) 287-4673 (HOPE)
Toll-Free Hotline: (888) 818-4673 (HOPE)
FAX: (408) 287-4676
E-mail: info@childquest.org
Website:
  http://www.childquest.org

Children of the Night
14530 Sylvan Street
Van Nuys, CA 91411
Phone: (818) 908-4474
Hotline: (800) 551-1300
FAX: (818) 908-1468
E-mail:
  llee@childrenofthenight.org
Website:
  http://www.childrenofthenight.org

Interstate Association for Stolen Children, Inc.
7024 Amberwick Way
Citrus Heights, CA 95621
Phone: 916-965-5959
FAX: 916-965-5961
E-mail: iasckids@pacbell.net
Website:
http://www.geocities.com/Capitol Hill/6042/

The Polly Klaas® Foundation, Inc.
P.O. Box 800
Petaluma, CA 94953
Phone: (707) 769-1334
Toll-Free Hotline: (800) 587-4357
FAX: (707) 769-4019
E-mail: pklaasfdtn@aol.com
Website:
http://www.pollyklaas.org

Vanished Children's Alliance, Inc.
2095 Park Avenue
San Jose, CA 95126
Phone: (408) 296-1113
FAX: (408) 296-1117
Toll-Free Hotline: (800) 826-4743 (VANISHED)
E-mail: info@vca.org
Website: http://www.vca.org

COLORADO

Missing Children's Task Force
P.O. Box 261141
Littleton, CO 80163
Phone: (303) 588-2909
E-mail: childfinders@qwest.net
Website:
http://www.childfinders.org

CONNECTICUT

The Paul & Lisa Program, Inc.
P.O. Box 348
Westbrook, CT 06498
Phone: (860) 767-7660
FAX: (860) 767-3122
E-mail:
paulandlisaprogram@snet.net
Website:
http://www.paulandlisa.org

FLORIDA

A Child Is Missing, Inc.
500 S.E. 17th Street, Room 101
Fort Lauderdale, FL 33316
Phone: (954) 763-1288
Toll-Free Hotline: (888) US5-ACIM
FAX: (954) 763-4481
E-mail: acim@mindspring.com
Website:
http://www.achildismissing.org

Child Watch of North America, Inc.
Don Wood, Executive Director
7380 Sand Lake Road, Suite 500
Orlando, FL 32819
Phone: (407) 290-5100
Toll-Free Hotline: (800) 928-2445; (888) CHILDWATCH
FAX: (407) 290-1613
E-mail: info@childwatch.org
Website:
http://www.childwatch.org

Jimmy Ryce Center for Victims of Predatory Abduction, Inc.
1111 Kane Concourse, Suite 305
Bay Harbor Islands, FL 33154
Phone: (305) 864-7477
Toll-Free Hotline: (800) 546-7923

FAX: (305) 864-7008
E-mail: misujim@netrox.net or
employerlawyer@yahoo.com
Website: www.jimmyryce.org

Missing Children Center, Inc.
Joan Thompson, Executive
Director
276 E. Highway 434
Winter Springs, FL 32708
Phone: (407) 327-4403
Toll-Free Hotline: (800) 330-1907
FAX: (407) 327-4514
E-mail: mccijoan@aol.com
Website:
www.missingchildrencenterinc.
org

Voice for the Children, Inc.
411 Wilder Street
West Palm Beach, FL 33405
Phone: (561) 833-0290
Toll-Free Hotline: (800) 28-HELP
ME (*children only*)
FAX: (561) 835-9367
E-mail: mvoice4@aol.com
Website:
http:/www.voice4thechildreninc.
org

KENTUCKY

**Exploited Children's Help
Organization, Inc.**
Lucy Lee, Executive Director
1500 Poplar Level Rd., Suite 2
Louisville, KY 40217
Phone: (502) 636-3670
FAX: (502) 636-3673
E-mail: echolou@aol.com
Website: http://www.echolou.org

MARYLAND

**Rachel Foundation for Family
Reintegration**
P.O. Box 368
Damascus, MD 20872
Phone: (202) 320-0848
FAX: (301) 840-9413
Website:
http://www.rachelfoundation.org

**Missing and Exploited
Children's Association
(MECA)**
Lutherville, MD
Phone: (410) 667-0718
Toll-Free Maryland: (888) 755-
6322 (MECA)
FAX: (410) 296-7812
E-mail: taavonjm@erols.com
Website: http://www.go.to/meca

MICHIGAN

**Missing Children's Network of
Michigan**
1600 Military Street, A-1
Port Huron, MI 48060
Phone: (810) 984-2911

MINNESOTA

**The Jacob Wetterling
Foundation**
P.O. Box 639
St. Joseph, MN 56374
Phone: (320) 363-0470
Toll-Free: (800) 325-HOPE
6600 France Avenue South, Suite
672
Edina, MN 55436
Phone: (952) 915-4779
E-mail: Jacob@uslink.net
Website: http://www.jwf.org

Missing Children–Minnesota
Ford Centre, Suite 570
420 North 5th Street,
Minneapolis, MN 55401
Phone: (612) 334-9449
Toll-Free Hotline: (888) 786-9355
(RUN-YELL)
E-mail: mssngchild@aol.com
Website:
http://www.missingchildrenmn.
org

MISSOURI

One Missing Link
Janis McCall, Executive Director
P.O. Box 10581
Springfield, MO 65808
Phone: (417) 886-5836
Toll-Free Hotline: (800) 555-7037
E-mail:
onemissinglinkinc@sbcglobal.net
Website:
http://www.onemissinglink.org

NEVADA

Nevada Child Seekers
25 TV5 Drive
Henderson, NV 89014
Phone: (702) 458-7009
E-mail:
jill@nevadachildseekers.org
Website:
www.nevadachildseekers.org

NEW YORK

Child Find of America
243 Main Street
P.O. Box 277
New Paltz, NY 12561
Phone: (845) 255-1848

E-mail: childfindamerica@aol.com
Website:
www.childfindofamerica.org

TENNESSEE

**Commission on Missing and
Exploited Children**
616 Adams Avenue
Memphis, TN 36105
Phone: (901) 405-8441
E-mail: comec@netten.net
Website: http://www.comec.org

TEXAS

Heidi Search Center
7900 No. IH 35
San Antonio, TX 78218
Phone: (210) 650-0428
Toll-Free Hotline: (800) 547-4435
FAX: (210) 650-3653
E-mail: heidisc@flash.net
Website:
www.heidisearchcenter.org

WASHINGTON

Operation Lookout
6320 Evergreen Way, Suite 201
Everett, WA 98203
Phone: (425) 771-7335
(800) 566-5688 (LOOKOUT)
(800) 782-7335 (SEEK)
E-mail: General Office:
lookoutfyi@operationallookout.org
Website:
http://www.operationlookout.org

WISCONSIN

Youth Educated in Safety, Inc.
P.O. Box 3124
Appleton, WI 54914-0124
Phone: (920) 734-5335
Toll-Free Hotline: (800) 272-7715
FAX: (920) 734-7077
E-mail: yes3124@aol.com
Website: www.yeswi.org

WYOMING

Christine Lamb Foundation
546 E. Adams
Powell, WY 82435
Phone: (307) 754-9261
E-mail: clamb@wavecom.net
Website: http://www.clamb.org

CANADA

Child Find Canada
1-1808 Main Street
Winnipeg, MB R2V 2A3
Phone: (204) 339-5584
FAX: (204) 339-5587
E-mail: childcan@aol.com
Website:
   http://www.childfindcanada.ca

Child Find Alberta Society
No. 101, 424-10 Street NW
Calgary, Alberta T2N 1V9
Phone: (403) 270-3463
Toll-Free Hotline: (800) 561-1733
E-mail: childab@aol.com
Website:
   http://www.childfind.ab.ca

Child Find Saskatchewan
202-3502 Taylor Street East
Saskatoon, SK S7H 5H9
Phone: (306) 955-0070

(800) 387-7962 (nationwide)
(800) 513-3463 (FIND)
   (provincial)
FAX: (306) 373-1311
E-mail: childsask@aol.com
Website: www.childfind.sk.ca

Child Find Ontario
295 Robinson Street, Suite 200
Oakville, ON L6J 1G7
(Regional offices in Kitchener,
   Barrie, and Sudbury)
Phone: (905) 842-5353
Toll-Free Hotline: (866) 543-8477
   (KID TIPS) in Canada
Toll-Free Hotline: (800) 387-
   7962, for sightings and case
   information
FAX: (905) 842-5383
E-mail: mail@childfindontario.ca
Website:
   http://www.ontario.childfind.ca

Child Find Nova Scotia
P.O. Box 523
Halifax, NS B3J 2R7
Phone: (902) 454-2030
Toll Free: (800) 682-9006
FAX: (902) 429-6749
E-mail: childns@aol.com
Website: www.childfind.ca

**Child Find Prince Edward
   Island**
549 North River Road
P.O. Box 21008
Charlottetown, PEI CIA 9H6
Phone: (902) 368-1678
FAX: (902) 368-1389
E-mail: childpei@aol.com
Website: http://www.childfind.ca

Child Find British Columbia
3673 Massey Drive
Prince George, British Columbia
V2N 4E6
Phone: (250) 562-3463
Toll-Free Hotline: (888) 689-3463
FAX: (250) 562-3467
E-mail: childbcpg@aol.com
Website:
http://www.childfindbc.com

**Child Find Newfoundland and
Labrador**
451 Kenmount Road
St. John's Newfoundland
A1B 3P9
Phone: (709) 738-4400
FAX: (809) 738-0550
E-mail: childnfld@aol.com
Website: www.childfind.ca

Child Find Manitoba
800 Portage Avenue
Winnipeg, MB R3G ON4
Phone: (204) 945-5735
Toll-Free Hotline: (800) 387-7962
FAX: (204) 948-2461
E-mail: childmb@aol.com
Website:
http://www.childfind.mb.ca

**Missing Children Society of
Canada**
Suite 219, 3501-23 Street NE
Calgary, Alberta T2E 6V8
Phone: (403) 291-0705
FAX: (403) 291-9728
Toll Free: (800) 661-6160
E-mail: info@mcsc.ca
Website: http://www.mcsc.ca

**Missing Children's Network
Canada**
376 Victoria Ave.
Westmount H3Z 1C3
Montreal, Quebec
Phone: (514) 843-4333
Toll-Free Hotline: (888) 692-4673
(HOPE)
FAX: (514) 843-8211
E-mail:
search@missingchildren.ca
Website:
http://www.missingchildren.ca

782-525-0379